# PathLight
## *Toward Global*
## *Awareness*

# PathLight
## Toward Global
## Awareness

### EDITED BY MEG CROSSMAN

YWAM
PUBLISHING

P.O. Box 55787 / Seattle, WA 98155

YWAM Publishing is the publishing ministry of Youth With A Mission. Youth With A Mission (YWAM) is an international missionary organization of Christians from many denominations dedicated to presenting Jesus Christ to this generation. To this end, YWAM has focused its efforts in three main areas: (1) training and equipping believers for their part in fulfilling the Great Commission (Matthew 28:19), (2) personal evangelism, and (3) mercy ministry (medical and relief work).

For a free catalog of books and materials, contact:
YWAM Publishing
P.O. Box 55787, Seattle, WA 98155
(425) 771-1153 or (800) 922-2143
www.ywampublishing.com

**PathLight: Toward Global Awareness**
Copyright © 2008 by Meg Bilby Crossman
Second Edition; first printing in 2003 under title *Perspectives Exposure: Discovering God's Heart for All Nations and Our Part in His Plan*

10 09 08     10 9 8 7 6 5 4 3 2 1

Published by Youth With A Mission Publishing
P.O. Box 55787
Seattle, WA 98155

ISBN 13: 978-1-57658-414-9
ISBN 10: 1-57658-414-3

Cover Design by Richard Kim
Cover Illustrations by Julie Bosacker

Printed in the United States of America.

# CONTENTS

# CONTENTS

# CONTENTS

## MAPS, CHARTS, AND GRAPHS

## ILLUSTRATIONS

# HOW TO USE THIS BOOK

## The purpose of *Pathlight*

This book has been developed to serve the needs of laymen and women and the local churches of which they are a part. It was originally constructed to make the material accessible to Senior Adults. However, it is also being used as material for Sunday school classes, preparation for short term teams, church training institutes, and women's ministries. It is constructed to introduce God's people to His work in the world in our generation.

PathLight includes five sections that shed light on God's heart for the Nations. We examine Kingdom principles from Biblical, Historical, Strategic, Cultural, and Partnership standpoints. We hope that many who use this book will be stirred to take additional entire courses to expand what they learn here.

## Using *Pathlight*

Although this material is divided into five sections, it can be broken down into ten or even more lessons if the leader so desires. In many locations, different speakers come to teach various segments of the material. Some classes are one hour long; others may last as long as an hour and a half or two hours.

Because this version of the material does not contain tests or homework, it is more malleable than longer courses. Suggestions for discussion questions, skits, video support, and other ways of enlivening the material can be downloaded from the Worldwide Perspectives or PathWays2 website. A Leaders Guide may be requested from Meg Crossman at megcrossman@cox.net.

## Suggestions for Class Experiences

Leaders often enhance the classroom experience with prayer walks, visits to various regional conferences, tours of nearby mission agencies, and support seminars of many kinds. Other groups visit local mosques or temples with the attitude of a learner. Your group may plan to invite members of various religions or international students from several countries to offer a discussion panel for the class.

If possible, as your group uses this material and tries various approaches to it, pleases send your comments, insights, and suggestions to us so we can improve it. The email address is megcrossman@cox.net. We welcome your input!

It is our prayer that this book may contribute in some way to awakening God's people to His relentless, invincible plans to love, bless and reach some from every nation. May all of us discover particular ways to participate in seeing His worthy Son receive the worship from all peoples that John described in Revelation 5!

Biblical
Exposure

Historical
Exposure

Strategic
Exposure

Cultural
Exposure

Partnership
Exposure

# ACKNOWLEDGMENTS

This book could not have been produced without the work of many faithful servants in the Kingdom. As originally developed for use with senior adults, it was the vision and prodding of Elmer and Jean Hiebert, longtime ministry activists among university students and internationals, that brought it into being.

Support from the staff of Perspectives Partnership, particularly Chuck Morgan, Barbara Rentz, and Tracy Evilsizor, made the beginning courses possible. The active coordinators of those initial offerings, Bill Kilgore, the Rev. Jerry McGhee, Renee Roelants, and Sandy Vivona, taught us a great deal.

Through the urging and encouragement of Harold Britton and the staff at Caleb Project, we decided to try to publish this volume. Their continuing involvement, advice, and advocacy for the material have been invaluable. Hours of formatting and planning came from Teri Moyer, who gave sacrificial labor in the midst of many difficulties and trials.

The Core Production Team all contributed a variety of essential services: Dick Ulmer, Scott Bauer, Debbie Tweeten, Julie Murphree, Barbara Rentz, and Renee Roelants. Editors labored exhaustively to improve the material: Keri Comer, Carey Lee, Shirley Miel. Any remaining errors are mine alone.

The support and understanding of my husband, Al, was invaluable. He is always my best critic and my strongest backer. There are more than forty committed intercessors who continually undergird this project with prayer. Without them nothing of value could have resulted.

It is the prayer of all of us that this book may effectively serve the movement, calling God's people to care for the nations and extend His Kingdom throughout the earth.

# Biblical Paths

## The Power of Story

Story is one of the earliest communications forms. It is found in every people and in every culture. It is still one that has great power. Even in these days of complex technology, elaborate media and multi-media, and impressive special effects, the ancient allure of a story still draws and affects us. Witness the worldwide popularity of film in our generation.

Story communicates principles in a comprehensible and memorable way. Story activates the imagination. Story is easily transmitted to others. Story often delivers the message with a force that figures, graphs, or principles can never produce. Jesus routinely used stories to declare eternal certainties in ways that the simplest people could grasp.

## The Bible—One Story

The Bible is not just a compilation of many stories. It is actually One commanding story. It is the story of our God and His actions and intentions. To many people, the Scriptures seem distant and sometimes elusive. They struggle to understand the intent of that Story and its relationship to their own time and daily lives. However, this story is no fiction or fable (even though such forms also have power). This is an actual account of God's action with and through His people. Understanding all of this Story can transform every part of our lives.

God's story is unique in many ways. It was written by a number of different people, living in a variety of cultures across centuries of time and in diverse circumstances. Yet it displays an incredible unity of purpose. It is as though one resounding voice—God's voice—is transmitted to us through all these varied voices. Our study seeks to go behind the accounts to discover that underlying Voice, to learn the cohesive Story, and to see His deliberate intent.

## Only an Exposure

This study will expose you to a fuller understanding story of our Father and His worldwide intentions. Using the writings of many different men and women of God, it will help you see the Bible as a unified story. It will help integrate the many stories from Scripture, with which you may already be familiar, into God's larger purpose.

This book is based on the curriculum called *PathWays to Global Understanding*. It cannot give you all the details of the story as told in the fuller class. However, it can introduce you to some of the concepts that will help you see God's Story and your connection to it.

## Why Is This Story Revealed?

God's story could only be known if He chose to reveal it—and He has! In giving us the Scriptures, He demonstrates Himself to be a person who wants to be *known*. His actions disclose the power and beauty and holiness of His character. He also makes clear that He wants others to know Him, not just know about Him. He reaches out to us with His word and He authorizes us to offer it to others, even to those who are very different from us.

## In This Class, We Will Study Five Facets of the Story:

▶ What do the Scriptures tell us about His story?

▶ How does His story operate through human history?

▶ What elements of the story are active in this generation?

▶ How can different cultures understand the story?

▶ Who has God called each of us to be in connecting to His global story?

## What New Questions Will We Probe?

In this opening section, we will take up the first question. We will look at articles that help us frame new questions:

▶ What is the reason God gave us the Bible?

▶ Where did His worldwide purposes begin to take shape?

▶ How are the stories of the Old Testament linked to these purposes?

▶ How did Jesus respond to these purposes and act upon them?

▶ What critical decision in Acts affects the way the Story goes forth?

▶ How does God intend His Kingdom to come and His will to be done?

Take the time to read each article carefully. Examine the verses that are cited. Keep a mind and heart open to new understandings that the Lord may want to give you. Above all, ask the Father to reveal Himself to you in new and richer dimensions.

This class is only an "Exposure" but it may provide some steppingstones for each reader to walk an exciting, challenging, and demanding pathway shining a stronger light on the purposes of God. Let your story begin to connect to His Story!

# The Bible in World Evangelization

*John R. W. Stott*

John R. W. Stott is known worldwide as a preacher, evangelist, and teacher of Scripture. Most of his years he served in various capacities at All Souls Church in London, as well as leading university missions on five continents. Retired now, he was one of the principal framers of the landmark Lausanne Covenant (1974).

Without the Bible world evangelization would be not only impossible but actually inconceivable. It is the Bible that lays upon us the responsibility to evangelize the world, gives us a gospel to proclaim, tells us how to proclaim it, and promises us that it is God's power for salvation to every believer.

It is, moreover, an observable fact of history, both past and contemporary, that the degree of the church's commitment to world evangelization is commensurate with the degree of its conviction about the authority of the Bible. Whenever Christians lose their confidence in the Bible, they also lose their zeal for evangelism. Conversely, whenever they are convinced about the Bible, then they are determined about evangelism.

Let me develop four reasons why the Bible is indispensable to world evangelization.

## Mandate for World Evangelization

First, the Bible gives us the *mandate* for world evangelization. We certainly need one. Two phenomena are everywhere on the increase. One is religious fanaticism, and the other, religious pluralism. The fanatic displays the kind of irrational zeal that (if it could) would use force to compel belief and eradicate disbelief. Religious pluralism encourages the opposite tendency.

Whenever the spirit of religious fanaticism or of its opposite, religious indifferentism, prevails, world evangelization is bitterly resented. Fanatics refuse to countenance what the rival evangelism represents, and pluralists its exclusive claims. The Christian evangelist is regarded as making an unwarrantable intrusion into other people's private affairs.

In the face of this opposition we need to be clear about the mandate the Bible gives us. It is not just the Great Commission (important as that is), but the entire biblical revelation. Let me rehearse it briefly.

There is but one living and true God, the Creator of the universe, the Lord of the nations, and the God of the spirits of all flesh. Some 4,000 years ago he called Abraham and made a covenant with him, promising not only to bless him but also through his posterity to bless all the families of the earth (Genesis 12:1–4). This biblical text is one of the foundation stones of the Christian mission. For Abraham's descendants (through whom all nations are being blessed) are Christ and the people of Christ. If by faith we belong to Christ, we are Abraham's spiritual children and have a responsibility to all mankind. So, too, the Old Testament prophets foretold how God would make his Christ the heir and the light of the nations (Psalm 2:8; Isaiah 42:6; 49:6).

> *The church's commitment to world evangelization is commensurate with the degree of its conviction about the authority of the Bible.*

When Jesus came, he endorsed these promises. True, during his own earthly ministry he was restricted "to the lost sheep of the house of Israel" (Matthew 10:6; 15:24), but he prophesied that many would "come from east and west, and from north and south," and would "sit at table with Abraham, Isaac, and Jacob in the kingdom of heaven" (Matthew 8:11; Luke 13:29). Further, after his resurrection and in anticipation of his ascension he made the tremendous claim that "all authority in heaven and on earth" had been given to him (Matthew 28:18). It was in consequence of his universal authority that he commanded his followers to make all nations his disciples, baptizing them into his new community and teaching them all his teaching (Matthew 28:19).

And this, when the Holy Spirit of truth and power had come upon them, the early Christians proceeded to do. They became the witnesses of Jesus, even to the ends of the earth (Acts 1:8). Moreover, they did it "for the sake of his name" (Romans 1:5; 3 John 7). They knew

Stott, J. R., (1992) The Bible in World Evangelization. In R.D. Winter & S.C. Hawthorne (Eds.). *Perspectives on the World Christian Movement: A Reader* (rev. ed.) (p. A3–9). Pasadena: William Carey Library.

that God had superexalted Jesus, enthroning him at his right hand and bestowing upon him the highest rank, in order that every tongue should confess his Lordship. They longed that Jesus should receive the honor due to his name. Besides, one day he would return in glory, to save, to judge, and to reign. So what was to fill the gap between his two comings? The worldwide mission of the church! Not till the gospel had reached the ends of the world, he said, would the end of history come (cf. Matthew 24:14; 28:20; Acts 1:8). The two ends would coincide.

> *The mandate the Bible gives is not just the Great Commission, but the entire biblical revelation.*

Our mandate for world evangelization, therefore, is the whole Bible. It is to be found in the creation of God (because of which all human beings are responsible to him), in the character of God (as outgoing, loving, compassionate, not willing that any should perish, desiring that all should come to repentance), in the promises of God (that all nations will be blessed through Abraham's seed and will become the Messiah's inheritance), in the Christ of God (now exalted with universal authority, to receive universal acclaim), in the Spirit of God (who convicts of sin, witnesses to Christ, and impels the church to evangelize), and in the Church of God (which is a multinational, missionary community, under orders to evangelize until Christ returns).

This global dimension of the Christian mission is irresistible. Individual Christians and local churches not committed to world evangelization are contradicting (either through blindness or through disobedience) an essential part of their God-given identity. The biblical mandate for world evangelization cannot be escaped.

## Message for World Evangelization

Secondly, the Bible gives us the *message* for world evangelization. The Lausanne Covenant defined evangelism in terms of the evangel. Paragraph four begins: "to evangelize is to spread the good news that Jesus Christ died for our sins and was raised from the dead according to the Scriptures, and that as the reigning Lord he now offers the forgiveness of sins and the liberating gift of the Spirit to all who repent and believe."

Our message comes out of the Bible. As we turn to the Bible for our message, however, we are confronted with a dilemma. On the one hand the message is given to us. We are not left to invent it; it has been entrusted to us as a precious "deposit," which we, like faithful stewards, are both to guard and to dispense to God's

household (1 Timothy 6:20; 2 Timothy 1:12–14; 2 Corinthians 4:1–2). On the other hand, it has not been given to us as a single, neat, mathematical formula, but rather in a rich diversity of formulations.

So there is only one gospel, on which all the apostles agreed (1 Corinthians 15:11), and Paul could call down the curse of God upon anybody—including himself—who preached a "different" gospel from the original apostolic gospel of God's grace (Galatians 1:6–8). Yet the apostles expressed this one gospel in various ways—now sacrificial (the shedding and sprinkling of Christ's blood), now messianic (the breaking in of God's promised rule), now legal (the Judge pronouncing the unrighteous righteous), now personal (the Father reconciling his wayward children), now salvific (the heavenly Liberator coming to rescue the helpless), now cosmic (the universal Lord claiming universal dominion); and this is only a selection.

The gospel is seen to be one, yet diverse. It is "given," yet culturally adapted to its audience. Once we grasp this, we shall be saved from making two mistakes. The first I will call "total fluidity." I recently heard an English church leader declare that there is no such thing as the gospel until we enter the situation in which we are to

> *The Church of God is a multinational missionary community, under orders to evangelize until Christ returns.*

witness. "We take nothing with us into the situation," he said; "we discover the gospel only when we have arrived there." Now I am in full agreement with the need to be sensitive to each situation, but if this was the point which the leader in question was wanting to make, he grossly overstated it. There is such a thing as a revealed or given gospel, which we have no liberty to falsify.

The second mistake I will call "total rigidity." In this case the evangelist behaves as if God had given a series of precise formulas that we have to repeat and certain images that we must invariably employ. This leads to bondage to words or images or both. Some evangelists lapse into the use of stale jargon, while others feel obliged on every occasion to mention "the blood of Christ" or "justification by faith" or "the kingdom of God" or some other image.

Between these two extremes there is a third and better way. It combines commitment to the fact of revelation with commitment to the task of contextualization. It accepts that only the biblical formulations of the gospel are permanently normative, and that every attempt to proclaim the gospel in modern idiom must justify itself as an authentic expression of the biblical gospel.

If it refuses to jettison the biblical formulations, it also refuses to recite them in a wooden and unimaginative way. On the contrary, we have to engage in the continuous struggle (by prayer, study, and discussion) to relate the gospel to the given situation. Since it comes from God, we must guard it; since it is intended for modern men and women, we must interpret it. We have to combine fidelity (constantly studying the biblical text) with sensitivity (constantly studying the contemporary scene). Only then can we hope to relate the Word to the world, the gospel to the context, Scripture to culture.

## Model for World Evangelization

Thirdly, the Bible gives us the *model* for world evangelization. In addition to a message (what we are to say) we need a model (how we are to say it). The Bible supplies this too, for the Bible does not just *contain* the gospel; it *is* the gospel. Through the Bible God is evangelizing, that is, communicating the good news to the world. You will recall Paul's statement about Genesis 12:3, that "the scripture...preached the gospel beforehand to Abraham" (Galatians 3:8; RSV). All Scripture preaches the gospel; God evangelizes through it.

If, then, Scripture is itself divine evangelization, we can learn how to preach the gospel by considering how God has done it. He has given us in the process of biblical inspiration a beautiful evangelistic model.

*It is the greatness of God's condescension to reveal his sublime truth through the vocabulary and grammar of human language, through human beings, human images, and human cultures.*

What strikes us immediately is the greatness of God's condescension. He had sublime truth to reveal about himself and his Christ, his mercy and his justice, and his full salvation. And he chose to make this disclosure through the vocabulary and grammar of human language, through human beings, human images, and human cultures.

*The message is given to us not as a single, neat, mathematical formula, but in a rich diversity of formulations. The gospel is thus seen to be one, yet diverse. It is "given," yet culturally adapted to its audience.*

Yet through this lowly medium of human words and images, God was speaking of his own Word. Our evangelical doctrine of the inspiration of Scripture emphasizes its double authorship. Men spoke and God spoke. Men spoke from God (2 Peter 1:21) and God spoke through men (Hebrews 1:1). The words spoken and written were equally his and theirs. He decided what he wanted to say, yet did not smother their human personalities. They used their faculties freely, yet did not distort the divine message. Christians want to assert something similar about the Incarnation, the climax of the self-communicating God. "The Word became flesh" (John 1:14). That is, God's eternal Word, who from eternity was with God and was God, the agent through whom the universe was created, became a human being, with all the particularity of a first-century Palestinian Jew. He became little, weak, poor, and vulnerable. He experienced pain and hunger and exposed himself to temptation. Yet when he became one of us, he did not cease to be himself. He remained forever the eternal Word or Son of God.

Essentially the same principle is illustrated in both the inspiration of the Scripture and the incarnation of the Son. The Word became flesh. The divine was communicated through the human. He identified with us, though without surrendering his own identity. And this principle of "identification without loss of identity" is the model for all evangelism, especially cross-cultural evangelism.

Some of us refuse to identify with the people we claim to be serving. We stay aloof. We hold on desperately to our own cultural inheritance in the mistaken notion that it is an indispensable part of our identity. We are unwilling to let it go. Not only do we maintain our own cultural practices with fierce tenacity, but we treat the cultural inheritance of the land of our adoption without the respect it deserves. We thus practice a double kind of cultural imperialism, imposing our own culture on others and despising theirs. But this was not the way of Christ, who emptied himself of his glory and humbled himself to serve.

Other cross-cultural messengers of the gospel make the opposite mistake. So determined are they to identify with the people to whom they go that they surrender even their Christian standards and values. But again this was not Christ's way, since in becoming human he remained truly divine. The Lausanne Covenant expressed the principle in these words: "Christ's evangelists must humbly seek to empty themselves of all but their personal authenticity, in order to become the servants of others" (paragraph 10).

We have to wrestle with the reasons why people reject the gospel, and in particular give due weight to the cultural factors. Some people reject the gospel not because they perceive it to be false, but because they perceive it to be alien.

Dr. René Padilla was criticized at Lausanne* [*the 1974 Congress on World Evangelization—ed.*] for saying that the gospel some European and North American missionaries have exported was a "culture-Christianity," a Christian message that is distorted by the materialistic, consumer culture of the West. It was hurtful to us to hear him say this, but of course he was quite right. All of us need to subject our gospel to more critical scrutiny, and in a cross-cultural situation, visiting evangelists need humbly to seek the help of local Christians in order to discern the cultural distortions of their message.

*S*ome people reject the gospel not because they perceive it to be false, but because they perceive it to be alien. Others reject the gospel because they perceive it to be a threat to their own culture.

Others reject the gospel because they perceive it to be a threat to their own culture. Of course Christ challenges every culture. Whenever we present the gospel to Hindus or Buddhists, Jews or Muslims, secularists or Marxists, Jesus Christ confronts them with his demand to dislodge whatever has thus far secured their allegiance and replace it with himself. He is Lord of every person and every culture. That threat, that confrontation, cannot be avoided. But does the gospel we proclaim present people with other threats that are unnecessary because it calls for the abolition of harmless customs or appears destructive of national art, architecture, music, and festivals, or because we who share it are culture-proud and culture-blind?

To sum up, when God spoke to us in Scripture, he used human language, and when he spoke to us

in Christ, he assumed human flesh. In order to reveal himself, he both emptied and humbled himself. That is the model of evangelism that the Bible supplies. There is self-emptying and self-humbling in all authentic evangelism; without it we contradict the gospel and misrepresent the Christ we proclaim.

*T*his principle of "identification without loss of identity" is the model for all evangelism, especially cross-cultural evangelism.

## Power for World Evangelization

Fourthly, the Bible gives us the *power* for world evangelization. It is hardly necessary for me to emphasize our need for power, for we know how feeble our human resources are in comparison with the magnitude of the task. We also know how armor-plated are the defenses of the human heart. Worse still, we know the personal reality, malevolence, and might of the Devil and of the demonic forces at his command.

Sophisticated people may ridicule our belief, and caricature it, too, in order to make their ridicule more plausible. But we evangelical Christians are naive enough to believe what Jesus and his apostles taught. To us it is a fact of great solemnity that, in John's expression, "the whole world is in the power of the evil one" (1 John 5:19). For until they are liberated by Jesus Christ and transferred into his kingdom, all men and women are the slaves of Satan. Moreover, we see his power in the contemporary world—in the darkness of idolatry and of the fear of spirits, in superstition and fatalism, in devotion to gods which are no gods, in the selfish materialism of the West, in the spread of atheistic communism, in the proliferation of irrational cults, in violence and aggression, and in the widespread declension from absolute standards of goodness and truth. These things are the work of him who is called in Scripture a liar, a deceiver, a slanderer, and a murderer.

So Christian conversion and regeneration remain miracles of God's grace. They are the culmination of a power struggle between Christ and Satan or (in vivid, apocalyptic imagery) between the Lamb and the Dragon. The plundering of the strong man's palace is possible only because he has been bound by the One who is stronger

---

* The Lausanne Covenant—this declaration of commitment to reach all nations was approved by Christian delegates from many nations who participated in the Congress on World Evangelization that met in Lausanne, Switzerland, in July of 1974.

still and who by his death and resurrection disarmed and discarded the principalities and powers of evil (Matthew 12:27–29; Luke 11:20–22; Colossians 2:15).

**To us it is a fact of great solemnity that "the whole world is in the power of the evil one."**

How then shall we enter into Christ's victory and overthrow the Devil's power? Let Luther answer our question: *ein wörtlein will ihn fällen* ("one little word will knock him down"). There is power in the Word of God and in the preaching of the gospel. Perhaps the most dramatic expression of this in the New Testament is to be found in 2 Corinthians 4. Paul portrays "the god of this world" as having "blinded the minds of the un-believers, to keep them from seeing the light of the gospel of the glory of Christ…" (v. 4).

If human minds are blinded, how then can they ever see? Only by the creative Word of God. For it is the God who said "let light shine out of darkness" who has shone in our hearts to "give the light of the knowledge of the glory of God in the face of Jesus Christ" (v. 6). The apostle thus likens the unregenerate heart to the dark, primeval chaos and attributes regeneration to the divine fiat, "Let there be light."

If then Satan blinds people's minds and God shines into people's hearts, what can we hope to contribute to this encounter? Would it not be more modest for us to retire from the field of conflict and leave them to fight it out? No, this is not the conclusion Paul reaches.

On the contrary, in between verses 4 and 6, which describe the activities of God and Satan, verse 5 describes the work of the evangelist: "We preach….Jesus Christ as Lord." Since the light which the Devil wants to prevent people seeing and which God shines into them is the gospel, we had better preach it! Preaching the gospel, far from being unnecessary, is indispensable. It is the God-appointed means by which the prince of darkness is defeated and the light comes streaming into people's

hearts. There is power in God's gospel—his power for salvation (Romans 1:16).

We may be very weak. I sometimes wish we were weaker. Faced with the forces of evil, we are often tempted to put on a show of Christian strength and engage in a little evangelical saber rattling. But it is in our weakness that Christ's strength is made perfect and it is words of human weakness that the Spirit endorses with his power. So it is when we are weak that we are strong (1 Corinthians 2:1–5; 2 Corinthians 12:9–10).

## Let It Loose in the World!

Let us not consume all our energies arguing about the Word of God; let's start using it. It will prove its divine origin by its divine power. Let's let it loose in the world! If only every Christian missionary and evangelist proclaimed the biblical gospel with faithfulness and sensitivity, and every Christian preacher were a faithful expositor of God's Word! Then God would display his saving power.

**Without the Bible we have no gospel to take to the nations, no warrant to take it to them, no idea of how to set about the task, and no hope of any success.**

Without the Bible world evangelization is impossible. For without the Bible we have no gospel to take to the nations, no warrant to take it to them, no idea of how to set about the task, and no hope of any success. It is the Bible that gives us the mandate, the message, the model, and the power we need for world evangelization. So let's seek to repossess it by diligent study and meditation. Let's heed its summons, grasp its message, follow its directions, and trust its power. Let's lift up our voices and make it known. ◼

---

**We are a people of destiny in Jesus.**
**God calls us to share with him in his mission.**
**We are never closer to God**
**than when our lives are involved with this mission.**

*Patrick Johnstone*

# The Living God Is a Missionary God

*John R. W. Stott*

Millions of people in today's world are extremely hostile to the Christian missionary enterprise. They regard it as politically disruptive (because it loosens the cement that binds the national culture) and religiously narrowminded (because it makes exclusive claims for Jesus), while those who are involved in it are thought to suffer from an arrogant imperialism. And the attempt to convert people to Christ is rejected as an unpardonable interference in their private lives. "My religion is my own affair," they say. "Mind your own business, and leave me alone to mind mine."

It is essential, therefore, for Christians to understand the grounds on which the Christian mission rests. Only then shall we be able to persevere in the missionary task, with courage and humility, in spite of the world's misunderstanding and opposition. More precisely, biblical Christians need biblical incentives. For we believe the Bible to be the revelation of God and of his will. So we ask: Has he revealed in Scripture that "mission" is his will for his people? Only then shall we be satisfied. For then it becomes a matter of obeying God, whatever others may think or say. Here we shall focus on the Old Testament, though the entire Bible is rich in evidence for the missionary purpose of God.

## The Call of Abraham

Our story begins about four thousand years ago with a man called Abraham, or more accurately, Abram, as he was called at that time. Here is the account of God's call to Abraham:

> Now the LORD said to Abram, "Go from your country and your kindred and your father's house to the land that I will show you. And I will make of you a great nation, and I will bless you, and make your name great, so that you will be a blessing. I will bless those who bless you, and the one who curses you I will curse; and in you all the families of the earth shall be blessed." So Abram went, as the LORD had told him; and Lot went with him. Abram was seventy-five years old when he departed from Haran. (Genesis 12:1–4).

God made a promise (a composite promise, as we shall see) to Abraham. And an understanding of that promise is indispensable to an understanding of the Bible and of the Christian mission. These are perhaps the most unifying verses in the Bible; the whole of God's purpose is encapsulated here.

God made a promise to Abraham. An understanding of that promise is indispensable to an understanding of Christian mission. These are perhaps the most unifying verses in the Bible.

By way of introduction we shall need to consider the setting of God's promise, the context in which it came to be given. Then we shall divide the rest of our study into two. First, *the promise* (exactly what it was that God said he would do) and second—at greater length—*its fulfillment* (how God has kept and will keep his promise). We start, however, with the setting.

Genesis 12 begins: "Now the LORD said to Abram." It sounds abrupt for an opening of a new chapter. We are prompted to ask, "Who is this 'Lord' who spoke to Abraham?" and "Who is this 'Abraham' to whom he spoke?" They are not introduced into the text out of the blue. A great deal lies behind these words. They are a key tht opens up the whole of Scripture. The previous eleven chapters lead up to them; the rest of the Bible follows and fulfills them.

What, then, is the background to this text? It is this. "The Lord" who chose and called Abraham is the same Lord who in the beginning created the heavens and the earth and who climaxed his creative work by making man and woman unique creatures in his own likeness. In other words, we should never allow ourselves to forget that the Bible begins with the universe, not with the planet earth; then with the earth, not with Palestine, then with Adam the father of the human race, not with Abraham the father of the chosen race. Since, then, God is the Creator of the universe, the earth, and all mankind, we must never demote him to the status of a tribal deity or petty godling like Chemosh, the god of the Moabites, or Milcom (or Molech), the god of the Ammonites, or Baal, the male deity, or Ashtoreth, the female deity, of the Canaanites. Nor must we suppose that God chose Abraham and his descendants because he had lost

---

Stott, J. R. W. (1992) Taken from *You Can Tell the World*, James E. Berney, ed. Copyright 1979 by InterVarsity Christian Fellowship/USA. Used by permission of InterVarsity Press, P.O. Box 1400, Downers Grove, IL 60515.

interest in other peoples or given them up. Election is not a synonym for elitism. On the contrary, as we shall soon see, God chose one man and his family in order, through them, to bless *all* the families of the earth.

> **S**ince God is the Creator of the universe, the earth, and all mankind, we must never demote him to the status of a tribal deity or petty godling.

We are bound, therefore, to be deeply offended when Christianity is relegated to one chapter in a book on the world's religions as if it were one option among many, or when people speak of "the Christian God" as if there were others! No, there is only one living and true God, who has revealed himself fully and finally in his only Son Jesus Christ. Monotheism lies at the basis of mission. As Paul wrote to Timothy, "There is one God, and there is one mediator between God and men, the man Christ Jesus" (1 Timothy 2:5).

The Genesis record moves on from the creation of all things by the one God and of human beings in his likeness to our rebellion against our own Creator and to God's judgment upon his rebel creatures—a judgment which is relieved, however, by his first gospel promise, that one day the woman's seed would "bruise," indeed "crush," the serpent's head (3:15).

The following eight chapters (Genesis 4–11) describe the devastating results of the Fall in terms of the progressive alienation of human beings from God and from our fellow human beings. This was the setting in which God's call and promise came to Abraham. All around was moral deterioration, darkness, and dispersal. Society was steadily disintegrating. Yet God the Creator did not abandon the human beings he had made in his own likeness (Genesis 9:6). Out of the prevailing godlessness he called one man and his family and promised to bless not only them but through them the whole world. The scattering would not proceed unchecked; a grand process of ingathering would now begin.

## The Promise

What then was the promise that God made to Abraham? It was a composite promise consisting of several parts.

*First*, **it was the promise of a posterity.** He was to go from his kindred and his father's house, and in exchange for the loss of his family, God would make of him "a great nation." Later, in order to indicate this, God changed his name from "Abram" ("exalted father") to "Abraham" ("father of a multitude")

because, he said to him, "I have made you the father of a multitude of nations" (17:5).

*Second*, **it was the promise of a land.** God's call seems to have come to him in two stages, first in Ur of the Chaldees while his father was still alive (11:31; 15:7) and then in Haran after his father had died (11:32; 12:1). At all events he was to leave his own land, and in return God would show him another country.

*Third*, **it was the promise of a blessing.** Five times the words *bless* and *blessing* occur in 12:2–3. The blessing God promised Abraham would spill over upon all mankind. A posterity, a land, and a blessing. Each of these promises is elaborated in the chapters that follow Abraham's call.

*First*, *the land*. After Abraham had generously allowed his nephew Lot to choose where he wanted to settle (he selected the fertile Jordan valley), God said to Abraham: "Lift up your eyes and look from the place where you are, northward and southward and eastward and westward; for all the land which you see, I will give to you and to your descendants for ever" (13:14–15).

*Second*, *the posterity*. Sometime later God gave Abraham another visual aid, telling him to look now not to the earth but to the sky. On a clear, dark night he took him outside his tent and said to him, "Look toward heaven and number the stars." What a ludicrous command! Perhaps Abraham started, "1, 2, 3, 5, 10, 20, 30…," but he must soon have given up. It was an impossible task. Then God said to him: "So shall your descendants be." And we read: "He believed the Lord." Although he was probably by now in his eighties, and although he and Sarah were still childless, he yet believed God's promise and God "reckoned it to him as righteousness." That is, because he trusted God, God accepted him as righteous in his sight.

> **G**od chose one man and his family in order, through them, to bless all the families of the earth.

*Third*, *the blessing*. "I will bless you." Already God has accepted Abraham as righteous or (to borrow the New Testament expression) has "justified him by faith." No greater blessing is conceivable. It is the foundation blessing of the covenant of grace, which a few years later God went on to elaborate to Abraham: "I will establish my covenant between me and you and your descendants after you…for an everlasting covenant, to be God to you and to your descendants after you…and I will be their God" (17:7–8). And he gave them circumcision as the outward and visible sign of his gracious covenant or pledge to be their God. It is the first time in Scripture that we hear the covenant formula that is repeated many times later: "I will be their God and they shall be my people."

A land, a posterity, a blessing. "But what has all that to do with mission?" For that let us turn now from the promise to the fulfillment.

*God has accepted Abraham as righteous, has "justified him by faith." No greater blessing is conceivable. It is the foundation blessing of the covenant.*

## The Fulfillment

The whole question of the fulfillment of Old Testament prophecy is a difficult one in which there is often misunderstanding and not a little disagreement. Of particular importance is the principle, with which I think all of us will agree, that the New Testament writers themselves understood Old Testament prophecy to have not a *single* but usually a *triple* fulfillment—past, present, and future. The past fulfillment was an immediate or historical fulfillment in the life of the nation of Israel. The present is an intermediate or gospel fulfillment in Christ and his church. The future will be an ultimate or eschatological fulfillment in the new heaven and the new earth.

**God's promise to Abraham received an immediate historical fulfillment in his physical descendants, the people of Israel.**

God's promise to Abraham of a numerous, indeed of an innumerable, posterity was confirmed to his son Isaac (26:4, "as the stars of heaven") and his grandson Jacob (32:12, "as the sand of the sea"). Gradually the promise began to come literally true. Perhaps we could pick out some of the stages in this development.

The first concerns the years of slavery in Egypt, of which it is written, "The descendants of Israel were fruitful and increased greatly; they multiplied and grew exceedingly strong; so that the land was filled with them" (Exodus 1:7; cf. Acts 7:17). The next stage I will mention came several hundred years later when King Solomon called Israel "a great people that cannot be numbered or counted for multitude" (1 Kings 3:8). A third stage was

some three hundred fifty years after Solomon; Jeremiah warned Israel of impending judgment and captivity, and then added this divine promise of restoration: "As the host of heaven cannot be numbered and the sands of the sea cannot be measured so I will multiply the descendants of David my servant" (Jeremiah 33:22).

So much for Abraham's posterity; what about the land? Again we note with worship and gratitude God's faithfulness to his promise. For it was in remembrance of his promise to Abraham, Isaac and Jacob that he first rescued his people from their Egyptian slavery and gave them the territory that came on that account to be called "the promised land" (Exodus 2:24; 3:6; 32:13), and then restored them to it some seven hundred years later after their captivity in Babylon. Nevertheless, neither Abraham nor his physical descendants fully inherited the land. As Hebrews 11 puts it, they "died in faith *not* having received what was promised." Instead, as "strangers and exiles on the earth" they "looked forward to the city which has foundations, whose builder and maker is God" (see Hebrews 11:8–16, 39–40).

God kept his promises about the posterity and the land, at least in part. Now what about the blessing? Well, at Sinai God confirmed and clarified his covenant with Abraham and pledged himself to be Israel's God (for example, Exodus 19:3–6). And throughout the rest of the Old Testament, God continued to bless the obedient while the disobedient fell under his judgment.

Perhaps the most dramatic example comes at the beginning of Hosea's prophecy, in which Hosea is told to give his three children names that describe God's awful and progressive judgment on Israel. His firstborn (a boy) he called "Jezreel," meaning "God will scatter." Next came a daughter, "Lo-ruhamah," meaning "not pitied," for God said he would no longer pity or forgive his people. Lastly he had another son, "Lo-ammi," meaning

*New Testament writers themselves understood Old Testament prophecy to have not a single but usually a triple fulfillment—past, present and future.*

"not my people," for God said they were not now his people. What terrible names for the chosen people of God! They sound like a devastating contradiction of God's eternal promise to Abraham.

But God does not stop there. For beyond the coming judgment there would be a restoration, which is described in words that once more echo the promise to Abraham: "Yet the number of the people of Israel shall be like thesand of the sea, which can be neither measured

Abraham, the man of faith, believed God for an Offspring, but he also believed God for the Far Horizons—all families. He accepted God's covenant blessing and acted in confidence that this blessing should be extended to all families of the earth. This is why Paul could say in Galatians 3:8 that Abraham had the gospel preached to him beforehand when God told him his offspring would bless all the nations.

*Mary Filidis, YWAM*

nor numbered" (Hosea 1:10). And then the judgments implicit in the names of Hosea's children would be reversed. There would be a gathering instead of a scattering ("Jezreel" is ambiguous and can imply either), "not pitied" would be "pitied", and "not my people" would become "sons of the living God" (1:10–2:1).

The wonderful thing is that the apostles Paul and Peter both quote these verses from Hosea. They see their fulfillment not just in a further multiplication of Israel but in the inclusion of the Gentiles in the community of Jesus: "Once you were no people but now you are God's people; once you had not received mercy but now you have received mercy" (1 Peter 2:9–10; cf. Romans 9:25–26).

This New Testament perspective is essential as we read the Old Testament prophecies. For what we miss in the Old Testament is any clear explanation of just *how* God's promised blessing would overflow from Abraham and his descendants to "all families of the earth." Although Israel is described as "a light to lighten the nations" and has a mission to "bring forth justice to the nations" (Isaiah 42:1–4, 6; 49:6), we do not actually see this happening. It is only in the Lord Jesus himself that these prophecies are fulfilled, for only in his day are the nations actually included in the redeemed community. To this we now turn.

**God's promise to Abraham receives an intermediate or gospel fulfillment in Christ and his church.**

Almost the first word of the whole New Testament is the word Abraham. For Matthew's Gospel begins, "The book of the genealogy of Jesus Christ, the son of David,

*This New Testament perspective is essential as we read the Old Testament prophecies for any clear explanation of how God's promised blessing would overflow from Abraham and his descendants to "all families of the earth."*

the son of Abraham. Abraham was the father of Isaac..." So it is right back to Abraham that Matthew traces the beginning not just of the genealogy but of the gospel of Jesus Christ. He knows that what he is recording is the fulfillment of God's ancient promises to Abraham made some two thousand years previously. (See also Luke 1:45–55, 67–75.)

Yet from the start Matthew recognizes that it isn't just *physical* descent from Abraham that qualifies people to inherit the promises, but a kind of *spiritual* descent, namely, repentance and faith in the coming Messiah. This was John the Baptist's message to crowds who flocked to hear him: "Do not presume to say to yourselves, 'We have Abraham as our father,' for I tell you God is able from these stones to raise up children to Abraham" (Matthew 3:9; Luke 3:8; cf. John 8:33–40). The implications of his words would have shocked his hearers, since "it was the current belief that no descendant of Abraham could be lost."[1]

And God has raised up children to Abraham, if not from stones, then from an equally unlikely source, namely, the Gentiles! So Matthew, although the most Jewish of all four Gospel writers, later records Jesus as having said, "I tell you, many will come from east and west and sit at table with Abraham, Isaac, and Jacob in the kingdom of heaven, while the sons of the kingdom will be thrown into the outer darkness" (8:11–12; cf. Luke 13:28–29).

It is hard for us to grasp how shocking, how completely topsy-turvy, these words would have sounded to the Jewish hearers of John the Baptist and Jesus. *They* were the descendants of Abraham, so *they* had a title to the promises that God made to Abraham. Who then were these outsiders who were to share in the promises, even apparently usurp them, while they themselves would be disqualified? They were indignant. They had quite forgotten that part of God's covenant with Abraham promised an overspill of blessing to *all* the nations of the earth. Now the Jews had to learn that it was in relation to Jesus the Messiah, who was himself seed of Abraham, that all the nations would be blessed.

The apostle Peter seems at least to have begun to grasp this in his second sermon, just after Pentecost. In it he addressed a Jewish crowd with the words, "You are the sons...of the covenant which God gave to your fathers, saying to Abraham, 'And in your posterity shall all the families of the earth be blessed.' God, having raised up his servant [Jesus], sent him to you first, to bless you in turning every one of you from your wickedness" (Acts 3:25–26). It is a very notable statement because he interprets the blessing in the moral terms of repentance and righteousness and because, if Jesus was sent "first" to the Jews, he was presumably sent next to the Gentiles, whose "families of the earth" had been "far off" (cf. Acts 2:39) but were now to share in the blessing.

Negatively, Paul declares with great boldness, "Not all who are descended from Israel belong to Israel, and not all are children of Abraham because they are his descendants" (Romans 9:6–7).

> **T**o Paul, God's eternal but secret purpose was revealed; to make Jews and Gentiles partakers of the promise through the gospel.

Who then are the true descendants of Abraham, the true beneficiaries of God's promises to him? Paul does not leave us in any doubt. They are believers in Christ, of whatever race. In Romans 4 he points out that Abraham not only received justification by faith but also received this blessing *before he had been circumcised*. Therefore Abraham is the father of all those who, whether circumcised or uncircumcised (that is, Jews or Gentiles), "follow the example of [his] faith" (Romans 4:9–12). If we "share the faith of Abraham," then "he is the father of us all, as it is written, 'I have made you the father of many nations'" (vv. 16–17). Thus neither physical descent from Abraham nor physical circumcision as a Jew makes a person a true child of Abraham, but rather faith. Abraham's real descendants are believers in Jesus Christ, whether racially they happen to be Jews or Gentiles.

What then is the "land" that Abraham's descendants inherit? The letter to the Hebrews refers to a "rest" which God's people enter now by faith (Hebrews 4:3). And in a most remarkable expression Paul refers to "the promise to Abraham and his descendants, that they should *inherit the world*" (Romans 4:13). One can only assume he means the same thing as when to the Corinthians he writes that in Christ "all things are yours, whether Paul or Apollos or Cephas or the world or life or death or the present or the future, all are yours" (1 Corinthians 3:21–23). Christians, by God's wonderful grace, are joint heirs with Christ of the universe.

> **T**he Apostle Peter seems to grasp this in his second sermon. If Jesus was sent "first" to the Jews, he was presumably sent next to the Gentiles, whose "families of the earth" had been "far off" but were now to share in the blessing.

It was given to the apostle Paul, however, to bring this wonderful theme to its full development. For he was called and appointed to be the apostle to the Gentiles, and to him was revealed God's eternal but hitherto secret purpose, to make Jews and Gentiles "fellow heirs, members of the same body, and partakers of the promise in Christ Jesus through the gospel" (Ephesians 3:6).

Somewhat similar teaching, both about the nature of the promised blessing and about its beneficiaries, is given by Paul in Galatians 3. He first repeats how Abraham was justified by faith, and then continues, "So you see that it is men of faith who are the sons of Abraham" and who therefore "are blessed with Abraham who had faith" (vv. 6–9). What then is the blessing with which all the nations were to be blessed (v. 8)? In a word, it is the blessing of salvation. We were under the curse of the law, but Christ has redeemed us from it by becoming

> **What then is the blessing with which all the nations were to be blessed? In a word, it is the blessing of salvation.**

a curse in our place, in order "that in Christ Jesus the blessing of Abraham might come upon the Gentiles, that we might receive the promise of the Spirit through faith" (vv. 10–14). Christ bore our curse that we might inherit Abraham's blessing, the blessing of justification (v. 8) and of the indwelling Holy Spirit (v. 14). Paul sums it up in the last verse of the chapter (v. 29): "If you are Christ's, then you are Abraham's offspring, heirs according to promise."

But we have not quite finished yet. There is a third stage of fulfillment still to come.

**God's promise to Abraham will receive an ultimate or eschatological fulfillment in the final destiny of all the redeemed.**

In the book of Revelation there is one more reference to God's promise to Abraham (7:9 ff.). John sees in a vision "a great multitude which no man could number." It is an international throng, drawn "from every nation, from all tribes and peoples and tongues." And they are "standing before the throne," the symbol of God's kingly reign. That is, his kingdom has finally come, and they are enjoying all the blessings of his gracious rule. He shelters them with his presence. Their wilderness days of hunger, thirst, and scorching heat are over. They have entered the promised land at last, described now not as "a land flowing with milk and honey" but as a land irrigated from "springs of living water" that never dry up. But how did they come to inherit these blessings? Partly because they have "come out of great tribulation" (evidently a reference to the Christian life with all its trials and sufferings), but mostly because "they have washed their robes and made them white in the blood of the Lamb," that is, they have been cleansed from sin and clothed with righteousness through the merits of the death of Jesus Christ alone. "*Therefore* are they before the throne of God."

Speaking personally, I find it extremely moving to glimpse this final fulfillment in a future eternity of that ancient promise of God to Abraham. All the essential elements of the promise may be detected. For here are the spiritual descendants of Abraham, a "great multitude which no man could number," as countless as the sand on the seashore and as the stars in the night sky. Here too are "all the families of the earth" being blessed, for the numberless multitude is composed of people from every nation. Here also is the promised land, namely, all the rich blessings that flow from God's gracious rule. And here above all is Jesus Christ, the seed of Abraham, who shed his blood for our redemption and who bestows his blessings on all those who call on him to be saved.

## Conclusion

Let me try to summarize what we learn about God from his promise to Abraham and its fulfillment.

*First, he is the God of history.* History is not a random flow of events. For God is working out in time a plan that he conceived in a past eternity and will consummate in a future eternity. In this historical process Jesus Christ as the seed of Abraham is the key figure. We belong to his spiritual lineage. If we have received the blessings of justification by faith, acceptance with God, and of the indwelling Spirit, then we are beneficiaries today of a promise made to Abraham four thousand years ago.

*Second, he is the God of the covenant.* That is, God is gracious enough to make promises, and he always keeps the promise he makes. Not that he always fulfills his promises immediately. Abraham and Sarah "died in faith *not* having received what was promised, but having seen it and greeted it from afar" (Hebrews 11:13). That is, although Isaac was born to them in fulfillment of the promise, their seed was not yet numerous, nor was the land given to them, nor were the nations blessed. All God's promises come true, but they are inherited "through faith *and patience* " (Hebrews 6:12). We have to be content to wait for God's time.

*Third, he is the God of blessing.* "I will bless you,"

> **History is not a random flow of events. For God is working out in time a plan that he conceived in a past eternity and will consummate in a future eternity.**

he said to Abraham (Genesis 12:2). "God...sent him [Jesus] to you first, to bless you," echoed Peter (Acts 3:26). God's attitude to his people is positive, constructive, enriching. Judgment is his "strange work"

(Isaiah 28:21). His principal and characteristic work is to bless people with salvation.

*Fourth, he is the God of mercy.* I have always derived much comfort from Revelation 7:9 that the company of the redeemed in heaven will be "a great multitude which no man could number." I do not profess to know how this can be, since Christians have always seemed to be a rather small minority. But Scripture states it for our comfort. Although no biblical Christian can be a universalist (believing that all mankind will ultimately be saved), since Scripture teaches the awful reality and eternity of hell, yet a biblical Christian can—even must—assert that the redeemed will somehow be an international throng so immense as to be countless. For God's promise is going to be fulfilled, and Abraham's seed is going to be as innumerable as the dust of the earth, the stars of the sky, and the sand on the seashore.

*Fifth, he is the God of mission.* The nations are not gathered in automatically. If God has promised to bless "all the families of the earth," he has promised to do so "through Abraham's seed" (Genesis 12:3; 22:18). Now we are Abraham's seed by faith, and the earth's families will be blessed only if we go to them with the gospel. That is God's plain purpose.

I pray that these words, "all the families of the earth," may be written on our hearts. It is this expression more than any other that reveals the living God of the Bible to be a missionary God. It is this expression too that condemns all our petty parochialism and narrow nationalism, our racial pride (whether white or black), our condescending paternalism and arrogant imperialism. How dare we adopt a hostile or scornful or even indifferent attitude to any person of another color or culture if our God is the God of "all the families of the earth"? We need to become global Christians with a global vision, for we have a global God.

> **I** pray that these words, "all the families of the earth," may be written on our hearts. It is this expression more than any other that reveals the living God of the Bible to be a missionary God.

So may God help us never to forget his four-thousand-year-old promise to Abraham: "By you and your descendants *all* the nations of the earth shall be blessed."

## End Notes

[1] J. Jeremias, *Jesus' Promise to the Nations*, SCM Press, 1958, p. 48.

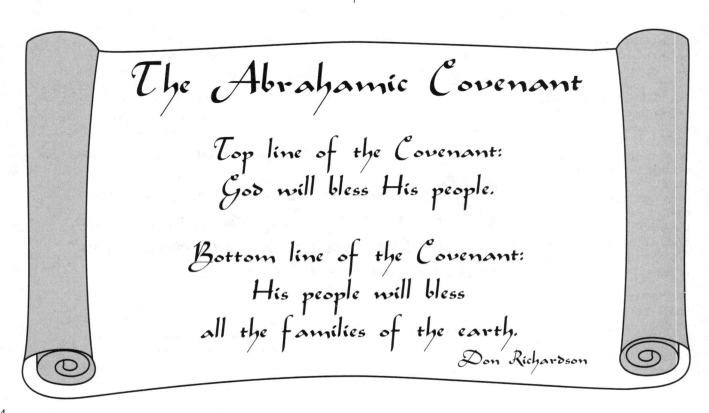

The Abrahamic Covenant

Top line of the Covenant:
God will bless His people.

Bottom line of the Covenant:
His people will bless
all the families of the earth.

Don Richardson

# A Mind for Missions: The Old Testament Scriptures

*Paul Borthwick*

Paul Borthwick serves on the staff of Development Associates International, a training group dedicated to the character and ministry development of leaders in the under-resourced world. A resource person, speaker, and author, he teaches missions at Gordon College and serves as Urbana/Missions Associate with InterVarsity Christian Fellowship.

Our God is a missionary God. He demonstrated this in His creation and in His pursuit of man after the Fall.

## Abraham

As a result of Adam's sin, human civilization began outside of a fellowship with God. Humanity populated the earth, fulfilling the mandate found in Genesis 1:28, but without God's intended perfection. So in time God destroyed the earth because of man's wickedness (Genesis 6:5–7), but He redeemed Noah and his family because of their righteousness (Genesis 7:1). Later, confusion reigned at the Tower of Babel (Genesis 11).

Yet in the midst of this profusion of sin, and out of the increased distance that was building between God and man, God called Abram (Genesis 12:1–3). God made a covenant with Abram, promising him that he would be the agent of God's redemption to all the earth. Through Abram God promised that "all peoples on earth will be blessed" (Genesis 12:3).

God's call to Abraham is repeated in Genesis 17:1–7, where God establishes the "everlasting covenant" with Abraham and his descendants. Through Abraham and his descendants, God again took the initiative to bring His blessing and redemption to all the earth.

## The Law

God wanted to bring His message of blessing and redemption to all the earth through Abraham's physical descendants, the people of Israel. But their sinfulness required the establishment of the Law.

Even in the Law, which is usually considered to be a revelation specifically for the people of Israel, God demonstrates His love for all who are not redeemed. At the outset of the Ten Commandments, God establishes that there is one God in all the earth: "You shall have no other gods before Me" (Exodus 20:3). The people of Israel were called to be witnesses of this one true God: "Israel wasn't great because of the number of people or the wars it won or the cities it built—Israel was great because God called the nation to demonstrate His character and love to the nations around it."[1] Thus the righteousness of the Law was intended to set Israel apart (see Leviticus 20:22–26; Deuteronomy 7:6–8; 14:2; 28:1). Later God made it plain that Israel's selection was to lead others to "acknowledge the Lord" (Isaiah 19:21), but the initial call of the mission was that one nation would know Him.

> *Israel wasn't great because of the number of people or the wars it won or the cities it built—Israel was great because God called the nation to demonstrate His character and love to the nations around it.*

In the Law, God also actively reminds the Israelites to be concerned and compassionate toward the "aliens" and "strangers" because they themselves had been aliens in Egypt when God redeemed them (see Exodus 22:21, Leviticus 19:33–34; Deuteronomy 10:17–19).

The Law, then, witnesses to the fact that the descendants of Abraham—through whom all the nations of the earth were to be blessed—were to be set apart. They were to live out the righteousness of the one true God, whose glory they were to declare in the whole earth (see Numbers 14:21; Deuteronomy 28:10).

## The Prophets

When the people of Israel rebelled against God, He raised up prophets as "missionaries, echoing the call of God."[2] The earlier prophets—like Elijah and Elisha—stood before rebellious and pagan kings, exhorted them to worship the one true God, and handed down God's judgment on those who chose to rebel. The later prophets spoke and wrote as God's voice, calling the people back into fellowship with Him. Their purpose in restoring the people of Israel to fellowship with God was so that the Israelites could be God's witnesses in the world.

Borthwick, Paul (1987). *A Mind for Missions* (pp. 25–31; 37–38). Colorado Springs, Colorado: Navpress.

William Dyrness clarifies the prophets' purpose:

> By the time we come to the prophets it is clear that the calling of Israel as a nation is for the sake of the whole world...Israel then is to be preserved (cf. Esther) so that she can mediate God's promises for his creation as a whole. They are to exhibit a people, institutions, and a land which will reflect God's glory so that this can one day be communicated to the whole earth and to all peoples.[3]

With God's redemptive purpose clearly in mind, the prophets spoke and wrote. Isaiah spoke with the vision that "the whole earth is full of His glory" (Isaiah 6:3) and predicted, like Habakkuk in Habakkuk 2:14, that the day would come when "the earth will be full of the knowledge of the LORD as the waters cover the sea" (Isaiah 11:9). Through Isaiah, God promised the people of Israel that they would be "a covenant for the people and a light for the Gentiles" (Isaiah 42:6, see also 60:3). In Isaiah 52:10 we plainly see God's worldwide purpose: "The LORD will lay bare His holy arm in the sight of all the nations, and all the ends of the earth will see the salvation of our God" (see also Isaiah 45:22–23).

*Israel was to exhibit a people, institutions, and a land which will reflect God's glory so that this can one day be communicated to the whole earth and to all peoples.*

While Isaiah is the most outspoken prophet regarding God's commission to the people of Israel to be a "light of revelation to the Gentiles," others like Habakkuk and Micah echo the same message. In Micah 5:4–5, for example, we read, "And they will live securely, for then His greatness will reach to the ends of the earth. And He will be their peace."

## The Psalms

The writers of the Psalms likewise reflect a worldwide understanding of God's purposes. When referring to God at work in the world, their overriding theme was that God's name should be declared in all the earth. For example, in Psalm 33:8 we see that all the earth is urged to worship God; in Psalm 67:1–2 God is asked to work in such a way that His power and His name would be known throughout the earth; in Psalm 96:3 God's worshipers are exhorted to be witnesses to God's glory throughout the whole earth; and in Psalm 145:8–13 the psalmist testifies that God's people will themselves speak of God in such a way that "all men may know of your mighty acts" (verse 12).

The declaration of God's name throughout the earth is ultimately summed up in Psalm 2:8, which is a prophecy of God's work through Jesus Christ: "Ask of Me, and I will make the nations Your inheritance, the ends of the earth Your possession."

## Missionaries

The Old Testament's "universal motif" is demonstrated not only through the Scriptures themselves but also through the people presented in Scripture. Elisha's work, for example, demonstrated God's redemption to Gentiles like the Shunammite woman. (2 Kings 4:8 ff.) and Naaman the Syrian (2 Kings 5). Esther served as God's missionary to her Gentile captors, and Joseph was God's agent of redemption in Egypt (Genesis 50:20). The fact that God is a missionary God, however, is nowhere more evident in the Old Testament than in the lives of Daniel and Jonah, two "witnesses" to pagan kingdoms.

As God's messenger, Daniel's ministry brought him in touch with four pagan kings—Nebuchadnezzar, Belshazzar, Cyrus, and Darius. Daniel's witness was consistent and convicting, to the point that Nebuchadnezzar of Babylon was seemingly converted (Daniel 4:34–37). Daniel himself saw the universal aspect of God's dominion in a vision where "one like a son of man" was given "authority, glory and sovereign power; all peoples, nations and men of every language worshiped him" (Daniel 7:13–14). Perhaps the greatest testimony to Daniel's work as a missionary in a pagan land occurred after God's hand saved him from the lions. When King Darius saw what Daniel's God had done, he ordered "all the peoples, nations and men of every language throughout the land" to "fear and reverence the God of Daniel" (Daniel 6:25–27). In these instances, God worked to bring His redemption to non-Israelites through one Israelite who was being a "light to the nations" as God intended.

## Summary

Our God is a missionary God. He prepared His people Israel, as children of Abraham, to be a blessing to all nations. In the Old Testament, God's people made choices that kept them from fulfilling His perfect plan, but they could not stop His purposes from being plainly stated. God was in the business of redemption, and He would accomplish His purposes through His Messiah. As William Dyrness observes, "The Old Testament prepares a universal message for what will become in the New Testament a universal mission."[4]

## The Basis of Mission Is to Reveal the Glory of God

Scripture teaches that there is one all-powerful, all-glorious, perfect, and holy God who desires that all of

*I*n the Old Testament, God's people made choices that kept them from fulfilling His perfect plan, but they could not stop His purposes from being plainly stated.

His creation experience His glory. But through Adam's sin, His creation has fallen, and now the glorious God seeks our redemption. This means that the work of mission is God's. He will work to accomplish His purposes (see Isaiah 55:11 and Daniel 4:35). He chooses to use us but is not dependent on us (see Job 38:4; Isaiah 66:1–2; and Luke 17:10). God is not in a rush; He has not lost control of the world; His ultimate purposes are not being thwarted; He is still all-powerful, all-glorious, and still seeks to bring humanity back to Himself so that we might experience His glory (see 2 Corinthians 4:6).

The great missionary to the North American Indians, David Brainerd, knew this glorious God of the Bible. His vision of God motivated his vision for missions: "Brainerd prays for his friends and his enemies. But this act of prayer rises out of a higher vision. God must be known, and not simply by name. God's name was well-known, even in the wilds of New Jersey. God must be known as GOD! To Brainerd that was the great thing. Even Christ's kingdom serves that end. Let God be known! To know God is the great essential. And to make Him known was Brainerd's task."[5]

A. W. Tozer, a great leader and writer from the Christian and Missionary Alliance, was fully committed to a missions vision but feared that through our efforts to exhort action in missions we would diminish the worship of the Almighty. He wrote, "We commonly represent God as a busy, eager, somewhat frustrated Father hurrying about seeking help to carry out His benevolent plan to bring peace and salvation to the world...Too many missionary appeals are based upon this fancied frustration of Almighty God."[6] Tozer is saying, in effect, "Don't get interested in missions out of some delusion that God is in trouble. He is still the Creator of the ends of the earth, the great Redeemer, the Almighty."

Serious study of Scripture helps keep our perspective straight. Scripture reveals that the one true God calls us into missions to declare His glory. Therefore, knowing Him is our top priority, and making Him known is then a natural result. ▣

*G*od must be known, and not simply by name. God must be known as GOD! To Brainerd that was the great thing.

## End Notes

1   Sam Wilson and Gordon Aeschliman, *The Hidden Half* (Monrovia, California: MARC, 1984), page 38.

2   William Dyrness, *Let the Earth Rejoice* (Westchester, Illinois: Crossway Books, 1983), page 95.

3   Dyrness, pages 115–116.

4   Dyrness, page 117.

5   Tom Wells, *A Vision for Missions* (Carlisle, Pennsylvania: Banner of Truth, 1985) page 123.

6   Tozer, as quoted by Wells, page 35.

**Joseph became a blessing not just to Egypt and his own Hebrew family.** "And all the countries came to Egypt to buy grain from Joseph because the famine was severe in all the world."       *Genesis 41:57 NIV*

**The Exodus revealed the Lord.** "I will gain glory for myself through Pharaoh and all his army, and **the Egyptians will know that I am the Lord.**"       *Exodus 14:4 NIV*

**The conquest of Canaan would reveal Him to all.** "He did this **so that all the peoples of the earth might know** that the hand of the Lord is powerful and so that you might always fear the Lord."       *Joshua 4:24 NIV*

**God judged His people because of the Nations.** "You have been more unruly than the nations around you... You have not even conformed to the standards of the nations around you. Therefore...I will inflict punishment on you **in the sight of the nations.**"       *Ezekiel 5:7–8 NIV*

# Israel - The Strategic Land Bridge

EUROPE

ASIA

ISRAEL
Jerusalem

DESERT

AFRICA

"This is Jerusalem:
I have set her in the midst of
the nations and the countries
all around her."    Ezekiel 5:5

PERS_1P

Global Mapping International (719) 531-3599, 8/99

## A Significant Location

As small as Israel was, it was set in a strategic geographic corridor. Because of the deserts to the east, all the viable trading routes passed through its territory. That significantly increased the interaction of Israel with the surrounding peoples. Traders were, in effect, the bearers of news throughout the ancient world, so the fortunes of Israel, for good or for ill, would quickly be heralded abroad.

Major political powers contended for possession of Israel's strategic location as well. For more than 1,000 years, all those who sought to build empires in that area had to conquer and subdue this land. Situated as it was "in the midst of the nations," it gave God's nation continual access to many different peoples.

The dynamic for Israel's witness included an "attractive" force—living in holiness and blessing would attract people to the Lord. It also involved an "expansive" force—their activities in proclaiming and interacting with various other peoples would take the message to those who had not heard.

Their opportunities were uncountable. Their message was simple and attractive. They could have easily fulfilled their covenant obligation and won innumerable individuals and nations. They could have thankfully responded to God's great blessings by giving them freely to other nations.

However, on most counts, as God's nation, they failed to take His blessings to the Gentiles, as He had commanded.

# A Man for All Peoples
*Don Richardson*

Don Richardson pioneered work among the Sawi Tribe of Irian Jaya for 15 years. Author of Peace Child, Lords of the Earth, Eternity in their Hearts, and Secrets of the Koran, Richardson is now Minister-at-Large for World Team. He speaks frequently for conferences and classes as well as doing seminars on the Biblical basis for God's work in the world.

Millions of Christians know, of course, that Jesus, at the end of His ministry, commanded His disciples to "go and make disciples of all [peoples]" (Matthew 28:19). We respectfully honor this last and most incredible command He gave with an august title—the Great Commission. And yet millions of us deep down in our hearts secretly believe, if our deeds are an accurate barometer of our beliefs (and Scripture says they are), that Jesus really uttered that awesome command without giving His disciples ample warning.

Read cursorily through the four Gospels and the Great Commission looks like a sort of after-thought paper-clipped onto the end of the main body of Jesus' teachings. It is almost as if our Lord, after divulging everything that was really close to His heart, snapped His fingers and said, "Oh yes, by the way, men, there's one more thing. I want you all to proclaim this message to everyone in the world, regardless of his language and culture. That is, of course, if you have the time and feel disposed."

Did Jesus hit His disciples with the Great Commission cold turkey? Did He just spring it on them at the last minute without fair warning and then slip away to heaven before they had a chance to interact with Him about its feasibility? Did He fail to provide reasonable demonstration on ways to fulfill it?

**Consider how compassionately Jesus exploited encounters with Gentiles and Samaritans to help His disciples think in cross-cultural terms.**

How often we Christians read the four Gospels without discerning the abundant evidence God has provided for an entirely opposite conclusion! Consider, for example, how compassionately Jesus exploited the following encounters with Gentiles and Samaritans to help His disciples think in cross-cultural terms.

## A Roman Centurion

On one occasion (Matt. 8:5–13) a Roman centurion, a Gentile, approached Jesus with a request on behalf of his paralyzed servant. Jews, on this occasion, urged Jesus to comply. "This man deserves to have you do this, because he loves our nation and has built our synagogue," they explained (Luke 7:4–5).

In fact, walls and pillars of a synagogue built probably by that very centurion still stand two thousand years later near the north shore of the Sea of Galilee! But notice the implication of the Jews' reasoning. They were saying, in effect, that if the centurion had not thus helped them, neither should Jesus help the centurion or his pitifully paralyzed servant! How clannish of them! Little wonder Jesus could not help sighing occasionally, "O unbelieving and perverse generation…how long shall I stay with you? How long shall I put up with you?" (Matthew 17:17).

Jesus responded to the centurion, "I will go and heal him." At that moment the centurion said something quite unexpected: "'Lord, I do not deserve to have you come under my roof. But just say the word, and my servant will be healed. For I myself am a man under authority, with soldiers under me….' When Jesus heard this, he was astonished," wrote Matthew. What was so astonishing? Simply this: the centurion's military experience had taught him something about authority. As water always flows downhill, so also authority always flows down an echelon (a chain of command). Whoever submits to authority from a higher level of an echelon is privileged also to wield authority over lower levels. Jesus, the centurion noticed, walked in perfect submission to God. Therefore Jesus must have perfect authority over everything below Him on the greatest echelon of all—the cosmos! *Ergo!* Jesus must possess an infallible ability to command the mere matter of the sick servant's body to adapt itself to a state of health!

"I tell you the truth," Jesus exclaimed, "I have not found anyone in Israel with such great faith!" As in many other discourses, Jesus exploited the occasion to teach His disciples that Gentiles have just as great a potential for faith as Jews! And they make just as valid objects for the grace of God, too!

Richardson, D. (1992) "A Man for All Peoples" from *Eternity in Their Hearts*, 1981, Regal Books, Ventura, Calif.

Determined to maximize the point, Jesus went on to say, "I say to you that many will come from the east and the west [Luke, a Gentile writer, adds in his parallel account, "and from the north and the south"] and will take their places at the feast with Abraham, Isaac and Jacob in the kingdom of heaven. But the subjects of the kingdom [this could only mean the Jews as God's chosen people] will be thrown outside, into the darkness, where there will be weeping and gnashing of teeth" (Matthew 8:7–12; Luke 13:28–29).

Feasts are usually called to celebrate. What would you guess that future feast attended by Abraham and a host of Gentile guests will celebrate?

Intimations of the Great Commission to follow could hardly have been clearer! Wait, there is still much more!

## A Canaanite Woman

Still later, a Canaanite woman from the region of Tyre and Sidon begged Jesus' mercy on behalf of her demon-possessed daughter. Jesus at first feigned indifference. His disciples, glad no doubt to see their Messiah turn a cold shoulder to a bothersome Gentile, concurred at once with what they thought were His true feelings. "Send her away," they argued, "for she keeps crying out after us" (see Matthew 15:21–28).

Little did they know that Jesus was setting them up. "I was sent only to the lost sheep of Israel," He said to the woman. Having already manifested an apparent insensitivity toward the woman, Jesus now manifests an apparent inconsistency also. He has already healed many Gentiles. On what basis does He now reject this one's plea? One can imagine the disciples nodding grimly. Still they did not suspect. Undissuaded, the Canaanite woman actually knelt at Jesus' feet, pleading, "Lord, help me!"

"It is not right to take the children's bread"— then He added the crusher—"and toss it to their dogs!" "Dogs" was a standard epithet Jews reserved for Gentiles, especially Gentiles who tried to intrude upon Jewish religious privacy and privilege. In other words, Jesus now complements His earlier "insensitivity" and "inconsistency" with even worse "cruelty."

Was this really the Savior of the world talking? No doubt His disciples thought His reference quite appropriate for the occasion. But just when their chests were swollen to the full with pride of race, the Canaanite woman must have caught a twinkle in Jesus' eye and realized the truth!

"Yes, Lord," she replied ever so humbly, not to mention subtly, "but even the dogs eat the crumbs that fall from their master's table!" (Matthew 15:21–27; see also Mark 7:26–30).

"Woman, you have great faith!" Jesus glowed. "Your request is granted!" No, He was not being fickle! This was what He intended to do all along. Immediately preceding this event, Jesus had taught His disciples about the difference between real versus figurative uncleanness. This was His way of driving the point home.

"And her daughter was healed from that very hour" Matthew records (v. 28).

*All men—not merely in spite of Jesus' humiliation, but because of it—would be drawn to Him as God's anointed deliverer.*

## A Samaritan Village

When on a later occasion Jesus and His band approached a certain Samaritan village, the Samaritans refused to welcome Him. James and John, two disciples whom Jesus nicknamed "sons of thunder" for their fiery tempers, were incensed. "Lord," they exclaimed indignantly (stamping their feet), "do you want us to call fire down from heaven to destroy them?"

Jesus turned and rebuked James and John. Some ancient manuscripts add that He said, "You do not know what kind of spirit you are of, for the Son of Man did not come to destroy men's lives, but to save them" (Luke 9:51–55, including footnote).

With those words, Jesus identified Himself as a Savior for Samaritans!

## Greeks at Jerusalem

Later on some Greeks came to a feast at Jerusalem and sought audience with Jesus. Philip and Andrew, two of Jesus' disciples, relayed the request to Jesus who, as usual, exploited the occasion to get another wedge in for the "all-peoples perspective": "But I, when I am lifted up from the earth, will draw all men to myself" (John 12:32). This prophecy foreshadowed the manner of Jesus' death—crucifixion! But it also foretold the effect! All men—not merely in spite of Jesus' humiliation, but because of it—would be drawn to Him as God's anointed deliverer. On the surface this statement could be interpreted to mean that everyone in the world will become a Christian. Since we know that this is quite unlikely, the statement probably means instead that some of all kinds of men will be drawn to Jesus when they learn that His death atoned for their sins. And that is exactly what the Abrahamic Covenant promised—not that all people would be blessed, but that all peoples would be represented in the blessing. Jesus' disciples thus gained still another fair warning of the Great Commission soon to follow!

## On the Road to Emmaus

Just as the disciples still did not believe Jesus' intimations of Gentile evangelism, so also they never really believed Him when He said He would rise from

*That is exactly what the Abrahamic Covenant promised—not that all people would be blessed, but that all peoples would be represented in the blessing.*

the dead. But He surprised them on both counts! Three days after His entombment He rose again! And one of His first encounters after resurrection began in incognito fashion with two of His disciples on a road leading to Emmaus (see Luke 24:13–49). During the opening exchange, the two disciples, still not recognizing Jesus, complained, "We had hoped that [Jesus] was the one who was going to redeem Israel" (v. 21); they did not add, "and make Israel a blessing to all peoples." A blind spot in their hearts still effectively obscured that part of the Abrahamic Covenant.

"How foolish you are," Jesus responded, "and how slow of heart to believe all that the prophets have spoken! Did not the Christ have to suffer these things and then enter his glory?" (vv. 25–26).

Then, beginning with the five "books of Moses and all the Prophets, he explained to them what was said in all the Scriptures concerning Himself." He had covered much of that ground before, but He went over it again—patiently (v. 27). And this time the two disciples' hearts burned within them as He opened the Scriptures (see v. 32). Was a wider perspective at last winning its way into their hearts?

*It was not an unfair command. The Old Testament foreshadowed it. Jesus' daily teaching anticipated it. Now He added the promise of His own authority bequeathed and His own presence in company—if they obeyed!*

Later they recognized Jesus, but at the same moment He vanished from their sight! They retraced their steps at once to Jerusalem, found the Eleven (as the disciples were called for a while after Judas' defection) and recounted their experience. But before they finished talking, Jesus Himself appeared among them, and the Eleven experienced the end of the story for themselves!

As unerringly as a swallow returning to its nest, Jesus returned to the Scriptures and their central theme:

"Then he opened their minds so they could understand the Scriptures. He told them, 'This is what is written: The Christ will suffer and rise from the dead on the third day, and repentance and forgiveness of sins will be preached in his name to all nations [*i.e., ethne*—peoples], beginning at Jerusalem. You are witnesses of these things'" (Luke 24:45–48).

## Go and Make Disciples

Notice, however, that He still did not command them to go. That would come a few days later, on a mountain in Galilee where—as far as the disciples were concerned—it all started. And here is the working of the command that the Abrahamic Covenant had already foreshadowed for 2,000 years, and which Jesus for three long years had been preparing His disciples to receive: "All authority in heaven and earth has been given to me. Therefore go and make disciples of all nations, baptizing them in the name of the Father and of the Son and of the Holy Spirit, and teaching them to obey [note the limitation that follows] everything I have commanded you. And surely I will be with you always, to the very end of the age" (Matthew 28:18–20).

It was not an unfair command. The Old Testament foreshadowed it. Jesus' daily teaching anticipated it. His frequent prejudice-free ministry among both Samaritans and Gentiles had given the disciples a real-life demonstration of how to carry it out. Now He added the promise of His own authority bequeathed and His own presence in company—if they obeyed!

Still later, moments before He ascended back into heaven from the Mount of Olives (near Bethany), He added a further promise: "You will receive power when the Holy Spirit comes on you; and you will be my witnesses..." Then followed Jesus' famous formula for the exocentric progression of the gospel: "...in Jerusalem, and in all Judea and Samaria, and to the ends of the earth" (Acts 1:8).

It was Jesus' last command. Without another word, and without waiting for any discussion of the proposal, He ascended into heaven to await His followers' complete obedience to it!

## Clannish Jews into Cross-Cultural Apostles?

Jesus knew, of course, that there was no hope of rescuing the majority of Jews in His time from blind self-centeredness any more than there is ever much hope of rescuing the majority of any people from the same plight! Throughout history, the majority of Jews focused so exclusively upon the top line of the Abrahamic Covenant that the bottom line became virtually invisible to them. It is probably not an exaggeration to describe their minds as hermetically sealed against any serious consideration of "the bottom line." That is why many Jews were determined to exploit Jesus' miraculous powers exclusively for their own benefit. But His covenant-based, all-peoples perspective clashed constantly with their own "our people" mentality. Even one of His disciples, as we have seen, betrayed Him in the context of this issue! The only hope, then, lay with these other eleven. If only Jesus could win them to the all-peoples perspective, the full promise of Abraham, and not just a truncated version, could still be fulfilled.

Question! Could even the Son of Man—without negating human free will—transform eleven men whose thought patterns were programmed from childhood to an extreme *ethnocentrism*?* The question may seem silly. Could not the Son of Man, who is also the omnipotent Son of God, do anything? The answer is yes, but—

human free will implies God's prior decision not to tamper with the metaphysical base of that free will. It also implies man's ability to reject the persuasion God uses to influence that free will while leaving its metaphysical base intact!

Persuasion, not compulsion, is what even He must rely upon! And persuasion, by its very definition, must be resistible! Yet the God who thus renders Himself resistible is so intelligent that He can overrule every consequence of His own self-limitation with ease! Working around and through human resistance as easily as through response, He still achieves His own eternal goals!

> *H*is covenant-based all-peoples perspective clashed constantly with their own "our people" mentality.

Ultimate suspense, then, does not hang upon the eventual success of God's design, for that success is assured. Ultimate suspense hangs rather upon questions like, who among the sons and daughters of men will recognize the day of God's privilege when it dawns around them? And which men and women, among those who discern that privilege, will choose to scorn it as Esau scorned his birthright? And finally, just how will God accomplish His goal when even the men and women who love Him and make His purpose theirs turn out to be spiritually vulnerable, physically weak, and oh so limited in understanding? ◼

## A Vital Understanding

A key verse in understanding God's plan for fulfilling His promise to Abraham is spoken by Jesus in Matthew 24. As He explains the cataclysmic signs that signal His return, He says **"And this gospel of the Kingdom will be preached as a witness to all nations" (v. 14 NIV).** The words "all the nations" are the same as in Matthew 28, when He commands "make disciples of all nations" (v. 19 NIV).

In the Greek, this phrase is *panta ta ethne.* "Ethne" is the root for our English word "ethnic." Jesus is not speaking of the political or geographical nations; He is speaking of all ethnic groups. Thus, when He tells His disciples, **"Nation shall rise against nation,"** (Matthew 24:7 NIV) He means, "Ethnic group shall rise against ethnic group." This is exactly what is happening in the former Yugoslavia, in the Caucasus, in Rwanda—not national wars, but bitter ethnic conflicts.

Matthew 24:14 is a key verse for world evangelization because it continues the covenant promise of blessing for "all peoples of the earth" (Genesis 12:3 NIV). It shows Jesus' authoritative backing to believe that there can be a completion of world evangelization. Most of all, it makes clear our assignment: proclaim the good news to every people, every *ethnos,* until He comes.

---

* Ethnocentrism: Cultural narrow-mindedness. The view that the way we do things in our culture is the only right way of doing things.

# Opening the Door
*Meg Crossman*

> Meg Crossman is Director Emeritus of PathWays Partnership, helping develop and support mobilization materials and classes. She edited a fuller version of this material called PathWays to Global Understanding.

## Paul Finds Surprising Response

The time came for Paul to undertake his journeys in response to God's initial directive at the time of his salvation, "Go! For I will send you far away to the Gentiles" (Acts 22:21 NASB). The church in Antioch sent him out with Barnabas as a partner. He added to his team as he went, incorporating believers from many cultures.

Paul implemented an interesting strategy. He went to major cities in the Mediterranean and spoke in Jewish synagogues. He took his message first to the people who were most equipped to understand the Old Testament prophecies about the Messiah.

Paul discovered that there was interest not only among some of the Jews living in Gentile countries but also among the Gentile "God-fearers." These were those Gentiles who had become disillusioned with the many licentious and idolatrous religions of the nations. Because of its moral superiority and historical grounding, they were attracted to the Jewish religion. They attached themselves to the synagogue in their city. (Historical note: at that time, the Jews may have constituted as much as 10% of the population of the Roman Empire.)

However, they struggled with undergoing circumcision and living by the extensive requirements of Jewish law. These people were naturally delighted with the message that salvation was available through faith in Jesus alone. Many of them became active followers of the Lord.

## Opening the Door

However, while this opened the door to Gentiles to become believers, it became a great stumbling block to the Jewish believers. Jews had always been willing to let Gentiles in—but only if they would become culturally Jewish. Paul was willing to let Gentile Christians keep their "gentileness"—their culture. As the equivalent of an ecclesiastical lawyer, Paul had the knowledge and ability to defend his contention that God did not require Gentiles to become Jews to enter His Kingdom. This controversy raged in the early church. The Council of Jerusalem was convened to take up the matter, as recorded in Acts 15.

This Council provided one of the defining moments in the early church. The implications of its decision resonate to this day. Their momentous conclusion made Christianity a movement that could encompass the peoples of the world rather than a limited Jewish sect.

> **P**aul had the ability to defend his contention that God did not require Gentiles to become Jews to enter His Kingdom.

Called before the leaders in Jerusalem, Paul and Barnabas gave a spirited defense of their ministry throughout the Gentile world. They explained their teaching and detailed its confirmation by signs and wonders. At last both Peter and James, the brother of the Lord, spoke out in favor of their approach. Quoting from Amos regarding God's plan to rebuild the tabernacle of David, James came to a critical resolution. The symbolic rebuilding of God's people had to happen "in order that the *rest of mankind* may seek the Lord, and *all the Gentiles* who are called by My name" (Acts 15:16–17 NASB; italics mine).

> **T**he watershed decision by the Jerusalem Council opened the door for great movements to God among peoples throughout the Roman world.

James determined that God's mercy in sending His Son to Israel was specifically linked to His desire to reach all nations. These apostolic leaders affirmed that faith in Jesus alone could save both Jews and Gentiles. They merely asked Gentile believers to refrain from behavior that would be extremely offensive to Jewish culture, so that Jewish believers would not be troubled by fellowshiping with them.

---

Taken from "The Reluctant Messengers," by Meg Crossman, *Worldwide Perspectives*, Meg Crossman, ed., 1996. Used by permission of William Carey Library, Pasadena, Calif.

The watershed decision by the Jerusalem Council opened the door for great movements to God among peoples throughout the Roman world. Rodney Stark, examining the first centuries of the Christian movement from the point of view of a social scientist, believes it also opened doors for many Jews living outside of Palestine. These were open to a message that did not require the stringent keeping of the law in order to please God. The many guidelines, which could be adhered to in their own country, were nearly impossible to keep in the Gentile urban centers. Stark argues for a significant, continuing influx of such Jews well into the 5th century. (Stark, *The Rise of Christianity: How the Obscure, Marginal Jesus Movement Became the Dominant Religious Force in the Western World in a Few Centuries.* See the chapter entitled, "The Mission to the Jews: Why It Probably Succeeded." Pgs. 49–72. Princeton University Press, Princeton, N.J. 1996.)

## Jewish Culture Honored, Too

Paul later demonstrated that he believed it was appropriate for Jews to be able to keep their culture as well. He personally circumcised Timothy in order to have him join their apostolic team (Acts 16:3). Timothy had a Jewish mother but a Greek father. According to Jewish reckoning, that made him a Jew. For the sake of Jews in that area, Paul showed that it was important to become "as a Jew, that I might win Jews (NASB)" a principle he developed more fully in 1 Cor. 9:19–23. He did not want Timothy's lack of circumcision to be a stumbling block to any Jews who met him.

> *For most of us, this is the reason our culture and our people were able to enter freely through the doorway of grace.*

For most of us, being able to keep our culture intact enabled us to freely enter the doorway of grace. If first-century Gentiles could be welcomed to worship Israel's God, how much more should all cultures be welcomed as believers, regardless of how different they are from us. We should actively support their right to keep God-honoring elements of their culture rather than expecting them to become like us. Having been blessed by God, we can and should extend His blessing and His welcome to all nations. ◼

**Miao:** Ethnic minorities in China's Yunan province alone comprise 13 million people in 27 distinct groups. In that closed Communist country, access to these groups is even more restricted, since Westerners are forbidden to enter the areas where they live. The church in China is beginning to get some vision for reaching them, but it needs training in order to be effective in a tribal culture.

The Miao people live high in the mountainous regions of China but are also found in Vietnam, Thailand, and Laos. Numbering nearly seven and a half million, they are subdivided into tribes who identify themselves by the predominant color in their national costume: Blue, Black, White, Red, and Flowery Miao.

It is unclear if there is any permanent work surviving from the mission outreach among them before the Communist takeover in China. Radio broadcasts are having an impact, and Mandarin Bibles have been taken in, but a living witness is needed. Hmong refugees who have become believers may be especially valuable in reaching them.

*Julie Bosacker, YWAM*

## God's Story May Be Surprising

Through the prism of various authors, we are seeing God's story in a new light. As always, God's ways are simple and yet His ways are infinitely profound. For many of us, these concepts may be new.

Believers know God is at work. Believers understand God wants to win people from all nations. However, it may surprise some to hear that His intentional purposes to reach all nations provides a "Genesis to Revelation" theme of Scripture. That this develops out of the opening verses of Genesis 12 may be unanticipated even for those who know the Bible well.

## God's Story Begins in His Covenant

The covenant God made with Abraham summarizes His intentions throughout history and into eternity. A few of its key components include:

- ▶ God, through Abraham, is making a nation for His good purposes.

- ▶ God will bless Abraham and his descendants in countless ways.

- ▶ God's desire is for His nation to extend blessings to all nations.

- ▶ God's people will find deep fulfillment as they link their lives to His Story.

Throughout the Old Testament, God brings His people again and again to the understanding that this is His relentless purpose and they have a role to play in achieving it.

## WE ARE BLESSED TO BE A BLESSING.

## God Confirms the Covenant Through Jesus

As the ultimate Offspring of Abraham, Jesus laid down His life to *confirm* the keeping of the Covenant Promise. He rises from the dead to *continue* the keeping of it, extending access to all. His last command is that His followers disciple the nations. This tells us:

- ▶ Jesus, in His life and person, is God's premiere blessing.

- ▶ Jesus offers everyone access to God's blessing: entry into the Father's Kingdom.

- ▶ We, as Abraham's descendants through the blessing, are now to offer it to others, even to the ends of the earth.

- ▶ As God's people, we tell His Story and live in His power in order to reach all nations with His blessing.

In the next chapter we will investigate how God's Story operates throughout human history.

# 2 Historical Paths

## Where Do History and God's Story Interact?

In the first chapter, John Stott told us,

> "History is not a random flow of events. For God is working out in time a plan which he conceived in a past eternity and will consummate in a future eternity. In this historical process...we are the beneficiaries today of a promise made to Abraham four thousand years ago." (See pg. 13.)

In what way does God's Story connect to History? How does it intersect with the calamities we see on the evening news? Does the covenant with Abraham still have a connection to our generation and the events swirling around us?

Much of history is obscured in the mist of the past. The light we can shine on it is dimmed by destruction from wars, floods, and fires. Many records were lost, obscured, or damaged. However, with what can be reconstructed, the import and relevance for us is seeing that God's Story actually provides *the reason* that History continues.

## How Is History Studied?

When we study history, we must make choices and establish criteria. We cannot study every single action of every single person in every single culture every day. We choose a "grid" of some kind in order to sort and classify what we want to learn from our study. We must decide which questions to ask about History in order to mine its value.

## Different Stories Can Be Seen in History

What are the questions that would interest students at West Point Military Academy? Perhaps they would ask:

▸ What kind of battles took place and where?

▸ What conditions affected those battles?

▸ Who were the Generals and how did they win or lose?

▸ What kind of strategies did they use and how did they implement them?

Their "grid," or their questions would cause them to study History in a particular way. This could bring out distinctive answers, which they might put to use.

Students of science would ask different set of questions. They might want to know:

▶ How did the study of nature begin?

▶ Who were the people who made important advances in science?

▶ What guidelines did scientists establish for their studies?

▶ What obstacles did they have to overcome?

While the raw material would be the same—the records of History—asking a different set of questions of that material would produce a different story and different insights.

## Where Is The Story in Church History?

Many books have been written and many classes given about church history. Our study will be somewhat different. Although the raw material is the same—the records of how the church developed from Pentecost until today—our set of questions is unique.

Most church history classes answer various broad questions:

▶ How did church doctrines develop?

▶ What church structures worked well, and where?

▶ How did church traditions and practices come about?

One missiologist looked at history and asked some unique questions:

▶ How did the Gospel grow from culture to culture?

▶ What barriers kept it from going into other cultures?

▶ What strategies were developed to overcome those barriers?

These questions give us a whole new outlook on church history. They gather some distinctive correlations within History to God's Story. They disclose the simple but profound ways God continues to work, whether it is with the obedience and cooperation of His people or in spite of their resistance.

These penetrating questions display History in a whole new light. The principles found in Scripture begin to "put on flesh" in a very enlightening fashion. The "dry bones" of History suddenly pulse with life. That changes the manner in which we read the newspaper or view the media. They light the path of our saga.

If you did not enjoy History in school, prepare to think again! Seeing the sweep of this Story may change your point of view.

# As the Waters Cover the Sea: His Glory Expands to the Nations

*Robert A. Blincoe*

> **Robert Blincoe is the U.S. Director of Frontiers, a ministry to the Muslim world. Author of Ethnic Realities and the Church: Lessons from Kurdistan, he worked among the Kurds in Turkey and northern Iraq for nine years.**

From Abraham to Jesus. From Jesus to the present day. Christ stands halfway between Abraham and our day. In this time, God relentlessly pursued His purpose: to redeem the peoples of the world. God's people took the message to diverse peoples and places. The history of Christian expansion is the record of how His glory came to the nations.

How did this come to pass? Among many reasons for its continuing expansion, one may be its innate transferability. Christianity, more than any religion, has outgrown every nationality with which it once seemed fully (even hopelessly) identified. It replants itself in distant cultures in completely unanticipated ways. As Ralph Winter says, "Christianity was the one religion that had no nationalism at its root."[1]

It is the nature of the gospel that each culture hears it first from someone beyond their own kind. D. T. Niles of Sri Lanka said, "It is a faith which must arrive from outside."[2] Someone crossed into your culture, or more likely your ancestor's culture, bringing the Good News of the Risen Lord. My ancestors, living near Hadrian's Wall in northern England, heard the gospel long centuries ago from missionaries who came across the sea. For some readers, the Good News arrived very recently. Despite frail messengers and flimsy mission structures, God passed on the faith. This is the greatest story ever told, and it is gloriously accelerating in our time.

Who imagined fifty years ago that Nigeria today would have more Anglican bishops than England? Who a century ago foresaw millions of Chinese coming to faith in a movement remarkably similar to that of the first three centuries of the Christian era? Who could have predicted during colonial rule that many missionaries would go to other cultures *from* Latin America, the Philippines, and India? Some who read this bring Good News to unreached peoples in our day, for "we have received grace and apostleship in order to bring about the obedience of faith among the ethne" (Romans 1:5).

## 0 to 400—From Jerusalem to Rome's Imperial Borders

To understand how the Good News entered hundreds of cultures and to discover our part in blessing all the families of the earth, we must begin when the missionaries were Jews.

## When the Missionaries Were Jews

Let us imagine a long-living, scholarly space visitor[3] who is able to visit Earth for field study every few centuries. Let us further assume that he wishes to pursue the study of Christianity.

His visit is to a group of the original Jerusalem Christians, about 37 a.d. He notes that *they are all Jews*; indeed, they are meeting in the Temple, where only Jews can enter. They offer animal sacrifices. They keep the seventh day free from work. They circumcise their male children. They carefully follow a succession of rituals and delight in the reading of old law books. What distinguishes them from other Jews is simply that they identify the figures of Messiah, Son of Man, and Suffering Servant (figures all described in those law books) with the recent prophet-teacher Jesus of Nazareth, whom they believe to have risen and inaugurated the last days.[4]

With this picture of early faith and practice, the space visitor returns home and writes a paper on "The Practice of Normal Jesus Religion in 37 a.d."

> *Christianity was the one religion that had no nationalism at its root.*

Winter, R. D. (1992) "The Kingdom Strikes Back: The Ten Epochs of Redemptive History." In R. D. Winter & S. C. Hawthorne (Eds.). *Perspectives on the World Christian Movement: A Reader* (rev. ed.) Pgs. B3–19. Pasadena: William Carey Library.

Don't miss the *Jewishness* of early Christian faith and practice. After Pentecost, Peter, James, and John

# Paul and Barnabas were de-Judaizing the gospel.

continued worshiping at the Temple and "thousands of Jews believed, all zealous for the Law" (Acts 21:20). The Jerusalem Fathers were content to remain Jewish in every way and to expect that Jewish believers would keep the Law. They even insisted on it (Acts 21:21–24).

However, other Jews (Paul and Barnabas) were giving the faith to Gentiles (ethné) without requiring them to become Jews. Paul and Barnabas were *de-Judaizing* the gospel. When challenged, Paul sharply disputed and debated the issue. The result was the watershed decision of the Jerusalem Council in Acts 15. There the Jerusalem fathers prayerfully decided to permit Paul's minority movement to continue: "We should not make it difficult for the *ethne* who are turning to God" (Acts 15:18—my paraphrase).

This was the opening that Paul and his small band had hoped to create. They carefully removed the cultural clothing from the gospel message and re-clothed it in non-Jewish words and concepts. Paul wrote what Peter could not: "To those who are without the law I become as though without the law, that I might win those who are without the law…This I do for the gospel's sake" (1 Corinthians 9:21, 23).

Peter, James, and John probably never foresaw hundreds of thousands of non-Jews pouring through this opening. Jewish believers would eventually become a tiny minority in a Mediterranean sea of Latin- and Greek-speaking, uncircumcised, pork-eating converts who would take the Good News to the varied peoples of the Roman Empire.

## What Attracted Gentiles?

What attracted thousands of Gentiles to Christianity? Sometimes the obvious needs to be stated: *The attraction was Jesus Himself.* He blessed and empowered men and women to live meaningfully in this world and to hope confidently in the next. Jesus was the living presence in every Christian gathering. No threat could stop His people from proclaiming His message and asserting that Jesus alone, not Caesar, was Lord (*kurios* in Greek—a term the emperor reserved for himself alone).

What a brutal world it was in which Christian virtues were displayed! It was a world where an emperor's son celebrated his birthday by watching animals tear people apart in the arena; where married life was usually a failure; where promiscuity, temple prostitutes, and homosexual practice were common; where the population decreased for the first three centuries of the Christian Era (simply because the world was too miserable a place to raise children); where so many newborn daughters were exposed and left to die that men greatly outnumbered women; and where callous enslavement of conquered peoples supported the lifestyle of the elite few. Even their religious practice was abhorrent: Roman deities did not promote morality among their followers but rather lewd, occult rites and costly ceremonies.

## The Fourth Century— the Good News Prevails

Persecution ceased and hardships eased when the emperor Constantine issued the Edict of Toleration a.d. 313. Whether he was personally converted or not, Constantine shrewdly consolidated his empire around the most vigorous belief system of his day. The

# Constantine shrewdly consolidated the empire around the most virile belief system of his day.

protection afforded by the emperor did greatly increase the church's discipleship of the general population as well as the influence of the church on public policy. For example, Constantine abolished gladiator combat in the arenas. Unfortunately, as Christianity became the state religion, nominal pagans simply became nominal church members.

The alien researcher pays a second visit to earth in 325 c.e. but not to Jerusalem. (Romans reduced that city to rubble while the early apostles were still alive.) Asking where all the Jesus believers are, the space visitor is told to visit the new capital of the empire, Constantinople.

His next visit to Earth is made about 325 c.e. He attends a great meeting of church leaders—the Council of Nicea. The company comes from all over the Mediterranean world and beyond it, but hardly one of them is Jewish. Indeed, in the whole they are rather hostile to the Jews.[6] They are horrified at the thought of animal sacrifices; when they talk about offering sacrifices, they mean bread and wine used rather as it was in the house meals our observer noticed in Jerusalem. Church leaders are not expected to marry, and indeed regard marriage as inferior, but they regard a parent who would circumcise his children as having betrayed his faith. They treat the seventh day as an ordinary working day; their special religious observances are on the first day of the week. They use the law books that the Jerusalem Christians used, in translation. They give equal value to another set of writings, not even composed when the Jerusalem Christians met.[7]

The space visitor marvels that, while their faith still centers on Jesus, their practice has changed dramatically and expanded significantly. Church leaders have *de-Judaized* the message, adapting the gospel to the Roman world. They took advantage of imperial roads and safety for travelers afforded by the *Pax Romana*, as well as the widespread use of two major languages—Latin and Greek—to bring the Good News to the largest cities of the Roman Empire between Spain and Babylon. However, though Christianity was declared the state religion of the Roman Empire, there was no official plan developed to evangelize nations beyond the Roman sphere. Farsighted missionaries were needed to create new church forms for peoples who had never been *Romanized*.

## Christian equals Roman: Calamity for the Mission of Christ

So closely did the Roman Empire come to identify with Christianity that in the fourth century the two terms Roman and Christian began to be used interchangeably.

The identities became conflated. There was little question of taking the faith to heathen barbarians. In the words of a leading modern authority, "Throughout the whole period of the Roman empire, not a single example is known of a man who was appointed bishop with the specific task of going beyond the frontier to a wholly pagan region in order to convert the barbarians living there."[8]

The Christianity that spread throughout the Roman world only extended to the imperial borders. In order to expand still farther, the gospel message needed to be *de-Romanized*. Not until the faith broke free from

its Roman cultural identity would it be able to bless other nations.

However, like early Jewish followers before them, Roman church leaders thought the whole world should adapt to their church practice. In North Africa, Augustine, a Berber bishop of Hippo (in today's Tunisia), believed that his fellow Berbers had to become culturally Roman before they could put their faith in Jesus. The Berbers, for the most part, resisted being culturally conquered by the pope just as their Carthaginian ancestors had resisted Caesar. Frederick Norris writes, "At the very moment when a Berber contextualization of the gospel needed strong pastoral guidance, Augustine's own Latin culture left him unable to see the possibilities."[9]

Because the church's outreach halted at Rome's imperial borders, its part in the biblical mandate to bless the nations nearly came to a standstill. Is this one reason for Rome's decline and fall? Indeed, in 430 a.d., Augustine lay dying in bed while barbarians besieged Hippo.

*H*owever, the irrepressible message of the Bible was taking root and thriving in places where Roman-Empire Christians had not imagined it could grow.

Would history have been different had his church preached the gospel of peace to those outside its borders? The light was dimming in the Latin half of the Roman Empire. However, the irrepressible message of the Bible was taking root and thriving in places where Romanized Christians had not imagined it could grow.

## Reaching the Goths

Germanic tribes called Goths began crossing into the Roman Empire in the third century a.d. They captured many Romans, including young Ulfilas and his family, and removed them from Cappadocia (now central Turkey) to north of the Danube River. Ulfilas was raised among them and, like Paul, became "bicultural." He probably found some Christians among the Goths. After studying in Constantinople, he was consecrated a bishop and returned to the north to evangelize the Goths. The mild form of Arianism that he taught may have made his message more palatable to Gothic tribes; because Arians were at odds with Roman theology, it may have been a positive factor in winning the Goths, who feared Rome.

Ulfilas preached boldly in what is now Romania, converting many during forty years of ministry. His greatest labor of love was giving the Goths their own alphabet and translating much of Scripture for them, the first major written work in any Germanic language. Accommodating his message to their lifestyle, he moved with them in their wagons, so it was said, "Those who had formerly used wagons for dwellings now use a wagon for a church."[10]

*It was a huge benefit to the citizens of Rome that earlier informal missionary effort had brought these peoples into at least a superficial Christian faith.*

Other Goths, suspecting Ulfilas might be an agent of Rome, resisted his message. In 348 a.d., after seven years of preaching, Ulfilas moved with his converts south of the Danube, to the protection of Roman legions. He continued preaching until his death, training many others for work among these so-called "barbarians." In 410 a.d., less than thirty years after his death, Gothic tribes, seeing the blessings which Roman cities contained, overran the Empire.

Ralph Winter points out that having some exposure to Christianity made a considerable difference in the way they carried out their invasions.

The only reason the city of Rome itself was not physically devastated by these invasions… was that these Gothic barbarians were, all things considered, really very respectful of life and property, especially that of the churches! It was a huge benefit to the citizens of Rome that the informal missionary effort—for which Latin Roman Christians could claim little credit—had brought these peoples into at least an acquaintance with Christian faith. Even secular Romans observed how lucky they were that the invaders held high certain standards of Christian morality.[11]

Within a short time, by the power of the gospel, the conquerors were conquered. Many of the invading barbarians embraced the faith of those whom they had overthrown.

## 400 to 800: Winning the Barbarians

The institutional church's influence began losing its hold in the fifth century. Waves of fierce peoples from central Asia pushed Germanic Goths and Vandals farther into the relative safety of the crumbling Roman Empire. With the exception of the monasteries, the light of faith and learning was nearly lost; Protestants are beginning to value the contribution that Benedict and others that followed him made:

The rise of monasticism was, after Christ's commission to his disciples, the most important—and in many ways the most beneficial—institutional event in the history of Christianity. For over a millennium, in the centuries between the reign of Constantine and the Protestant Reformation, almost everything in the church that approached the highest, noblest, and truest ideals of the gospel was done either by those who had chosen the monastic way or by those who had been inspired in their Christian life by the monks.[12]

Most of what we know of the ancient world, both in literature and technology (tanning, dyeing, masonry, weaving, bridge building) would have been lost without the scholarship of women and men working in various monasteries. These monastic movements revived the church and were the source of most missions outreach throughout the Dark Ages.

### Celts Light Up the Dark Ages

In spite of the darkness, God was actively moving. In an unexpected corner of non-Roman Europe, another form of Christianity took hold and pushed across Europe to win Germanic tribes. That corner was Ireland, with its inhabitants, the Celts. These were a people so callous that in previous years, both Julius Caesar and St. Jerome had recoiled from them because of their headhunting and cannibalism.

*The rise of monasticism was, and after Christ's commission to his disciples, the most important—and in many ways the most beneficial—institutional event in the history of Christianity.*

The third time the interplanetary traveler visits earth Rome lies in ruins. However, he finds vibrant faith in Ireland, far from the borders that once enclosed the Roman Empire:

A number of monks are gathered on a rocky coastline. Some are standing immobile, praying with their arms outstretched in the form of a cross. Others are going off in a small boat in doubtful weather with a

## However, in spite of the darkness, God was actually moving.

box of beautiful manuscripts and not much else to distribute themselves on islands in the Firth of Clyde, calling the astonished inhabitants to give up their worship of nature divinities and seek for joy in a future heavenly kingdom.[13]

Patrick was the principal missionary that God used to turn the Celts from pagan druidic rites to the living God. Born in Britain (not Ireland), Patrick's father was a deacon; his grandfather a Christian priest. Celtic raiders kidnapped Patrick when he was a teenager and sold him as a slave in Ireland. Patrick later gave thanks for this misfortune, which God used to bring him to personal faith. After years in slavery, Patrick received divine instructions in a dream, escaped, went home, and studied for the priesthood. A subsequent vision called him to return to Ireland.

Though his life could be forfeit there, he chose to obey. The fruit of his ministry: hundreds of thousands baptized and hundreds of churches started. He inspired a generation of leaders, such as Columba and Columbanus, who built missionary training centers like Iona and Lindisfarne that sent forth the *peregrini*—the wandering exiles—who vowed to take the gospel to the ends of the earth.

The Celtic missionaries were characterized by spontaneity, a lack of traditionalism, and rugged individualism. They went where others would not go, without credentials or material support. Self-reliant and trusting in God, they were able to accomplish much more than their numbers would warrant. Theirs was a monasticism that was ardently missionary; not seeking a place of retreat from the world but a place of preparation for mission.[14]

The Celtic church successfully re-evangelized England and continental Europe. Within two generations of their introduction to Christianity; the Celts taught themselves Greek, Latin, and Hebrew. They set themselves to the labor of lovingly translating and copying by hand the Bible and classic commentaries. In fact, more than half of the commentaries written between a.d. 650–850 were by Irishmen.

There is evidence of Celtic monasteries in Belgium, in the Alps, in Moravia, and even as far as Kiev. Women peregrini went out as well, and churches dedicated to their patron, Brigid, still stand in France, Germany, Austria, and Italy. Secular historian Thomas Cahill praised their work:

> Where they went, the Irish brought with them their books, many unseen in Europe for centuries and tied to their waists as signs of triumph, just as Irish heroes had once tied to their waists their enemies' heads. In the bays and valleys of their exile, they re-established literacy and breathed new life into the exhausted literary culture of Europe. And that is how the Irish saved civilization.[15]

Patrick and the Irish *de-Romanized* the gospel, adapting to forms and practices with which the Celts were more familiar. Celtic Christian priests (who could marry) retained the white robes of the Celtic druid priests. The diocese and the bishop were replaced by the monastery and the abbot. Church leadership passed from relative to younger relative along the pattern of Celtic tribal rule. Winter writes,

> Curiously, our phrase *Third World* comes from those days when Greek and Latin were the first two worlds and the barbarians to the north were the *Third World*. Using this phrase, barbarian Europe was won more by the witness and labors of "Third World Missionaries"—the Celts and Anglo-Saxon converts of the Celts—than by the efforts of missionaries deriving from Italy or Gaul.[16]

## Celtic monasticism was ardently missionary. The monastery was not a place of retreat from the world.

## 8th Century—the Gospel Throughout Western Europe

The Christian faith accelerated its expansion in the eighth century. Winfrid, England's greatest missionary, preached for three decades to the Saxons (in Germany) and Frisians in today's Holland. He won many converts by dramatically cutting down the Mighty Oak of Thor. However, he aroused suspicion that he was an agent of Charlemagne, sworn enemy of the Saxons, and was martyred in 754.

Charlemagne, king of the Germanic Franks, was the most powerful ruler of the Holy Roman Empire in 400 years. He re-established safety along the roads, consolidated all of Western Europe under his rule, and Christianized the Germanic tribes. After peace was established, a renaissance of culture flourished throughout Charlemagne's empire:

Efforts were made to raise the level of religious observance, morality, and the process of

*I*n most instances, conversion was a community affair; chieftains or kings led people in a kind of mass movement to baptism and faith.

justice throughout the empire…The spiritual and literary movement called the "Carolingian renaissance" had many centers, especially in the empire's monasteries… [Furthermore] Charles respected the traditional rights of the various peoples and tribes under his dominion as a matter of principle.[17]

But once more a people from beyond the reach of missionary effort came crashing into the Christian world and the cultural flourishing came to a sudden halt.

## 800 to 1200— Winning the Vikings

Suppose our intergalactic traveler returns again to earth in the early 900s. Where are the famed Irish monasteries? They lie in ruins. A people from the north, where the *peregini* seldom traveled, came to plunder their treasures. Waves of shock and horror reverberated through Christendom in a.d. 793 when Lindisfarne, the island-based Celtic mission training center, was ravaged.

Ruthless raiders, terrorizing populations by loosing vicious dogs before they attacked, were striking everywhere. Shallow-draft Viking ships sailed up the rivers to London, York, Rouen, and Hamburg. "God protect us from Norsemen and their Great Danes," was an oft-repeated prayer. These Northmen, proudly calling themselves *berserkers*, came in relentless waves, repeatedly assaulting Iona, Lindisfarne, and dozens of

other monastic sites. Because they had become centers of wealth, the monasteries were particular targets. Once again, when God's people did not share all the blessings that accompany God's truth, others came to wrest the blessings away from them.

Unlike the Barbarians, the Vikings had no exposure to the gospel. Their raids were savage and bloodthirsty. Then, in one of history's great reversals, the power of the gospel of salvation began to transform this warrior culture. Captives who went unwillingly to the north (priests, because they could read and write) as well as women (taken for wives, slaves, and concubines) brought with them their Christian faith. Little by little, the gospel took hold among their captors. Perhaps because they did not represent a political threat in any way, their witness was more easily absorbed into the Nordic culture.

Throughout the tenth, eleventh, and twelfth centuries, Christian faith advanced in the Scandinavian countries of Denmark, Norway, and Sweden. From preserved bodies exhumed from bogs in Denmark, it is clear that Scandinavian people practiced human sacrifice for 1000 years. However, "With the coming of Christianity, sacrifices at the bog sites ceased."[18] In countless ways the quality of life improved under Christian influence. King Olaf of Norway forbade the "exposure of newborn infants" and ordered that every spring, at the opening of the national assembly, "a slave should not be slain as heretofore, but freed."[19]

New faith expanded in many other directions. The monks Cyril and Methodius gave the Slavs a written language, the basis of the Cyrillic alphabet.

*C*aptives brought with them their faith; because they did not represent a political threat, their witness was more easily absorbed into the culture.

Their translation of the Bible became the inspiration for literacy in the Slavic world. Vladimir, ruler of Kiev, took the faith of the Orthodox, initiating the Russian Orthodox Church. Magyars invaded Hungary, killing the Christian population and burning their churches. However, they converted to Christianity in the tenth century. "Europe and Christianity were becoming synonymous."[20]

In most instances conversion was a communal affair. Chieftains or kings led people in a kind of mass movement to baptism and faith. In fact, community-wide movements, influenced by rulers, were the norm: "In Western Europe of this period, faith was adopted as the religion of the community, usually at the command or at least with the energetic assistance of the prince."[21] This top-down, worldly method greatly expanded Christianity between 900 and 1386, the year in which Lithuania became the last part of Europe to accept Christianity.

## The Rise of Islam

A third monotheistic religion arose in the seventh century. Influenced by both Jews and Christians, Mohammed proclaimed throughout Arabia the worship of Allah as the one God. Islam spread through North

> **C**hurches feared that their way of life would disappear entirely if they caused any annoyance or made any innovation.

Africa into Spain and half the Mediterranean countries. Christians fled to Sicily, to Spain, to Greece, to Gaul, even to Germany. Their exodus dealt a fatal blow to the Christianity of North Africa. Elsewhere, nominal Christians converted to Islam, in part to avoid the extra tax burden, in part because their military victories were so astounding. "For they appeared to prove that Islam was under the peculiar favour of God."[22]

Muslim rulers placed greater restrictions on Christian churches. It became nearly impossible to convert to Christianity. Churches under Islamic rule were perpetuated mostly along family lines; there was fear that this way of life could disappear entirely if there was any annoyance or innovation. Consequently, churches in Arab and Persian realms became extremely conservative.

## 1200 to 1600— Winning the Saracens*?

When our space traveler returns, he sees great numbers of peoples on the move. The roads of Europe are safe for the first time in centuries. However, they are filled with crusading armies. Under the banner of the cross, presuming to fulfill the desires of Christ, they overflow with zeal and passion to "save the Holy Land from the infidels."

History shows their undertaking to actually be the greatest perversion of mission motivation in history. Eight

Crusades began in a.d. 1095 and continued until a.d. 1350, leaving a terrible legacy and closing minds and hearts throughout the Middle East. There the very word Christian is hateful, even to this day. "Never before had any…group of nations in the name of Christ launched as energetic and sustained a campaign into foreign territory as did Europe in the tragic debacle of the Crusades."[23]

Ambition, greed, and fanaticism drove men to mercilessly spill blood in what they believed to be the honor of Christ. Muslim peoples paid a heavy price for these misguided Crusades, but they were not the only victims. Jews throughout Europe and Orthodox Christians in the Byzantine east were also pillaged in the frenzy for plunder and land. Winter points out that "Ironically, the mission of the Crusaders would not have been so appallingly negative had it not involved so high a component of abject Christian commitment. The great lesson of the Crusades is that goodwill, even sacrificial obedience to God, is no substitute for a clear understanding of His will."[24]

## 1600–2000—the Silent Age and the Age of Great Advance

Most Western Christians' knowledge of how His glory came to the nations begins with Martin Luther, and yet they seldom understand the role cultural issues played in the Protestant Reformation. During the same period, much spiritual reform took place in the Catholic tradition as well: a return to Scripture, a desire for holy living, and evangelical preaching. Why then did the northern states of Europe break away? Much of the underlying ferment had to do with differences between the Latin culture and the Teutonic, or German culture.

The northern revolt was prompted in part by the desire to experience worship and theology that reflected cultural practices familiar to the Germanic traditions. Luther, for example, wrote in the German vernacular and translated the Scriptures into the language of the ordinary person. He *de-Latinized* the gospel. Peoples who spoke the "romance languages" or were influenced by Latin culture largely stayed within the Latin liturgy and practice of the Catholic fold. Those who were Germanic

> **T**he great lesson of the Crusades is that goodwill, even sacrificial obedience to God, is no substitute for a clear understanding of His will.

were more likely to be sympathetic to the Reformation message.

Yet where were Protestant missions? Luther and Calvin believed in the universal claims of Jesus Christ on humanity. Why didn't the Protestant Reformation produce a great missions advance? For three hundred and fifty years the embarrassing problem went unresolved while Catholic missionaries followed their explorers to the ends of the earth: Matteo Ricci to China; Francis Xavier to India, China, and Japan; Junipero Serra and Bartholomew de las Casas to the

> *After a unique outpouring of the Holy Spirit in 1727, a prayer movement began that continued, day and night, for more than a hundred years.*

New World; and Alexander de Rhodes to Vietnam.

When Luther confiscated monasteries and shut them down, he took down the sails that the Holy Spirit had used to send missionaries for a thousand years. Without an organized structure, Protestants could only occupy the ground they already had. They were unequipped to send workers "to preach the gospel where Christ was not known" (Romans 15:20). The Lutheran faculty at Wittenberg actually condemned a layman, Justinian Welz, for proposing a new society for sending missionaries overseas.

## The Moravian Exception

One bright exception relieves the dismal Protestant record. Count Nikolaus Von Zinzendorf permitted a group of religious refugees from Moravia to settle on his estate in 1722. After a unique outpouring of the Holy Spirit in 1727, a prayer movement began that continued day and night for more than 100 years. Zinzendorf met "two native Greenlanders and a Negro slave from the West Indies. So impressed was he with their pleas for missionaries…that he himself returned home with a powerful sense of urgency."[25] Within a year, their first two missionaries went to the Virgin Islands.

The Moravian way was to send entire communities of skilled laborers to live among and teach non-Christians. Their missionaries were lay people who were trained for evangelism, not theology. They went as unsupported laborers and used their trades among the people they sought to win. In just twenty years, this tiny group sent out more missionaries than all Protestants had in 200 years.

## William Carey and the Means of Modern Missions

The Moravians inspired an English Baptist lay preacher to propose a radical way to implement obedience to Christ's Great Commission. His name was William Carey. He asked, "If the gospel is worthy of all acceptation, why is it not preached to all?" His proposal supplied the missing element to begin the Protestant mission advance: *organizations* to carry out the endeavor.

Carey's *Enquiry* furnished Protestants the motivation and the means to implement the evangelization of non-Christians throughout the world. His small book provided the big bang that started the modern mission expansion.

## The Twentieth Century—Colonial Era Ends

Two world wars in which Christians slaughtered millions of fellow Christians jolted many nations into action. They struggled for independence from countries that had been their colonial rulers. In what Winter termed, "the Twenty Five Unbelievable Years" (1945–1969) Western nations lost control over all but 5 percent of the non-Western world.[26] In the second half of the 20th century, dozens of countries declared their independence, set up their own governments, and joined the United Nations.

In the early 1990s, Russia's colonies broke free from Moscow's bear hug. Central Asian nations that had been virtually inaccessible were now available for witness. Would resistance to the religion of the colonizers now decrease? Would the nationalistic

> *In just twenty years, their tiny group sent out more missionaries than all the Protestants had in two hundred years.*

fervor that produced these changes also stir a desire in the church of the non-Western world to participate in spreading the gospel?

## The Twenty-First Century—De-Westernizing the Gospel?

The cultural flexibility that the Jerusalem Council permitted allows an ever-increasing diversity of Christian practice as the message reaches to the ends of the earth. Our space visitor returns again, in our day,

> …this time to Lagos, Nigeria. A white-robed group is dancing and chanting through the streets on their way to their church. They are inviting people to come and experience the power of God in their services. They claim that God has messages for particular individuals and that his power can be demonstrated in healing. They carry the same book as Christians of all ages. Their main concern is with power, as revealed in preaching, healing, and personal vision.[27]

Which of the time capsules the intergalactic visitor observed represents real Christianity? All of them. True to the spirit of Acts 15, we must not attach our own cultural assumptions to the gospel and declare them the truth to be proclaimed. The gospel takes root in a culture and indigenizes in ways far different from what the messenger may have experienced. The gospel is the

**More than any other of the faiths of mankind, Christianity has proved its capacity to outlast cultures with which it has seemed to be identified.**

liberator of every culture. Peoples everywhere, attracted to the person and teachings of Jesus, resist the message when it is entangled with alien values. The biblical pattern will now be to *de-westernize* the message. Our message must be Jesus, all of Jesus, more of Jesus, only Jesus, the savior of all people and the gatherer of the nations.

God will not be hindered in His relentless pursuit. Messengers will clearly preach Jesus and the cross, and "not make it difficult for the *ethne* that are coming to faith" by adding man-made rules. "More than any other of the faiths of mankind, Christianity has proved its capacity to outlast cultures with which it has seemed to be identified and some of which it has helped to create."[28]

The world has turned many times since Yahweh made His covenant with Abram, the moon-worshiper from Chaldea (Judges 24:1) forty centuries ago. From generation to generation, from Jerusalem to the ends of the earth, God woos rebellious humanity and wins nations from sin, Satan, and death. He invites the peoples to His coming banquet. That is the mission He

gave Abraham's children; that is the task He leaves for us today. Those who have opened their hearts to join Him in His relentless pursuit pray that the blessings that have come to us will soon come to all the peoples of the world. ◾

## End Notes

1. Winter, Ralph, and Steven C. Hawthorne, (ed.). *Perspectives on the World Christian Movement: A Reader* (Pasadena: William Carey Library, 1999), p. 201.

2. Niles, Daniel T., *Upon the Earth* (New York: McGraw-Hill, 1962), p 170.

3. I am indebted to Andrew Walls, whom Ralph Winter has called the foremost missiologist of our time, for his story of a space visitor who comes to study earth Christianity. See Walls's opening chapter in *The Missionary Movement in Christian History* (Maryknoll, N.Y.: Orbis Press, 1996).

4. Ibid, pp. 3–4.

5. At the council of Arles convened by Constantine in a.d. 314, three Bishops attended from England, indicative of the spread of the Christian movement even to the far reaches of the Roman Empire.

6. Rodney Stark questions the factual nature of oft-reported hostility of the early church to Jews. He makes the case that many diaspora Jews were attracted to Christianity because it freed them from the arduous requirements of Jewish ceremonial law (difficult to maintain outside of their homeland) while keeping them connected to their Biblical roots. Stark believes there was a significant influx of Jewish-background believers into the Christian community until well into the fifth century. See the chapter in his book entitled, "The Mission to the Jews: Why It Probably Succeeded," in *The Rise of Christianity: How the Obscure, Marginal Jesus Movement Became the Dominant Religious Force in the Western World in a Few Centuries* (Princeton, New Jersey: Princeton University Press, 1996) pp. 49–72.

7. Walls, pp. 3–4.

8. Fletcher, Richard, *The Barbarian Conversion* (New York: Henry Holt and Co., 1997), p. 25.

9. Anderson, Gerald H., *Biographical Dictionary of Christian Missions* (New York: Simon & Schuster MacMillan, 1998), p. 33.

10. Tucker, Ruth, quoting Ambrose of Milan, *From Jerusalem to Irian Jaya* (Grand Rapids: Zondervan Publishing House, 1983), p 37.

11. Winter, p. 202. Winter points out that, unlike the cruel practices of Angles, Saxons, and Frisians in Britain, the Gothic invading force did not kill the priests, ravage the women, or destroy the churches.

12. Noll, Mark A., *Turning Points: Decisive Moments in the History of Christianity* (Grand Rapids: Baker Books, 1997), p. 84.

13. Walls, p. 4.

14  Pierson, Paul. "The Celtic Missionary Movement" in *The Evangelical Dictionary of World Mission*, A. Scott Moreau, (ed.). (Grand Rapids: Baker Books, 2000), p. 170.

15  Winter, p. 204.

16  *Encyclopedia Brittanica*, (Chicago, 1991), p. 743.

17  *National Geographic*, March 1987, p. 404.

18  Latourette, Kenneth Scott, *A History of Christianity*, vol. 1 (New York: Harper and Row), p. 558.

19  Ibid., p. 401.

20  Ibid., p. 351.

21  Ibid., p. 289.

22  Winter, p. 20.

23  Ibid.

24  Tucker, p. 71.

25  Carey, William.

26  Winter, Ibid.

27  Walls, p. 5.

## Culture and the Reformation

Cultural issues played a larger part in the Protestant Reformation than many realize. Spiritual reform was taking place at this time in the Catholic tradition. Why then, did the northern states of Europe break away? Much of the underlying ferment had to do with differences between the Latin culture and the Teutonic or German culture.

The northern revolt was prompted, in part, by the desire to experience worship and theology that reflected familiar cultural practices. Luther, for example, wrote in the German vernacular and translated the Scriptures into the language of the ordinary person. Peoples who were Latin or influenced by Latin culture by and large stayed within the Catholic fold, with its Latin liturgy and practice. Those who were Germanic were more likely to be sympathetic to the Reformation message.

## Paul Was Still Right

Once again, the principle that Paul defended at the Council of Jerusalem in Acts 15 showed its power:

> *Peoples who become Christian must be allowed to have expressions of worship, leadership, theology, and practice that reflect their own culture.*

Conversion does not require the converts to follow the conventions of the sending culture. Once the basic foundation of truth is laid, the receiving culture must determine its own appropriate ways to communicate and celebrate God's truth. It must express its love for God within its own cultural framework.

It is these meaningful, culturally appropriate expressions of the message, or lack of them, that determine how easily the Gospel is extended within the new cultural basin.

# ERAS OF MODERN MISSION

| ERAS OF MODERN MISSION | First Era (1792–1910) | Second Era (1865–1980) | Third Era (1934–Present) |
|---|---|---|---|
| *Emphasis* | Coastlands of unreached continents | Interiors of unreached continents | Hidden and unreached peoples |
| *Pioneers* | William Carey | Hudson Taylor | Cameron Townsend<br><br>Donald McGavran |
| *Writings* | *An Enquiry Into the Obligation of Christians to Use Means for the Conversion of the Heathens* | *The Call to Service*<br><br>*China's Spiritual Needs and Claims* | *Tribes, Tongues, and Translators*<br><br>*The Bridges of God* |

JON LEWIS, WORLD MISSION

**Tibetan:** In the Himalayan mountains, the "Rooftop of the World," 2.2 million Tibetan people suffer under two assaults: from the Chinese and from the powers of darkness. The Chinese invaded in 1950 and have systematically sought to destroy their culture, religion, and ethnic identity. One hundred thousand, including the Dalai Lama, have fled the country.

The original religion, Bon, was steeped in occult practices. In the seventh century, Buddhism entered from India. Shamanistic rituals continue, with some of the darkest practices on earth. China, wanting to keep its oppression unpublicized, prefers to keep this region closed. Workers can only enter through tentmaker strategies.

Over sixty Tibetan-Buddhist peoples have been identified. The Tirvans of Mongolia, the Naxi of China, the Sherpas and Larkya of Nepal, and the Drukpas of Bhutan are among them. Two dozen refugee camps for Tibetans exist throughout India. Radio broadcasts are under attack. Many who work on translations have died. The need for urgent prayer is obvious and continual for this heart of darkness.

*Julie Bosacker, YWAM*

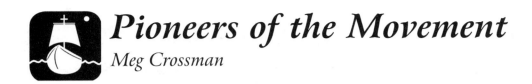

# Pioneers of the Movement
*Meg Crossman*

## WILLIAM CAREY:
## First Era of Modern Missions

### An Unlikely Voice

In 1792 the British (through the East India Company) had been in India for more than 150 years. In all that time, not one verse of Scripture had been translated into any native language. A humble shoemaker in rural England was stirred to concern for colonial peoples such as those in India. The reports of Captain Cook's explorations awakened him. He learned all he could about other countries. The plight of unevangelized continents so burdened him that he covered his walls with maps, praying while he repaired shoes.

That shoemaker, William Carey, was later to be called "the Father of Modern Missions." Though he had little formal education, he demonstrated linguistic gifts early on. He taught himself Greek by using a New Testament commentary. He also learned French and Dutch in a matter of weeks. Most of all, he began to ponder the responsibility of Christians to reach the unsaved with the Word of God.

> **W**illiam Carey began to ponder the responsibility of Christians to reach the unsaved with the Word of God.

There is a curiously modern quality to the writings of William Carey. This impoverished, part-time pastor, hoping to convince his tiny denomination to begin reaching other nations, wrote a small pamphlet: *An Enquiry into the Obligation of Christians to Use Means for the Conversion of the Heathen.* This "little book with the long name" produced an upheaval that reverberated throughout the Christian world. The following segments from that book summarize some of Carey's most significant concepts.[1]

> As our Blessed Lord has required us to pray that His kingdom may come and His will be done on earth as it is in heaven, it becomes us not only to express our desires of that event by word, but to use every lawful method to spread the knowledge of His name.

Carey saw that prayer required a response of obedience. He was convinced that in order to carry out our Kingdom obligation, the Church must become aware of the actual situation.

> **C**arey saw that prayer required a response of obedience.

### A Call to Action

With these thoughts in mind, Carey researched extensively the state of the unsaved world in his day. In more than twenty detailed demographic charts showing every continent, he compared the countries, the population, and their exposure to the gospel. His research convincingly demonstrated the tremendous need. After evaluating the compelling nature of the gathered information, he called the Church to act and discussed the problems that might hinder her:

> The impediments in the way of carrying the gospel among the heathen must arise, I think, from one or other of the following things:
>
>> either their distance from us,
>>
>> their barbarous and savage manner of living,
>>
>> the danger of being killed by them,
>>
>> the difficulty of procuring the necessities of life, or the unintelligibleness of their language.

Carey pointed out that none of these difficulties restrained the commercial interests. If people could go for gain, could they not go for God? Using a twist of irony, he reminded his readers that these hardships did not seem like deterrents "to the apostles and their successors, who went among the barbarous Germans and Gauls, and still more barbarous Britons!"

As far as being killed, Carey pointed out that usually acts of savagery are provoked by hostility, and that missionaries such as the Moravians were seldom molested. As for necessities of life, he suggested that it was both possible and wise to live like the local people. As for language, he believed that any person living amongst the people could learn sufficient language to communicate within two years.

## Overcoming Resistance at Home

One of the greatest obstacles Carey faced in motivating the Church toward her obligation was the then-popular theological opinion that the Great Commission was binding *only on the apostles*. Among other arguments to dispel this notion, Carey pointed out that:

If the command of Christ to teach all nations be restricted to the apostles, or those under the immediate inspiration of the Holy Ghost, then that of baptizing should be so, too; and every denomination of Christian, except the Quakers, do wrong in baptizing with water at all.

> *Carey pointed out that none of these difficulties restrained the commercial interests. If people could go for gain, could they not go for God?*

Finally, Carey dealt with an objection that is still current: "There is so much to be done here at home!" Although the language may seem stilted, the argument is still applicable:

It has been objected that there are multitudes in our own nation and within our immediate spheres of action, who are as ignorant as the South-Sea savages, and that therefore we have work enough at home, without going into other countries. That there are thousands in our own land as far from God as possible, I readily grant, and that this ought to excite us to ten-fold diligence to our work, and in attempts to spread divine knowledge amongst them is a certain fact; but that it ought to supercede all attempts to spread the Gospel in foreign parts seems to want proof. Our own countrymen have the means of grace, and may attend on the word preached if they choose it. They have the means of knowing the truth, and faithful ministers are placed in almost every part of the land, whose spheres of action might be much extended if their congregations were but more hearty and active in the cause; but with them the case is widely different, who have no Bible, no written language (which many of them have not), no ministers, no good civil government, nor any of those advantages which we have. Pity therefore, humanity, and much more Christianity, call loudly for every possible exertion to introduce the Gospel amongst them.

## The Use of Means

One of Carey's most important contributions was his concept of the use of "means":

Suppose a company of serious Christians, ministers and private persons, were to form themselves into a society, and make a number of rules respecting the regulation of the plan, and the persons who are to be employed as missionaries, the means of defraying the expense, etc., etc. This society must consist of persons whose hearts are in the work, men of serious religion, and possessing a spirit of perseverance; there must be a determination to not admit any person who is not of this description, or to retain him longer than he answers to it.

From such a society a *committee* might be appointed, whose business it should be to procure all the information they could upon the subject, to receive contributions, to enquire into the characters, tempers, abilities, and religious views of the missionaries, and also to provide them with necessaries for their undertakings.

## Carey Acts on His Own Proposal

Acting on these suggestions, the Baptist Missionary Society formed, first among many similar denominational missions agencies. Carey did not suggest to others what he was not willing to do himself. In 1793 he offered himself as a missionary for BMS. From this inauspicious beginning, the modern Protestant missions movement arose.

The hurdles Carey had to overcome in getting to the field parallel those with which missionaries contend today. First, he had to combat universalism and other theological objections. Next, he met severe resistance to his new idea for a "committee" or what would today be called a "mission agency." He struggled to raise his outgoing expenses, an overwhelming amount at the time.

> *Carey did not suggest to others what he was not willing to do himself.*

Once on the field, his promised support dried up, and he was forced to undertake secular employment, much like today's tentmakers.* His target country, India, was firmly "closed" to missionary work because of the opposition of the British East India Company. The population he wanted to reach was highly resistant to the Gospel. Although his supporting base was always marginal, the home group still attempted to control the work from England. All the while, he had to deal with intense personal and family stress.

*He had to combat universalism and other theological objections. He met severe resistance to his new idea for a "mission agency." He struggled to raise his outgoing expenses.*

Carey worked in India for eight years, continually harassed by hostile commercial interests. At last he was invited to found a base in Danish-held Serampore, near Calcutta. With co-workers, Joshua Marshman and William Ward (who, with Carey, came to be known as the Serampore Trio), he established a team that would serve together for many years. Even during this time, Carey supported his work almost entirely through his well-paid and prestigious position as Professor of Oriental Languages at Fort William College in Calcutta. The publication work of the team was financed largely through the sale of published materials.

In spite of personal tragedy (Carey's wife died insane, and several children perished as well) and ministry setbacks (a fire in 1812 destroyed priceless manuscripts and whole translations), Carey continued doggedly. He once said, "I can plod. I can persevere in any definite pursuit. To this I owe everything."[2]

Carey's life demonstrated his great watchword, "Expect great things *from* God; attempt great things *for* God." He translated the entire Bible into Bengali, Sanskrit, and Marathi. Together the team completed forty-six translations, New Testaments, and portions in various languages and dialects. Carey founded Seramapore College to train national leaders and church planters.

Carey died in 1834, but as Dr. Ruth Tucker says, "not before leaving his mark on India and on missions for all time. His influence in India went beyond his massive linguistic accomplishments.... He also made a notable impact on harmful Indian practices through his long struggle against widow burning and infanticide. But otherwise he sought to leave the culture intact."[3]

## HUDSON TAYLOR: Second Era of Modern Missions

Like Carey, the young Englishman who would launch the movement to the inland regions had an unprepossessing start. Hudson Taylor did not impress his fellow missionaries with his ideas. The church at home questioned his suitability to carry them out. God, however, was using another unknown visionary to begin a new mission thrust.

## The Call to Service

Before the age of sixteen, Hudson Taylor experienced a compelling call to China.

> Well do I remember, as in unreserved consecration I put myself, my life, my friends, my all, upon the altar, the deep solemnity that came over my soul with the assurance that my offering was accepted. The presence of God became unutterably real and blessed; and though but a child under sixteen, I remember stretching myself on the ground and lying there silent before Him with unspeakable awe and unspeakable joy.[4]

He began to learn about China and prepare himself to work there. While pursuing medical studies, Taylor began, in a disciplined way, to equip himself for missionary service. He trained himself to live simply and frugally. He practiced trusting God for practical provision, letting the Lord provide his needs, even when it was within his power and rights to ask it of others. "Move men through God by prayer alone" became his motto and deeply affected his philosophy of ministry.

*Carey's life demonstrated his great watchword, "Expect great things from God; attempt great things for God."*

I began to take more exercise in the open air to strengthen my physique. My feather bed I had taken away and sought to dispense with as many other home comforts as I could in order to prepare myself for rougher lines of life. I

---

*Tentmakers are committed Christians with marketable occupational skills who are working overseas while effectively sharing their faith in Jesus Christ. The term is taken from the apostle Paul's practice of making tents to help support himself during his missionary journeys (Acts 18:3).

began also to do what Christian work was in my power, in the way of tract distribution, Sunday school teaching, and visiting the poor and sick, as opportunity afforded.

More time was given in my solitude to the study of the Word of God, to visiting the poor, and to evangelistic work on summer evenings than would otherwise have been the case. Brought into contact in this way with many who were in distress, I soon saw the privilege of still further economising, and found it not difficult to give away much more than the proportion of my income I had at first intended.[5]

Besides living in very simple accommodations, Taylor periodically went through his books and his wardrobe, to see what he could give to others. As his guideline, he asked what he would be ashamed of still having, if the Lord were to return that day.

## A New Agency Needed

In 1854, he arrived in Shanghai, China. He worked with some missionaries there, but he began to take trips into the interior where no missionaries had yet gone. To make himself more acceptable to the Chinese, he adopted the dress of a Mandarin scholar,

including blacking his hair and constructing a pigtail. British colleagues were horrified, but the increase in effectiveness with the native peoples convinced Taylor of the wisdom of his actions. Even when he had to go home for health reasons, God used the apparent setback for ultimate good:

> To me it seemed a great calamity that failure of health compelled my relinquishing work for God in China, just when it was more fruitful than ever before;…. Little did I then realise that the long separation from China was a necessary step towards the formations of a work which God would bless as He has blessed the China Inland Mission.
>
> Months of earnest prayer and not a few abortive efforts had resulted in a deep conviction that a *special agency was essential* for the evangelisation of Inland China…. The grave difficulty of possibly interfering with existing missionary operations at home was foreseen; but it was concluded that, by simple trust in God, a suitable agency might be raised up and sustained without interfering injuriously with any existing work. I had also a growing conviction that God would have me to seek from Him the needed workers, and to go forth with them. But for a long time unbelief hindered my taking the first step.[6]

# ERAS OF MODERN MISSIONS

**SECOND ERA: INLAND
1865—1980**

- J. Hudson Taylor
- "Faith" Mission Agengies
- N. Americans prominent

**FIRST ERA: COASTLANDS
1792—1910**

- William Carey
- Denominational Agencies
- British & Europeans prominent

SECOND ERA

FIRST ERA

TRANSITION PERIOD

| 1792 | 1800 | 1810 | 1820 | 1830 | 1840 | 1850 | 1860 | 1865 | 1870 | 1880 | 1890 | 1900 | 1910 |

1792—Wm. Carey's Book published

1910—Edinburgh I Conference

1865—Hudson Taylor founds
China Inland Mission

*Jon Lewis, World Mission*

# ERAS OF MODERN MISSIONS

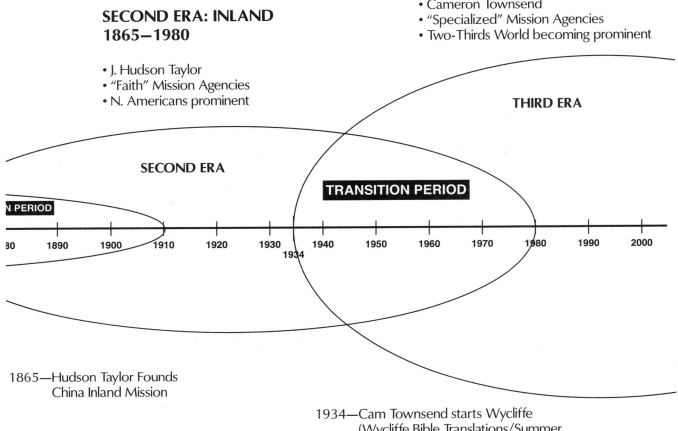

**THIRD ERA:**
**UNREACHED PEOPLES**
**1934—?**

• Donald McGavran
• Cameron Townsend
• "Specialized" Mission Agencies
• Two-Thirds World becoming prominent

**SECOND ERA: INLAND**
**1865—1980**

• J. Hudson Taylor
• "Faith" Mission Agencies
• N. Americans prominent

THIRD ERA

SECOND ERA

TRANSITION PERIOD

N PERIOD

80    1890    1900    1910    1920    1930    1940    1950    1960    1970    1980    1990    2000

1934

1865—Hudson Taylor Founds
China Inland Mission

1934—Cam Townsend starts Wycliffe
(Wycliffe Bible Translations/Summer
Institute of Linguistics)

*Jon Lewis, World Mission*

His great struggle in prayer centered not on God's ability to give workers, but on the dangers, difficulties, and trials that they might be called upon to face on the field. His inner conflict climaxed on a beach in Brighton, England.

On Sunday, June 25th, 1865, unable to bear the sight of a congregation of a thousand or more Christian people rejoicing in their own security, while millions were perishing for lack of knowledge, I wandered out on the sands alone, in great spiritual agony; and there the Lord conquered my unbelief, and I surrendered myself to God for this service. I told Him that all the responsibility as to issues and consequences must rest with Him; that as His servant, it was mine to obey and follow Him—His, to direct, to care for, and to guide me and those who might labour with me. Need I say that peace at once

flowed into my heart? There and then I asked Him for twenty-four fellow-workers, two for each of eleven inland provinces which were without a missionary, and two for Mongolia.[7]

Taylor's society was unique, developed around the experiences and person of its founder. It was not linked to a denomination. It appealed to the working classes instead of demanding years of study and training. Its headquarters was in China rather than far away in England, so it could be more responsive and more informed as to field situations. Like Taylor, the missionaries were to adopt Chinese dress.

Taylor gladly accepted single women and expected missionary wives to be full partners in the enterprise. Most distinctive of all, the missionaries were not to ask for funds but to trust God entirely for their needs, believing that "God's work done God's way will never lack for God's supply." From this principle came the appellation "faith missions."

*Like Carey, Taylor used charts and research, as well as Scriptural evidence in presenting his case.*

## Extending the Kingdom to China

Besides an extensive speaking schedule, Taylor mobilized many through the book written with his wife, Maria, called *China's Spiritual Needs and Claims.* Like Carey, he used charts and research, as well as Scriptural evidence in presenting his case.

> Think of the over eighty millions beyond the reach of Gospel in the seven provinces, where missionaries have longest laboured; think of the over 100 millions in the other eleven provinces of China proper, beyond the reach of the few missionaries labouring there; think of the over twenty millions who inhabit the vast regions of Manchuria, Mongolia, Thibet, and the Northwestern Dependencies, which exceed in extent the whole of Europe—an aggregate of over 200 millions beyond the reach of all existing agencies—and say, how shall
>
> > *God's name be hallowed by them,*
> > *His kingdom come among them, and*
> > *His will be done by them?*
>
> His name, and His attributes they have never heard. His kingdom is not proclaimed among them. His will is not made know to them![8]

Like Carey, Hudson and Maria saw the need for His Kingdom to come in China:

> We have now presented a brief and cursory view of the state and claims of China. To have entered into them at all in detail would have required for each province more time and space than we have devoted to the consideration of the whole empire. We have shewn how *God* has blest the efforts which have been put forth; and have endeavoured to lay before you the facilities that at present exist for the more extensive evangelisation of this country. We have sought to press the great command of our risen Savior, *"Go ye, into all the world, and preach the gospel to every creature,"* and

would point out that in the parable of our Lord, contained in Matt. 25, it was not a *stranger,* but a *servant;* not an *immoral* but an *unprofitable* one who was to be cast into outer darkness, where there is weeping and gnashing of teeth....

> We cannot but believe that the contemplation of these solemn facts has awakened in many the heartfelt prayer, "Lord, what wilt thou have me to do, that Thy name may be hallowed, Thy kingdom come, and Thy will be done in China?"[9]

In 1865 the China Inland Mission [now known as Overseas Missionary Fellowship] was officially organized, and the following year, he left with Maria, his four children, and fifteen recruits for China. While extensive work was done and the force of laborers grew, there were many problems to be overcome and dangers to be faced. Perhaps the worst incident occurred in 1900, when 153 missionaries and 53 missionary children were killed in the hostilities unleashed by the Boxer Rebellion. It was an overwhelming heartbreak to their aging leader.

Taylor lived to see a force of over 1,500 workers committed to the inland regions of China. His agency became a model for more than 40 new "faith missions." His vision for the inland regions stirred new zeal for the vast interior populations not only of China but of Africa, Asia, and Latin America as well.

## TOWNSEND and MCGAVRAN: Third Era of Modern Missions

Two very different men ushered in the Third Era. Cameron Townsend dropped out of college to go to work on the field. Donald McGavran, son and grandson of missionaries, left his parents' field to seek a secular career. Townsend gloried in the fact that he never had a degree. McGavran finished his Ph.D. in his thirties. Townsend served in Guatemala. McGavran returned to work in India. Once again, it was not from the institutional church, but from its periphery that new movements began.

*Taylor's vision for the inland regions stirred new zeal for the vast interior populations not only of China but of Africa, Asia, and Latin America as well.*

The impact of each man was extensive. Townsend's agency became the largest in the Protestant world. McGavran founded no agency, but his writings affected the thinking of much of the Church. These two very different men—captured by provocative insights, tempered by field experience—changed forever the face of world missions.

*T*ownsend's agency became the largest in the Protestant world. McGavran founded no agency, but his writings affected the thinking of much of the Church.

## Cameron Townsend: Visionary for Tribes and Translations

Cam Townsend, or "Uncle Cam" as he would affectionately come to be known, was led to the Lord by his deaf father, Will. Influenced by the Student Volunteer Movement, he left college before graduating and began selling Bibles in Guatemala. An Indian who could not read the Spanish testaments demanded to know, "Why, if your God is so smart, hasn't He learned our language?"

This challenge convicted Townsend. Although he had no background in linguistics, he determined that the 200,000 Cakchiquel natives should have written language and Scripture in their own dialect. It took ten demanding years. His words tell of his growing resolve:

"Don't be a fool," friends told me fifty years ago when I decided to translate the Word for the Cakchiquel Indians, a large tribe in Central America. "Those Indians aren't worth what it would take to learn their outlandish language and translate the Bible for them. They can't read anyhow. Let the Indians learn Spanish," they said.

My friends used these same arguments fourteen years later, when, after having seen the transformation the Word brought to the Cakchiquels, I dreamed of reaching all other tribes. When I included even the small primitive groups in Amazonia in my plan, my friends added other arguments, "They'll kill you," said one old, experienced missionary. "Those jungle tribes are dying out anyway. They kill each other as well as outsiders with their spears, or bows and arrows. If they don't kill you, malaria will get you, or your canoe will upset in the rapids and you'll be without supplies and a month away from the last jumping-off place. Forget the other tribes, and stay with the Cakchiquels."

But I couldn't forget them. And one day God gave me a verse that settled the matter for me. He said: "The Son of Man is come to save that which was lost. How think ye? If a man have a hundred sheep and one of them be gone astray, doth he not leave the ninety and nine, and goeth into the mountains and seeketh that which is gone astray? (Matthew 18:11–12)" That verse guided me; I went after the "one lost sheep," and four thousand young men and women have followed suit.[10]

## A New Agency Focus Required

As Townsend understood the need to develop a unique work with each tribal and language group, he was also forced to realize that a new agency was required. The complex work of translation necessitated a great degree of both specialization and support.

We call ourselves the "Wycliffe, Bible Translators," in memory of John Wycliffe who first gave the whole Bible to the speakers of English. Half our members are dedicated to linguistic and translation work among the tribespeople, bringing them the Word. The other half are support personnel; teachers, secretaries, pilots, mechanics, printers, doctors, nurses, accountants, and others who man the supply lines…. Our tools are linguistics and the Word, administered in love and in the spirit of service to all without discrimination.

*T*ownsend maintained that "the greatest missionary is the Bible in the mother tongue. It never needs a furlough, is never considered a foreigner."

Tribesmen formerly lost to the lifestream of their respective nations are being transformed by the Word. And whether the transformation occurs in the mountains of southern Mexico, the jungles of Amazonia, or the desert plains of Australia, it is a spectacular leap out of the old into the new.[11]

Following thirteen years with the Cakchiquel, Townsend spent seventeen years in Peru, then started pioneer work in Columbia. Even after fifty years of active service, he was excitedly exploring the possibility of translating in the Soviet Caucasus. That dream remained unfulfilled at his death, but with the newly opened doors in Russia, younger translators are now working to accomplish it.

**A**s Townsend understood the need to develop a unique work with each tribal and language group, he was also forced to realize that a new agency was required.

Townsend maintained that "the greatest missionary is the Bible in the mother tongue. It never needs a furlough, is never considered a foreigner."[12] His leadership and drive brought into being Wycliffe Bible Translators and the Summer Institute of Linguistics. Aviation support came through JAARS (Jungle Aviation and Radio Service). Through their service together, these organizations have seen more than 400 translations completed, each for a different tribe or language group. Wycliffe translators are currently at work in more than 700 language groups, dedicating some thirty translations each year.

With personnel from thirty or more countries, Wycliffe currently fields more than 6,000 people in eighty nations. Although Townsend continued to defend the value of non-degreed workers for translation work, Wycliffe today probably has more Ph.D.s than any other agency. Ruth Tucker credits him with being "The one individual most responsible for the twentieth century surge in Bible translation."[13] That surge produced not only his organization, but some twenty other translation ministries worldwide.

**M**cGavran suggested that peoples' cultural differences can actually suggest wiser strategies for advancing the kingdom. The uniqueness of each group can facilitate the work instead of hindering it.

## Donald McGavran: Voice for Hidden Peoples

At the same time, on the other side of the globe, Donald McGavran was beginning to ask some different questions. His answers would significantly change the way the church would think about missions.

Born in India, McGavran was determined not to become a third-generation missionary. God had other ideas. Although planning to pursue a career in law, McGavran surrendered to Christ in college through the Student Volunteer Movement. Eventually, he returned to work in India with his parents' agency. Beginning as the head of a mission school, he served in medical work, evangelistic programs, and translated the Gospel into Chhattisgarhi.

## Another Way of Looking at Missions

McGavran persistently looked, listened, and most of all, asked questions.

> His practical experience and his insatiable appetite to learn from other missionaries had made him realize the necessity of sound, well-reasoned mission theory, and he began dedicating his energies to that discipline. He had long realized that much of the work that was being carried out by missionaries was accomplishing very little toward the goal of world evangelization.[14]

With well-documented research, McGavran began to challenge the validity of the mission station* approach to field work. He asked the disquieting question, "How do *peoples* become Christian?" He began to contest the soundness of accepted methods such as evangelistic campaigns and one-by-one conversions. Applying the methods of sociological research, he searched for hard facts to document actual results.

It was McGavran's exposure to the uniqueness of various strata of society that started his quest for answers.

Nowhere but India, with its multi-layered caste system, could this issue have come into such sharp focus. The difficulties encountered in taking the Gospel from one caste to another forced him to unexplored conclusions. He suggested that, rightly understood, peoples' cultural differences can actually suggest wiser strategies for advancing the Kingdom. The uniqueness of each group can facilitate the work instead of hindering it.

---

* Mission station—an area where missionaries (and often their converts) lived and worked together. This usually separated them from the people they were trying to reach.

McGavran contended that the way peoples see themselves as a group (leading to the coining of his term "people group") must be taken into account in giving them the good news. Harnessing their natural networks, their kinship and relational ties, rather than breaking them, will produce more conversions and stronger churches. This insight led to another startling conclusion.

*The western style of individual decisions was unacceptable to the eastern mind and questionably productive for winning them.*

## Another Way of Thinking about Decisions

McGavran also recognized that *the way* decisions are made in most cultures was a vital key. He asserted that the western style of individual decisions was unacceptable to the eastern mind and questionably productive for winning them. Studying this "group mind" produced some riveting proposals.

To understand the psychology of the innumerable subsocieties which make up non-Christian nations, it is essential that the leaders of the churches and missions strive to see life from the point of view of a people to whom individual action is treachery. Among those who think corporately, only a rebel would strike out alone, without consultation and without companions. The individual does not think of himself as a self-sufficient unit, but a part of the group. His business affairs, his children's marriages, his personal problems, or the difficulties he has with his wife are properly settled by group thinking. *Peoples become Christian as their group-mind is brought into a life-giving relationship to Jesus as Lord.*

It is important to note that the group decision is not the sum of separate individual decisions. The leader makes sure that his followers will follow. The followers make sure that they are not ahead of each other. Husbands sound out wives. Sons pledge their fathers. "Will we as a group move if so-and-so does not come?" is a frequent question. As the group considers becoming Christian, tension mounts and excitement rises. Indeed, a prolonged informal vote–taking is under way. A change of religion involves community change. Only as its members move together does change become healthy and constructive.

Peoples become Christian as a wave of decision for Christ sweeps through the group mind, involving many individual decisions but being far more than merely their sum. This may be called a chain reaction. Each decision sets off others, and the sum total powerfully affects every individual. When conditions are right, not merely each sub-group, but the entire group concerned decides together.[15]

Needless to say, this analysis was both compelling and controversial. It provided the impetus for the rethinking of many strategies. It proposed the notion of encouraging movements of whole peoples to Christ.

## A Center for Research

From these questions, and the research done to explore them, McGavran began to develop the discipline now called "missiology." In 1961 he started the Institute of Church Growth, where "missiological research developed more fully than it had anywhere or anytime in the history of the Christian Church."[16] In 1965 McGavran became the founding dean of the School of World Mission at Fuller Theological Seminary.

His prolific writing exposed the entire missions world to his studies and theories. Although McGavran did not establish an agency, his research influenced all of them. Two principal results of his efforts were the Church Growth Movement (studying how expansion happens within groups where the church already exists) and the Frontier Mission Movement (developing ways to reach those groups where it does not exist).

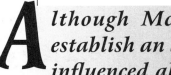

*Although McGavran did not establish an agency, his research influenced all of them.*

## A Whole New Era

Once again, while one era was at its peak, a new one commenced. Townsend and McGavran—one a college drop-out, the other a learned Ph.D.—each proposed a radical new way of thinking about missions. Though for different reasons, these two disparate individuals came to the similar conclusions at almost the same time. To be effective, missionaries needed to consider their task in terms of ethnic groups, now referred to as "peoples" or "people groups." With such perceptive insights, these two pioneers clarified the mission task in concepts that were no longer based on geography. This laid the groundwork for the development of missions from the

Two-thirds World. Through Townsend and McGavran, God moved His church into the Third Era of Modern Missions. ⬛

## End Notes

[1] Carey, William. *An Enquiry into the Obligation of Christians to Use Means for the Conversion of the Heathens.* (New Facsimile ed.) London: Carey Kingsgate Press. (Original work published in 1792.)

[2] Tucker, Ruth. *From Jerusalem to Irian Jaya.* Grand Rapids, Mich.: Zondervan. Pg.120.

[3] Tucker, ibid. Pg. 120.

[4] Taylor, J. H. (n.d.). *A Retrospect.* Philadelphia: China Inland Mission. Pgs.10–14

[5] Taylor, ibid.

[6] Taylor, ibid. Pgs. 105–109.

[7] Taylor, ibid.

[8] Taylor, J. H. *China's Spiritual Needs and Claims.* 1895 Philadelphia: China Inland Mission. Pg. 38.

[9] Taylor, ibid. Pgs. 47–48.

[10] Townsend, Wm. Cameron. (1963) "Tribes, tongues, and translators." In Wycliffe Bible Translators, Inc., in cooperation with the Summer Institute of Linguistics, *Who Brought the Word.* Santa, Ana, Calif.: Wycliffe. Pg. 7.

[11] Townsend, ibid. Pg. 8.

[12] Hefley, J., & Hefley, M. (1974). *Uncle Cam.* Waco, Tex.: Word. Pg. 182.

[13] Tucker, Ruth A. *From Jerusalem to Irian Jaya.* Grand Rapids, Mich.: Zondervan. Pg 351.

[14] Tucker, ibid. Pg. 476.

[15] McGavran, Donald. *(1955.) The Bridges of God: a study in the strategy of missions.* New York: Friendship Press. Pg 13.

[16] Tucker, Ruth. ibid. Pg. 477.

**Ladakhi:** The Ladakhi of Northern India are descended from Tibetan emigrants. They inhabit the largest region of Kashmir, the only state in India with a Muslim majority. Continual conflict over Kashmir between India and Pakistan has produced two wars, and a third one threatens.

About half of the 60,000 Ladakhi people are still in the grip of Lamaistic Buddhism. Members of the two different sects distinguish themselves by their headgear: some wear yellow hats, some red. They practiced polyandry (the marriage of one woman to several husbands) in the past, but now a number of them have become Muslim. As Muslims, some have become polygamous, and the population is increasing.

Moravians translated the Tibetan New Testament into Ladakh years ago, but little fruit has resulted. The lack of a Christian presence in Kashmir, coupled with the continued warfare, makes evangelism difficult. The church in India is seeking to develop prayer and engagement strategies to reach these people.

*Julie Bosacker, YWAM*

# GOD'S PATHS THROUGH HISTORY

John Rowell, an experienced missions leader, teaches, "History is the scaffolding on which the promises of God are displayed!" The sweep of history we have covered is staggering and challenging and encouraging, all at once. *The reason history continues* is that God's plans are still being carried out. (See Mt. 24:14).

## Principles of God's Work

In tracing 2,000 years of the expansion of Christianity, we observe the working of God throughout. Within the framework of this examination, there are exhilarating insights and serious warnings.

The Good News moved into various cultural "clusters." It flowed along natural kinship and friendship lines. It impacted the connected and related cultures in myriad ways. Yet, what mattered most was *whether the Gospel was taken beyond themselves* to dissimilar and distant cultures. There the lasting vitality of that "cluster" was most deeply affected.

## Three Eras of Gospel Advance

In the last two hundred years, three overlapping eras of cross-cultural activity took the Gospel from Europe and the Americas to far distant nations.

Initially, William Carey wrote and modeled the need to reach the nations.

Hudson Taylor *awakened* concern.

More recently, Cam Townsend and Donald McGavran conveyed the need to *understand* each people group.

Inspired by such visionaries, each era, fueled by research and prayer, mobilized God's people to advance the Kingdom further.

These advances continue as many churches send workers across cultural barriers. Now two-thirds world of churches are making strategic contributions to the advancing force. Each has a valued part to play.

## What Must Now Be Done?

In this new millenium, God's people must ask:

▶ What work is still ahead and how can it be undertaken?

▶ What should be the particular contribution of this generation?

▶ What will it take to complete the work Jesus left us to do?

George Eldon Ladd challenges us to consider this:

For the ultimate meaning of modern civilization and the destiny of human history, you and I are more important that the United Nations. From the perspective of eternity, the mission of the Church is more important than the march of armies or the actions of the world's capitals, because it is in the accomplishment of this mission that the divine purpose for human history is accomplished." (Ladd, *The Gospel of the Kingdom*. Grand Rapids, Mich.: Eerdmans. Pg. 135)

Like Carey, Taylor, Townsend and McGavran, let us do research and commit ourselves to prayer. Like them, let us commit our resources to act on what we know. None can do this alone. Alongside brothers and sisters around the world, vital paths appear for all within God's relentless purposes.

# 3 Strategic Paths

## What Now?

The account of God working through History is full of stirring examples and convicting challenges. Now, in our generation, we must grasp the full sweep of what yet needs to be done. What light does this shed on our path today? How will God choose to fulfill His purposes now? How can we connect and cooperate with the current move of the Lord?

Scripture tells us that "David...served his own generation, by the will of God" (Acts 13:36). Each of us can only serve one generation—that one into which we were born. Each generation has unique characteristics. In each season, God is moving along distinct and creative paths. He created each of us for the singular moment in which we live.

When we understand where we are and what needs to be done, we can become like the men of Issachar who "understood the times and knew what Israel ought to do" (I Chr. 12:32). Combining research and prayer like the pioneers who have gone before us, we can contribute effectively. Alert to what God is doing, we can discover ways to join Him.

## What Next?

Here are some of the strategic questions this chapter will begin to answer:

▸ Who are "unreached peoples" and why is it vital to understand them?

▸ How can they be reached?

▸ Where are cross-cultural workers now serving, and where are they needed?

▸ What strategies are essential to extending the Kingdom throughout the earth?

## Is Strategy Scriptural?

Some people wonder if having a strategy shows a lack of faith in God's leading. Not so! God gave strategies to Moses for organizing and leading Israel as He formed them into a nation. Paul had a strategy for reaching the Gentiles and establishing churches across the Roman Empire.

In his second letter to Timothy, Paul urges the young leader to learn from three vocations that always employ strategy: the soldier, the farmer, and the athlete. All of these positions must use planning to accomplish their goals. Each of them must gather suitable particulars and sort through them wisely. Each must seek practical ways to realize a desired end.

Let us examine the information in this chapter as we begin to shed light on God's strategic paths toward the nations.

# The Task at Hand: World Evangelization
*Edward R. Dayton*

Edward R. Dayton was an aerospace engineer who joined World Vision International, becoming their VP-at-large and a leader in the Lausanne Movement. He founded MARC, the missions research arm of WVI, and authored significant studies on reaching the world, particularly *Strategies for World Evangelization*.

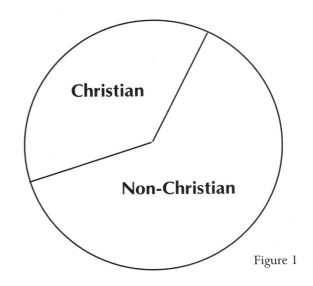

Figure 1

There are now more than 6.0 billion people in the world; almost one-third call themselves Christians. That includes all Protestants, Catholics, and Orthodox. But more than 4.1 billion others do not follow Christ. If we divided up the world between those who call themselves Christians and those who do not, the division would look something like Figure 1.

Although the number of Christians in the world is growing, the percentage of Christians to non–Christians has remained more or less constant for the past fifty years. But what do we think about a world in which there are more than 4.1 billion people who need to know the saving power of Jesus Christ?

*Jesus came to them (the disciples) and said, "All authority in heaven and on earth has been given to me. Therefore go and make disciples of all nations, baptizing them in the name of the Father and of the Son and of the Holy Spirit, and teaching them to obey everything I have commanded you. And surely I am with you always, to the very end of the age." (Matthew*

**I**f the world is to be evangelized, the Church should seek to bring God's name glory by sharing His love cross-culturally.

*28:18–20, NIV).*

The Lord Jesus Christ has commanded His church to make disciples of every nation. This responsibility has been given to His church, His body. Every Christian in every local church, in every country of the world, is called to be a witness of the saving power of Jesus Christ. No matter who we are and where we are, if we claim Jesus as Lord, God commands us to proclaim our faith by what we say and how we live.

Therefore God has set apart certain men and women to go cross-culturally from where they live to reach those villages, towns, and cities where there is no gospel witness. They follow in the footsteps of those early apostles who were set apart for the work to which the Holy Spirit had called them:

*In the church at Antioch there were prophets and teachers: Barnabas, Simeon called Niger, Lucius of Cyrene, Manaen (who had been brought up with Herod the tetrarch) and Saul. While they were worshiping the Lord and fasting, the Holy Spirit said, "Set apart for me Barnabas and Saul for the work to which I have called them." (Acts 13:1–2, NIV).*

God set apart two pastors of the church in Antioch to go into cross-cultural ministry. However, if the world is to be evangelized today, and if every person in the world is to have an opportunity to know Jesus Christ as Lord and Savior, then the Church should seek to bring God's name glory by sharing His love cross-culturally.

The whole Church needs to see that God has given to us the responsibility of reaching this world. We need to uncover God's approach and God's way for reaching these people.

## Defining World Evangelization

What do we mean by world evangelization? The following definition has been adopted by the Lausanne Committee for World Evangelization:*

**NATURE:** The nature of evangelization is the communication of the good news.

Dayton, E. R. (1990). *The Task at Hand: World Evangelization*, Monrovia, Calif.: Missions Advanced Research & Communication Center
* The Lausanne Committee for World Evangelization is an international movement for the purpose of encouraging Christians and churches everywhere to pray, study, plan, and work for the evangelization of the world.

**PURPOSE:** The purpose of evangelization is to give individuals and groups a valid opportunity to accept Jesus Christ.

**GOAL:** The goal of evangelization is men and women who accept Jesus Christ as Lord and Savior, and serve Him in the fellowship of His Church.

Only the Lord really knows whether a man or a woman has given true allegiance to Jesus Christ. But it is the nature of evangelization that the good news, the gospel, should be shared.

It is the purpose of evangelization that ultimately every individual and group of people in the world should have an opportunity to accept or reject Jesus Christ as Lord and Savior. But if this is to be carried out in any meaningful way, we need a measurable goal. Thus we state that the goal of world evangelization is that men and women should not only come to accept Jesus Christ as Lord and Savior but also come to serve Him in the fellowship of His church. This includes seeing culturally relevant churches established among every nation, tribe, people, and language.

## That Everyone May Hear

How do we think about evangelizing the entire world? Somehow that seems like too big a responsibility in a world that every day grows more complex, a world torn by disasters, political upheaval, and starving people.

How do you even think about a world like that?

**The Countries of the World:**

One way to think about it is in terms of the world's countries. While these countries are geographical locations, we are not talking about the nations that the Bible describes; rather, we are talking about geographical territories that break up language groups and cultures. For example, the Kurdish nation is located in Iran, Iraq, Turkey, and the former Soviet Union. There is not a country called Kurdistan, but there is a nation filled with Kurds that God desires to be with Him.

> *The goal of world evangelization includes seeing culturally relevant churches established among every nation, tribe, people, and language.*

In 2000 the U.S. government *World Factbook* said there were over 267 countries in the world. They come in all sizes. They range from an estimated 1.2 billion people in China down to only 1,876 in Niue, South Pacific. That tremendous variation shows the difficulty of talking about world evangelization in terms of countries. It is one thing to evangelize Niue; it is quite another to reach the 1.2 billion people of China.

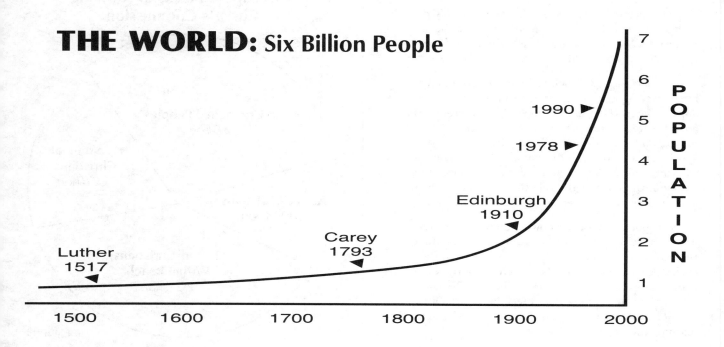

# THE WORLD: Six Billion People

Luther 1517
Carey 1793
Edinburgh 1910
1978 ►
1990 ►

POPULATION

7 6 5 4 3 2 1

1500 1600 1700 1800 1900 2000

## The Religions of the World

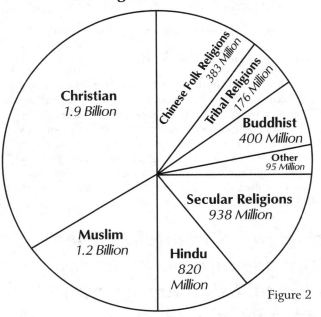

Figure 2

### The Religions of the World

Another way to think about the world is in terms of its religions. Figure 2 shows the approximate distribution of the peoples of the world by different religions in 2000.

*Those who acknowledge Jesus Christ* number approximately 1.9 billion people. (This number includes many individuals who are Christian in name only, going to church once a year and never really knowing Christ.)

The second largest religion in the world is *Islam*, with an estimated 1.2 billion Muslims. With the majority in India, there are some 820 million *Hindus* found all over the world.

*"Secular religions"* (such as Marxism, Communism, humanism, agnosticism, and atheism) include approximately 938 million people. *Chinese folk-religionists* are estimated to number 383 million. There are 400 million *Buddhists* (mostly in Japan, Thailand, Tibet, and Myanmar, formerly Burma) and 176 million *tribal religionists* (mostly in the South Pacific) who worship nature or the spirit world. All other religions of the world make up the balance.

It is not so important how accurate any of these numbers are. In terms of proportions and magnitude, they are accurate enough to give us a picture of the challenge that approximately 68 percent of the world's people do not acknowledge Jesus Christ as the Lord. But it is obvious that, though this breakdown helps us, it still does not give us the basis for a workable strategy for reaching the world.

## Three Major Tasks

Fulfilling Christ's Commission involves three major tasks for the Church today. They vary in complexity and difficulty, but all three are tremendously important:

1. First, we need to evangelize the millions of nominal Christians we have included in the "1.9 billion Christians." There are people all over the world, particularly in Western countries, who have been baptized and have joined a local church but have little understanding of the saving power of Jesus Christ, and even less of what it means to serve Him.

2. Second, we need to evangelize 2.2 billion non-Christians with whom we are in immediate contact. We need to find ways to share with our non-Christian friends and neighbors the gracious love of their Heavenly Father and His desire to make them citizens of His kingdom.

3. Third, we need to discover the more than 2 billion people who are unreached by any Christian witness and to develop strategies for reaching them. *This is the major task of the Church.* Today less than ten percent of all missionaries are attempting to reach these 2 billion people. To put it another way, we need to see churches planted among these 2 billion people, churches that can then get on with the responsibility of evangelizing people who speak the same language, people "just like them."

### Three Major Tasks in Fulfilling Christ's Commission

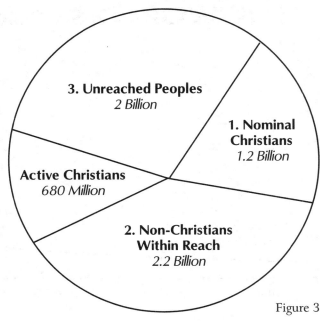

Figure 3

## The Challenge of Unreached Peoples

Of the approximately 4.2 billion people who are not Christians, only a little over 2.2 billion live within cultures where there are Christians who know Jesus and who can share His love. To put that another way, no matter how earnest all the local churches in the world are in reaching out to their near neighbors (people like them), only one-third of the non-Christians in the world can be reached by Christians who speak their language and understand their culture.

The other people of the world are not only unchurched, they are living in places around the world where there are no Christians to communicate Christ to them in their own language or culture. They live their lives every day without knowing or hearing about Christ, without any effective witness to the saving power of Jesus Christ. We need to say it over and over:

*How, then, can they call on the one they have not believed in? And how can they believe in the one of whom they have not heard? And how can they hear without someone preaching to them? And how can they preach unless they are sent? As it is written, "How beautiful are the feet of those who bring good news!" (Romans 10:14–15, NIV).*

## How Do You Evangelize the World?

God is in the business of redeeming this world. This is His business. Our responsibility is to become involved with Him in carrying out His good purposes for the world.

One way of thinking about reaching that world is ONE PEOPLE GROUP AT A TIME, not one country at time, because countries vary so much. India, with its over 1 billion people has eighteen official languages and thousands of castes, tribes, and other social groups. Certainly, reaching India is quite a different responsibility from reaching Niue with its 1,867 people.

Not one religion at a time. Not only are most of the major religions of the world huge in numbers of adherents, they are also spread out through many different people groups. There are more Buddhists in the world today than the total population of the world at the time of Christ!

## What Is a People Group?

Let us use an illustration to explain what we mean by a people group. Assume for a moment that this block of figures on this page represents all the people living in the United States.

# ONE PEOPLE GROUP

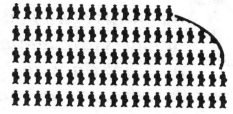

**LANGUAGE**

**ETHNIC GROUP**

**REGION**

**SOCIAL RELATIONSHIPS**

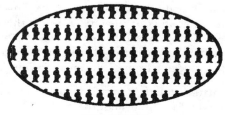

**RELIGION**

Figure 4

First, your language is English. Who are the people with whom you have been communicating naturally in English? Which ones do not speak the language? Let us draw a "boundary" that represents language.

Do you live among different ethnic groups? Which one is yours? ❑ Hispanic? ❑ Indian? ❑ White? ☑ Black? ❑ Asian? Notice how in Figure 4 the boundary is reduced because of your ethnic group.

**T**wo-thirds of all non-Christians are living in places around the world where there are no Christians to communicate Christ to them in their own language or culture.

You live on the south side of Chicago. For many people, where they live and the people they live close to determine who they consider to be part of their group. Again, in our illustration your group is becoming better defined by country or region.

Being black, do you relate to some people better than others? Do you think of yourself as belonging to a particular class or caste? Perhaps you think of yourself as belonging to a specific occupation or profession. Your parents came to America from Libya, North Africa. You relate best with other North Africans. Another boundary goes up because of social relationships.

What kind of people do you worship with? In other words, what is your religion? For many people, religion is one of the primary ways they identify themselves with a group. You happen to be a Muslim like your parents. A boundary of religion is formed.

All these boundaries are both inclusive and exclusive. They define a particular people group. And they exclude those people who are not part of the people group.

Every country is filled with people groups. At first glance we may believe that all the people in our country are "just like us." But closer examination will show a vast mosaic of differences. Take, for example, the city of greater Los Angeles. The numbers of Asians, Hispanics, and Blacks have been rising so fast that by the year 2000 there will not be an ethnic white majority. This will change the whole look of the city. Already there is not just one Asian community but Koreans, Chinese, Japanese, etc. In the schools, teachers learn Spanish to speak to their students from Latin American countries.

The situation in Los Angeles is duplicated in cities, as well as rural areas, throughout the world.

## What Is an Unreached People Group?

We have defined a people group. From our illustration we can perhaps already see how targeting our evangelistic efforts on a particular people group will help focus our attention toward planting churches among these people. But our evangelistic efforts must include a strategic plan for reaching those people groups who have never heard the gospel of Jesus Christ, the unreached people groups.

In other words, unreached people groups lack a church that has the numbers and strength to reach their own people. Obviously, if there are no Christians within this group, there will be none who can share the gospel with them. And this is the situation in which we find over 2.2 billion people of the world. They are the people groups in which there is no church that is able to tell them the good news of Jesus Christ.

The world we need to be concerned with is the world of unreached people groups. Some are large. Some are small.

## World Evangelization in Sight

To think about the world in terms of reaching 3.6 billion people is more than most minds can comprehend. To think about reaching approximately 935 million Muslims seems like an impossible responsibility. To think about evangelizing all of India seems incomprehensible.

But when we recognize that God may be calling us to bring the gospel to one particular people group, then the assignment becomes understandable and definable. It may be the group in which we now find ourselves. It may be a people group somewhat different from us but nearby. It may be one of the unreached people groups that are separated from us by boundaries of geography, culture, language, or a combination of these and other things.

The 2.2 billion unreached people will only be reached when Christians cross cultural barriers and engage in long-term ministries that lead to the establishment of individual churches among every nation, tribe, people, and language.

When we think about the world as divided up into people groups, then we can have a manageable strategy. Then the Holy Spirit can help us to believe it is possible to take the whole gospel to the whole world.

## The Mystery of Evangelization*

Planning strategies for evangelization is no substitute for the powerful presence and action of the Holy Spirit! If anything, the more carefully and prayerfully we try to think through the evangelization of a specific group, the more keenly we feel our dependence upon God.

There is a *mystery* to evangelization. The Spirit moves as He sees fit (John 3:8). It is God who is at work to do His perfect will. In ways that we cannot understand, He uses imperfect, sinful men and women to communicate His love and the good news of salvation through His beloved Son to all who will receive Him.

There is a *mystery* to what happens as the Holy Spirit transforms lives of individuals and nations. We can many times see only the *results* of the Spirit's work. The finger of God writes across the pages of history, and we can see what He has done. But so often we are unable to understand fully what has happened.

But there is *mystery* too in the fact that God has charged His Church to go into all the world to preach and make disciples, trusting Him for results and yet at the same time praying, dreaming, anticipating, longing into the future. And as we respond to the command of God's Word and the prompting of His Spirit within us, we are expected to bring our *total being* to bear on the task before us, to think, to pray, and to plan. Jesus spoke to this when He said that a man should not start to build a tower or engage an enemy without first considering the possible outcomes (Luke 14:28). It was said of the early Church that they outlived, outdied, and outthought the Roman Empire.

There is a *mystery* about God's action in society through the society itself. Many times God uses changes in the society to prepare people to receive His Word.

Finally, there is *mystery* about the person of the evangelist. The Word of God has as much to say about what we are to *be* as what we are to *do*. The gospel is proclaimed through the spoken word. People cannot come to a knowledge of the Savior unless they hear (or read) that He is. But they are often attracted to Him by the love they find among His disciples.

> **I**t is God who is at work to use imperfect, sinful men and women to communicate His love and salvation.

Remember, each disciple is called upon to see himself or herself as part of a larger body (1 Corinthians 12:12). Within that body each has a special place, and in the process of evangelization different persons play their special role at different times. "I planted, Apollos watered, but God gave the increase" (1 Corinthians 3:6, NKJV).

Let us then use *all* the gifts that God has given us, both individually and corporately. Let us try to think God's thoughts after Him. Let us attempt to uncover God's strategy—to think about the people to whom we may be called, to earnestly consider their needs, to take into account all that God might do to reach them. Let us make certain that we are clean vessels, fit for His use. And then let us go forward believing that God will be faithful and GIVE HIM THE GLORY. 🔲

*Julie Bosacker, YWAM*

**Thai:** In Bangkok, known as the sin capital of Asia, there are 700,000 female and 100,000 male prostitutes. Many have been kidnapped or sold into prostitution slavery. A major industry of Thailand, over 2 million people derive their income from this despicable trade. As AIDS becomes rampant, younger and younger children are sought.

Thais are proud that their nation, a constitutional monarchy, retained its freedom when countries all around them were colonized and invaded. Yet the Buddhist nation of Thailand has never found the freedom of redemption in Christ. Not only the corruption of the sex trade but a complex culture of spirit appeasement and occultism keep this land in bondage. Prayer and well-contextualized ministry are needed for a breakthrough.

* Dayton, E. R. (1978). "To Reach the Unreached." In C. P. Wagner & E. R. Dayton (Eds., ) *Unreached Peoples '79* (pp. 25–31). Elgin, Ill.; David C. Cook.

# To See With New Eyes
## Andy Jackson

Andrew Jackson is the founder and leader of the International Turkey Network. He serves as Pastor of Discipleship and Leadership Development in a local church. He is the author of The Lost Land of the Bible: A Christian Travel and Prayer Guide Through the Ancient Biblical Land of Turkey.

In every forward advance, God gives some people a passion for the frontiers. They see what others do not see. Often, they come from the edges of the church rather than from an institutional setting. With a fresh point of view, they go beyond conventional categories and can challenge the prevailing status quo. Their compelling concerns envision a future unformed and yet unfolding. They look beyond *what is* and call others to see *what could be*.

In the past, it has sometimes been unproven younger leaders with emergent ideas who set an unexpected bearing or altered course. Other times, it is those who ask piercing questions, pushing toward objectives that may have been obscured. Breakthrough insights—in "fullness of time" moments—can provide motivation and stimulus for Kingdom expansion. By examining earlier movements and how they began, God's people can prepare for future movements that He will yet release.

## Societies

In 1792, William Carey, an unpretentious shoemaker serving as a lay pastor in a tiny denomination, called believers to see differently. He articulated clearly their responsibility before God

**Breakthrough insights can provide motivation and stimulus for Kingdom expansion.**

to reach distant nations. His booklet, the *Enquiry*, presented radical questions to the Christians of his day. Followers of Christ, he insisted, must conscientiously do all in their power to see God's Kingdom come and His will be done in every land. Following the example of the "Trading Societies" working in many countries, Carey advocated that believers put together organizations or "societies" to initiate and sustain long-term missionary efforts.

A small group of his friends took up this challenge and formed the Baptist Missionary Society. However, Carey's research and his prayers brought him to a still more personal crisis. He concluded that he must not only advocate these ideas but also act upon them. As the Baptist Missionary Society's first envoy, Carey sailed for India, serving forty years without a furlough. In her book, *From Jerusalem to Irian Jaya*, Ruth Tucker says,

Carey was ahead of his time in missionary methodology. He had an awesome respect for the Indian culture and he never tried to import Western substitutes.... His goal was to build an indigenous church 'by means of native preachers' and by providing the Scriptures in the native tongue.... But it was not just in India where Carey's influence was felt. His work was being closely followed not only in

Diane Buchanan

**E-1 evangelism** is reaching out to people within one's own language and culture. The major barrier to be overcome is the "Stained-Glass Barrier"—finding ways to make the message relevant to the target group. E-1 evangelism will always be the most powerful because the messenger understands the culture within which the message is given.

Winter, R. D. (1992) *The New Macedonia*. In R. D. Winter & S. C. Hawthorne (Eds.). *Perspectives on the World Christian Movement: A Reader* (rev. ed.) (pp. B157–175). Pasadena: William Carey Library.

England, but also on the Continent and in America where the inspiration derived from his daring example outweighed in importance all his accomplishments in India.

In response to Carey's powerful example, many similar societies, usually denominationally linked, were established. The societies began to develop clear plans for effective work, and in spite of daunting hardships, a great stream of missionaries gradually set off toward the distant nations of India, China, and Africa. William Carey had helped them to see with new eyes.

## Cultures

In the 1860s another young man began to envision a wider way of seeing. Hudson Taylor looked at the work being done in China, he perceived something more. Evangelism and ministry were active in Shanghai, Canton, and Hong Kong, but what of the multiplied provinces further inland? What could be done there? Who would go beyond the coastal enclaves to extend the Kingdom?

Hudson and his wife Maria (herself a child of missionaries) organized for the undertaking through prayer and painstaking research. They began to exhort God's people to reach the *entire* nation. Their radical idea was not only to take the Gospel into the untouched districts but to do so in the garb of Confucian scholars and teachers. They planned to pair their messengers with Chinese workers—teams of "outsiders and insiders" who would enter into Chinese culture in every way possible.

The Taylor's suggestions shocked and dismayed many seasoned missionaries. These missionaries believed an essential part of their task was to "civilize" the Chinese, and the Taylor's proposals seemed to be a step backwards. Yet before long, brave souls—women

*Diane Buchanan*

**E-2 Evangelism** is reaching out to a culture that is somewhat different but with some similarities. It often requires learning a new language. There will always be cultural distinctives to be considered. The message must be contextualized, and the congregations planted must be appropriate to that culture.

Ordinary laymen and women were recruited, not just ordained workers. Because they were not linked to any specific denomination, the China Inland Mission accepted all. Other groups, later called "Faith Missions," organized to move toward interior regions in India, Myanmar (then Burma) and Africa. Latin America became a focus of concern as well. It was a time of resourceful insight and innovative advance.

udson and his wife Maria organized for the undertaking through prayer and painstaking research.

and men—caught the vision and joined this daring venture.

No other missionary...has had a wider vision and...a more systemized plan of evangelizing a broad geographical area than Hudson Taylor.... The China Inland Mission was his creation and the pacesetter of future faith missions. In his own lifetime the missionary force under him totaled more than eight hundred and...it continued to grow.

## Languages

Around 1919, the Lord began to awaken another way of looking at God's world. Cameron Townsend was working as a bookseller in rural Guatemala. Through a translator, a Cakchiquel Indian man asked Townsend, "If your God is so powerful, why doesn't He speak *my* language?"

This man's insistent question provoked a group of workers, later known as the "Chichicastenango Twelve" to deliberate as to how to give the Scriptures to the tribes of Guatemala. They represented several different agencies, yet they felt compelled to commit themselves to tribal work in the native languages of Guatemala. Townsend, one of the twelve, went to live among the Cakchiquel. Within ten years he gave them a written language and translated a New Testament for them.

As a consequence of this experience, Cameron Townsend founded an organization to do the same for other languages. He advocated for groups with small populations to receive Scripture in their mother tongue. That organization, Wycliffe Bible Translators, now includes 7,000 members working in countries around the world. Many similar partner agencies established in other nations work alongside them.

*Every culture is infected with "people blindness." They do not readily notice the presence or needs of other groups.*

## Peoples

Donald McGavran, serving in India, saw that there were major social and economic barriers to the spread of the Gospel. The caste system was a primary example, but his research also led him to examine other barriers. He began asking, "How do *peoples* become Christian?" He found many examples of multi-individual, mutually-interdependent decisions that swept large numbers into the Kingdom. By documenting them, he showed that the concept of a "people movement," though strange to the Western mind, was quite valid. His work came to be known as the Church Growth Movement.

In 1974, Ralph Winter, who had been taught by the studies of McGavran but took them further, stunned the Lausanne Congress. He confronted them with the reality of unreached people groups. Winter held that these people groups (often blending ethnic and linguistic identity with social and cultural factors) were, by all *ordinary* means, outside the reach of the Gospel. A new frontier became visible.

This paradigm summarizes some of Winter's thinking. With "E" representing "Evangelism," it expresses the distance and barriers that needed to be crossed for a people to hear the Gospel.

| | |
|---|---|
| Nominal Christians in the same culture | E-0 |
| Unbelievers in the same culture | E-1 |
| Unbelievers in a somewhat different culture | E-2 |
| Unbelievers in a very different culture | E-3 |

Unreached Peoples in cultures at an E-2 or E-3 distance from believers would require a deliberate cross-cultural initiative for them to be won and discipled. Winter's goal was to see within every culture an indigenous, viable church-planting movement. Church clusters of this kind could ultimately reach their own people.

These helpful distinctions parallel the assignment Jesus gave in Acts 1:8. E-1 represents Jerusalem and Judea; E-2 represents Samaria, and E-3 represents the ends of the earth. Winter's synopsis made it clear that while E-1 will always be valuable as well as the *most powerful* (because it takes place within the same culture) E-3 is the *most essential* (if all nations are to be won).

E-3 is also the most often neglected. Because a group is still unreached, it is often unknown. No one is there to recruit workers, prayer, or help for them. While workers may still be needed in E-2 areas, only deliberately crossing barriers towards E-3 groups will allow the unreached to receive a witness.

Winter pointed out that every culture is infected with "people blindness." They are so aware of their own group (those who look like them and hold the same worldview they do) that they do not readily notice the presence or needs of other groups. Even if these groups are nearby, churches may fail to examine how they might reach them. God was stretching His church to see beyond geography, beyond language, beyond ethnic and cultural blindness, into the segmented but overlapping *"ethne"* (the Greek word for nations used in Mt. 24:14) or peoples.

## Church Planting Movements

Building on these concepts, David Garrison of the Southern Baptist International Mission Board, as well as others, began to look into expanding movements within a people group. Garrison's group tried to discover the principles that nurtured such developments. Multiple elements, from committed prayer to a wide dissemination of the message led to successful church-planting movements, or CPMs as they came to be called.

These movements were founded in local leadership with reproducible gatherings. It became apparent that not only *could* this happen, it was possible to replicate it in other settings. No one could guarantee that following these principles would produce a "Church Planting Movement." However, workers could take steps that would not undermine the chances of it happening.

## What Breakthroughs May Lie Ahead?

Carey, the Taylors, Townsend, McGavran, Winter, and Garrison—all of them were given fresh ways to look at the world. Through richer and deeper insights, the Holy Spirit spurred the Church towards wider understanding. Though such movements might begin in unimposing ways or with unimpressive people, they have led to momentous shifts.

God will undoubtedly release unanticipated breakthroughs in the 21st century. Will they come from the West or the Two-Thirds world? From societies or agencies, from churches or from denominations, or perhaps from another ordinary or unexpected person? Which of the changing currents that swirl around our planet will open doors or close them? Which trends will affect the progress of the Kingdom? Which are going to work against it? It is time to be attentive and watchful.

## The Global Church

Because of the extensive work of earlier generations, the center of Global Christianity is shifting. Encouraging reports of movements toward Jesus Christ come from Africa, Latin America, India, and areas of Asia. The transfer from a geographically-centered Christendom to a "disappearing center" is disconcerting for some and heartening for others!

Vibrant and growing churches in these parts of the world are steadily advancing the Kingdom within their countries. Besides evangelizing their own people, young and emerging churches are making progress in sending out cross-cultural workers. The challenges they face may be significant but the openings are remarkable. It cannot be forgotten that the need of many nations is compelling.

The Korean church is dedicated and fervent, assigning cross-cultural workers to go and supporting them with zealous prayer. Latin Americans from Mexico to Argentina are setting off for North Africa and doing fruitful work in Middle Eastern countries. Indian believers are finding entrance to unreached groups

underground church in China is sending out workers through their "Back to Jerusalem" initiative.

In these endeavors, partnerships with Western churches can be beneficial, but they may contain special pitfalls for both sides. As Thom Wolf of Global Spectrum says, "To be effective together, the West must give up its arrogance and the Majority World must give up its resentments." Will each pay their price to rightly reflect Christ?

## Globalization: Blessing or Blight?

Globalization is one of the most powerful forces in the 21st century. It produces upheavals in nearly every sphere: economic, cultural, ethnic, political, and religious. How will these seismic changes on our planet that affect the way the Church will serve? Many peoples experience these effects as negative. Traditional boundaries are undermined or even erased. Can a rightly understood Biblical worldview offer a rationale for valuing and preserving the best in culture?

Individuals and nations worldwide are becoming ever more interconnected. Communication through the Internet can link cross-cultural workers to people outside normal reach. Access to research on peoples or topics can be found more readily. Bibles in many languages can be downloaded without having to go through customs. At the same time, the Internet may be a security nightmare for people trying to enter restricted or closed countries. The same tools that officials use to identify illegal immigrants may also endanger workers bringing in the Gospel.

Ease of travel makes it possible to reach almost any area of the world within 36–48 hours. More and more individuals visit and interact with other cultures through business, science and education. However, this openness for travel has also provided channels for the worst in smuggling and human trafficking.

Professionals are invited into increasingly diverse sectors. Scientists, lawyers, professors, businessmen and women, engineers, and many others can use their broad capacities to share their faith with colleagues and clients. There seems to be no skill that cannot be employed to open doors. Instead of building their own organizations, many are finding ways to work with those already in place, winning the people within them.

One educator uses her teaching expertise to serve among university professors in a Central Asian country. Returning again and again, she helps them gain the competence they

*No one could guarantee these principles would produce a "Church Planting Movement." However, they could take steps that would not undermine it.*

within their own borders. Gateways into difficult-to-reach places are available for Filipinos. Even the need to succeed. Her repeated visits and deepening relationships facilitate many on their journey toward the Lord.

Business and entrepreneurial initiatives may relieve some of the global unemployment upheaval. Connecting with field workers, businessmen can survey local needs and provide startup ideas and capital for small businesses. Apple growers from Yakima, Washington work alongside Uyghur people who grow the same kinds of apples. Not only are they exchanging practical insights, the Yakima growers are opening markets for their friends while they share their faith.

Multi-cultural partnerships can be especially productive. A Denver man who was worked on the field in Guatemala wants to link coffee growers there with a Himalayan nation. Their skills and experiences could assist beleaguered believers in a part of the world distant from theirs. A western church helped finance the travel costs to Sri Lanka for a Filipino believer seeking to learn strategies for reaching Muslims under a more experienced practitioner. This internship for the Filipino believer has now placed him and his wife among Muslims in a West African nation together with a New Zealander.

At the same time, globalization is bringing people from other nations to jobs as skilled workers in Christianized countries. Relationships built during transitional adjustments can bear long-lasting fruit. An interesting professional magazine with a Christian base is published for Indians who work outside India. On the other hand, an Indian believer actively reaches out to people who are working in the increasingly popular India-based call centers that provide worldwide computer service and support.

## Constant Change

The lightning speed of change in this century can make it difficult to rely on any consistent strategy. Doors that are open for a season may swiftly and unexpectedly close. Nations in the former Soviet Central Asia (Kazakhstan, Turkmenistan, Tajikistan, Khyrghistan, and Uzbekistan) have been approachable since the fall of communism. Currently, however, governmental hostility to Christian witness, as well as the lure of consumerism, are serious hazards to productive undertakings there.

In other situations, doors may fly open in moment, as they did following the tsunami in Asia. Regions that were inaccessible were suddenly in great need of the world's compassion. Some groups were ready to take action with concrete help at a moment's notice; others lagged behind, concerned but unprepared.

Perhaps these kinds of sudden openings are all for the good. Many leaders in the non-Western world have resisted what they perceive to be a "managerial missiology" In the west. No one is hurt by having to depend more closely on the Lord's direction when "business plans" cannot be utilized. Churches are being urged to set aside a significant percentage of their mission budget for God's plan, with the readiness to move whenever He provides an opening.

> **E**ven young and emerging churches are making progress in sending out cross-cultural workers.

> **T**he same tools that officials use to identify illegal immigrants may also endanger workers bringing in the Gospel.

## Beyond Translations

Bible societies around the globe continue to translate the Scriptures. Yet a new horizon beckons here, too. Serious consideration is being given to reaching Oral Peoples. One method has been through "chronological Bible storytelling"—presenting the message beginning in Genesis, not in the New Testament. With a presentation that takes place over several months' time using pictures and drama, the chronological method is effective, particularly among tribal people.

> *God's purpose for His people*
> *in being light for the nations of this world*
> *is also His command to us*
> *to bring salvation to the ends of the earth.*
>
> *David Filbeck*

Many people are not literate and may never be, so "storytelling" as a strategy may suit these people more appropriately. It is a relaxed way to convey truths of Scripture to listeners rather than preaching or lecturing. It was the method Jesus used, after all. It paves the way for questions and discussion. Film may be a form of storytelling, like the widely distributed Jesus film. It provides another useful approach that many people are utilizing.

"Storying" is an interesting and unique method: speaking an account exactly from Scripture by memory. This allows a community of listeners to receive it and discuss its meaning without an outside worker explaining it. This may help separate the Biblical account from the culture of the one who recites it. It is not unusual to have it spoken multiple times for the same gathering until they capture it themselves.

Although a great number of people do not read, they may be highly skilled at memorization. Once they have received and learned the account, they may have natural openings to pass on the message to others. Oral peoples possess valuable skills in this arena.

When the concept is clear to them, these groups can employ the arts to express what they've learned. Music and drama are especially powerful vehicles to extend the message. Wycliffe is exploring ways to offer translations orally—a valuable example of how to adjust strategies to newly envisioned realities.

## Movement of Peoples

Many factors contribute to the extensive relocation of peoples throughout the earth. Urbanization will be a continuing magnet. Rural peoples come to the cities in search of a better life or are forced there, fleeing from a failing one. Urbanization contributes to widespread social breakdown. A film shot clandestinely in China documents the exploitation of migrants once they arrive in the cities:

"The largest migration of people in history is taking place right now [in China]. 130 million peasants, mostly young women, have left their villages in search of jobs.... They comprise the world's largest pool of cheap labor."

Workers in the sweatshops in China, Myanmar, Cambodia, and Viet Nam are kept in shameful conditions and paid a pittance. Yet they supply the inexpensive clothing and goods that fill stores in developed countries. Many migrants must live in slums, trash heaps, or ghettoes, seldom able to rise to any other level.

Refugees and immigrants affect the world dramatically. Vulnerable and suffering people may be left to linger in camps for years and even generations, as is the case with the Sarahawi people in Western Sahara or the Palestinians. Refugees in the southern Sudan

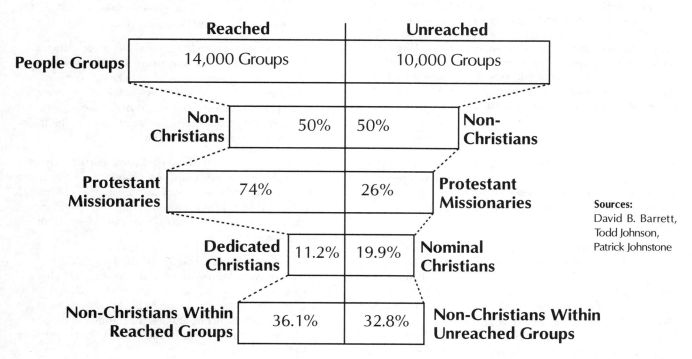

# THE GREAT IMBALANCE

|  | Reached | Unreached |  |
|---|---|---|---|
| **People Groups** | 14,000 Groups | 10,000 Groups |  |
| **Non-Christians** | 50% | 50% | **Non-Christians** |
| **Protestant Missionaries** | 74% | 26% | **Protestant Missionaries** |
| **Dedicated Christians** | 11.2% | 19.9% | **Nominal Christians** |
| **Non-Christians Within Reached Groups** | 36.1% | 32.8% | **Non-Christians Within Unreached Groups** |

Sources:
David B. Barrett,
Todd Johnson,
Patrick Johnstone

*What an imbalance!* Adapted from Winter, R. D. (1992): "The Task Remaining: All Humanity in Mission Perspective" in R. D. Winter & S. C. Hawthorne (Eds.). *Perspectives on the World Christian Movement: A Reader* (rev. ed.) Pg.188–189. Pasadena: William Carey Library. (1992)

*Diane Buchanan*

**E-3 evangelism** is the most difficult, but the most urgent. It requires penetrating and engaging a culture that is distant and very different from that of the messenger, even if it's geographically nearby. Language—maybe several languages—must be learned and the intricacies of the culture understood. It takes teamwork, sensitivity, endurance, time, and prayer. No unreached people group will be won until someone undertakes E-2 or E-3 evangelism.

are the focus of intense international concern. Finding answers or giving protection to these devastated people is a seeming quagmire of complexity. The world wades through a policy impasse trying to bring a solution to light.

Immigrants from countries which were colonized in the last century had easy acess to come as low-skilled workers to the colonizer's country. This now creates some exceptional challenges. Britain and most of Europe is staggering under an immigrant population that could become the majority. Few Christian "societies" are exploring ways to reach and win these new (or not so new—some are now second or even third generation) residents.

While refugees and immigrants are better known, internally displaced peoples or IDPs are under the radar. When famine, drought, or civil unrest force a family from their land, they may seek shelter with nearby relatives. Often this overwhelms each family's resources. Little or no international aid is available for them, as can be the case for immigrants or refugees.

The increase of poverty and oppression as a result of globalization cannot be ignored. It often enriches the few who already have too much and makes even poorer those who struggle desperately to survive. Can God's people find ways to work for justice and use their multiple blessings to lift those with the greatest needs? Can the poorest be shown God's intentions to use them to bless others as well?

These factors break down the "neat" segmentation of peoples. As the distinctive groups which might be the focus of a singular strategy grow fewer, people group thinking may be less appropriate. Will innovative strategies effectively discover and contact these intersections of groups in an increasingly urbanized and traumatized world?

## Worldwide Tribulations

Terrorism, rearing its ugly head all around the world, is having a chilling effect on efforts to reach the nations. Persecution of those who follow Christ can come from extremism and radical nationalism. Because these movements are seldom visible, they are all the more dangerous. Many people view those who worship Jesus as traitors to their own families and nations. Harsh measures are taken against them, as well as those who send people to work among them.

Government restrictions make it more difficult for international students to get into Western universities. Suspicion and anxiety may keep believers from befriending those who do come. Some in the West fear cross-cultural options that might make them vulnerable. However, dangerous scenarios often provide the most advantageous moments to serve.

Violent and hate-filled civil wars, particularly in Africa, South America, and Asia, fuel the fires of a new tribalism. In the worst cases they even lead to genocide. Young children, pressed into militias or cloistered in madrassas, are often raised without the gentling influence of women.

The scourge and tragedy of the HIV/AIDS is affecting every family in sub-Saharan Africa. Whole societies crumble without the teachers, traders, leaders, and parents necessary to maintain a stable social structure. Africa is not alone—the pandemic is also proliferating throughout India, Russia, Southeast Asia, and Central America.

Churches are stepping up to work among HIV/AIDS sufferers, seeing them with eyes of concern rather than judgment. A hospital in Malawi offers care to the wealthy in one area. It then uses the income from that work to fund its care for the destitute in the rest of the hospital. In Uganda, two homes for children, the most innocent victims of AIDS, are supported by the art of the local people. In places such as restaurants, the art is displayed and sold. A portion of the price goes to the artist; the rest supports the work with children.

## Arts and Ideas

Creative strategies develop in collaborations with national believers. Those who are insiders in the culture are likely to know the best ways to be effective. Taking time to listen to one another before acting is far wiser than arriving with prepared solutions.

Artistic messages of all kinds are stirring and memorable. The arts convey spiritual issues not always captured by abstract ideas. Concepts captured artistically through drama, pictures, video, song, dance, and poetry often enlighten and remain when words have been forgotten. Some of the most compelling arise from the least expected places. Persecuted believers in China and those who have suffered greatly in South Africa and Northern Ireland are producing powerfully moving songs that touch the worldwide church.

A guide at the famous Hermitage museum in Russia was showing Rembrandt's depiction of the return of the prodigal son. She clearly had no understanding of the purpose of the painting or the story it embodied. When a believer on the tour explained it to her, she dissolved into tears. In another case, with the approval of the government of a communist nation, an ongoing Internet program uses a class on the art of western Europe to showcase images of the life of Christ.

## Local Church Inventiveness

A pastor in Fort Worth, Texas, went to meet with imams in highly dangerous border areas of Afghanistan. Forming relationships with these tribal leaders led to natural opportunities to speak of his Kingdom viewpoint. The practical service of the church in response to expressed local needs backed up those beliefs

Even the poorest churches see ways to impact the society around them. One small Cambodian church offered to clean up the deplorable conditions in a notorious prison hospital. Not only did they change the environment for the ailing prisoners, the restriction against sharing the Good News with all the inmates was lifted.

Providing clean water is an imperative throughout the world. A pastor and his son are developing an inventive technology for cleansing water. A simple "bio-sand" water filter can be made in Cambodian villages. It both purifies water and gives the villagers an income source.

In order to supply safe, hygienic drinking water for all, various groups offer training in how to drill wells. Another organization teaches construction of a simple windmill from cloth and wood to continue the pumping of water without mechanical measures. On every level, water will continue to be a critical discussion.

Without question, local churches are coming to the fore in strategic endeavors. They boldly attempt new approaches, affecting all the spheres of life. They can learn from mistakes and achievements, and then teach others. Bob Moffitt of Harvest Foundation states,

The local church is the most visible and permanent representation of God's kingdom in any community. More than any other institution, it can reflect God's concern in each domain of man's need. [[/ex]]

## Civilizations in Conflict

While these examples of Kingdom work are encouraging and valuable, they are still micro-issues in a world full of macro-concerns. Samuel Huntington, in his book, The Clash of Civilizations and the Remaking of the World Order, concludes that our world is experiencing a great revitalization of major historic civilizations. He defines a civilization as "the broadest cultural entity" crossing national boundaries. Among key elements that make up a civilization, he identifies religion as the characteristic feature. In fact, some suggest his material could realistically be called "The Clash of Spiritualities."

Huntington's theory is that the interaction and tension between these civilizations will be the source of the most serious conflicts in the 21st Century. Huntington's view is that Western or "Christian" civilizations will encounter confrontations either with the Islamic world or with the Asian (especially Chinese) world. This is not merely about economic, military, or political conflict. The polarizations that produce these clashes come from much larger worldview collisions.

Those from different civilizations usually grasp only the surface features of the others. Negative and overly simplified images of the opposing group lead to responses of intense apprehension and hatred. Huntington's hypothesis seems to be supported by daily news bulletins. This places Francis Schaeffer's question "How shall we then live?" at the center point of the global discussion.

Wherever God's people find themselves, there will be worldview issues to confront. It is no longer the task of the religious professionals alone to speak to them. Every believer, in whatever domain of life they serve, must understand how to meet them head-on. In a globalized world, these questions will be inevitable.

## It Will Be Done

The One who sits in the heavens still laughs at the kings and rulers of the earth who conspire to oppose Him. In the 1930s it was said that Communism would take over Latin America. The Pentecostal outpouring through the church overcame that prediction. In the 1950s it seemed unlikely that the church in China would survive. Everyone now knows how woefully that forecast failed.

Immense challenges face the church today. Those who would desire to see the glory of God must face this certainty: glory in Scripture is inexorably linked with suffering. The experience of the underground church of China experience reveals that, as does the record of history. A smug expectation that resources, finances, or assets can allow any part of the church to bypass suffering would be terribly mistaken. Those who have experienced martyrdom and persecution have much to teach the comfortable world.

Yet, if rightly understood, this news is heartening! In her book, The Great Commission, Rose Dowsett explains how, throughout the chronicle of the ages, the Kingdom advances most effectively in weakness.

Woven through the bright cloth of...amazing growth...was the persistent thread of weakness and vulnerability. It was costly to be a disciple, and those who sought to bring others into God's family were under no illusion about that. Suffering was normative, not an aberration.

In the 21st century, too, through poor, foolish and despised vessels, the Lord will find ways to confound the great and the mighty.

No one knows where or to whom the next insights will be given. They will come on the worldview level and on the lowest levels. Setbacks are sure to come as well, even from within. Often those who resist the next move of God may be those who were used in the last move of God. Hearts prepared for the unexpected are more likely to be ready for the surprises of the Lord.

Reaching the nations is still God's relentless purpose. His purposes continue to unfold and He watches over them to see them accomplished. Each generation receives unique assignments to walk alongside those purposes. What assignment, what insights will this generation receive? Whatever they may be, they will call for both risk and faith.

The Lord spoke to Habbakuk, "Look among the nations and watch! For I will work a work in your days which you would not believe, though it were told you." (Hab.1:5). A creative God continues to guide His people with innovative ideas and preparations. Believers prepared for obedience will see with new eyes as the Father unveils His intentions. ◪

# Essentials of a Church

*George Patterson*

**George Patterson** teaches in the Division of Intercultural Studies at Western Seminary in Portland, Oregon. He coaches and trains missionaries to multiply churches in many areas of the world. He worked for 21 years in northern Honduras through a program of Theological Education and Evangelism by Extension.

## Teach and Practice Obedience to Jesus' Commands in Love, Above and Before All Else

Jesus, after affirming His deity and total authority on earth, commissioned His Church to make disciples who obey all His commands (Matthew 28:18–20). So His commands take priority over all other institutional rules (even that hallowed *Church Constitution and Bylaws*). This obedience is always in love. If we obey God for any other reason, it becomes sheer legalism; God hates that.

> *Obedience is always in love. If we obey God for any other reason, it becomes sheer legalism; God hates that.*

## Start Right Out with Obedience to Jesus' Basic Commands

To plant churches in a pioneer field, aim for each community to have a group of believers in Christ committed to obey His commands. This definition of a church might get a D minus where you studied theology, but *the more you add to it, the harder it will be for the churches you start to reproduce.* We asked our converts to memorize the following list of Christ's basic commands:

1. Repent and believe: Mark 1:15

2. Be baptized (and continue in the new life it initiates): Matthew 28:18–20; Acts 2:38; Romans 6:1–11

3. Love God and neighbor in a practical way: Matthew 22:37–40

4. Celebrate the Lord's Supper: Luke 22:17–20

5. Pray: Matthew 6:5–15

6. Give: Matthew 6:19–21; Luke 6:38

7. Disciple others: Matthew 28:18–20

Memorize them; you can neither be nor make obedient disciples unless they are basic to your Christian experience. They are the ABCs of both discipling and church planting.

## Define Evangelism Objectives in Terms of Obedience

Do not simply preach for "decisions"; make obedient disciples. Only disciples produce a church that multiplies itself spontaneously within a culture. Consider the two commands: "Repent and believe," and "Be baptized." In western culture a man stands alone before his God and "decides" for Christ. But in other cultures sincere conversion needs interaction with family and friends. Faith, repentance, and immediate baptism of the entire family or group—not an invitation to make a decision—is the norm (Acts 2:36–41; 8:11; 10:44–48; 16:13–15, 29–34; 18:8). Repentance goes deeper than a decision; it is a permanent change wrought by God's Spirit. We are born all over again. Few purely intellectual decisions in any culture lead to permanent, obedient discipleship.

We found that when we baptized repentant believers reasonably soon, without requiring a long doctrinal course first, the great majority then responded to our training in obedient discipleship. The detailed doctrine came later. Teaching heavy theology *before* one learns loving, childlike obedience is dangerous. It leaves him assuming that Christianity is having Scripturally correct doctrine, and he leaves it at that. He becomes a passive learner of the Word rather than an active disciple. Balanced discipling activates mind, heart, and hands. It integrates Word, Care, Task. It learns, loves, serves. Emphasizing one of the three at the expense of the others yields spiritually unbalanced believers, not disciples.

> *The first weeks of new life will determine whether they are Bible-centered, active, loving disciples.*

The new members of the first New Testament Church in Jerusalem obeyed all of the basic commands of Christ from the very beginning. After repentance and

Patterson, G. (1999). From "The Spontaneous Multiplication of Churches." In R. D. Winter & S. C. Hawthorne (Eds.). *Perspectives on the World Christian Movement: A Reader* (rev. ed.). (Pgs. 601–602; 604). Pasadena: William Carey Library.

baptism they learned the apostle's doctrine (Word), broke bread, prayed and fellowshiped (Care) and gave and witnessed, adding new members every day (Task): Acts 2:41–47. We also must teach each new convert from the very beginning to obey all these commands in love (John 15:15). Don't wait to start obeying Christ! The first few weeks of their new life in Christ are the most impressionable; they will determine more than any other time of teaching whether or not they are (and make) Bible-centered, active, loving *disciples*.

## Orient Your Teaching to Loving Obedience

We taught our pastors to orient all church activity to New Testament commands. As they taught the Word of God, they accustomed their people to discern three levels of authority for all that they did as a body of disciples.

1. **New Testament Commands.** These carry all the authority of heaven. They include the commands of Jesus as well as those of the inspired apostles in the Epistles that apply only to baptized, more mature Christians who are already members of a church. We don't vote on them nor argue about doing them. They always take precedence over any human organization's rules.

2. **Apostolic Practices (Not Commanded).** We cannot enforce these as laws because Christ alone has authority to make laws for His own church, His body. Nor can we prohibit their practice because they have apostolic precedent. Examples include: holding possessions in common, laying hands on converts, celebrating the Lord's Supper frequently in homes using one cup, baptizing the same day of conversion, Sunday worship.

3. **Human Customs.** Practices not mentioned in the New Testament have only the authority of a group's voluntary agreement. If it involves discipline, the agreement is recognized in heaven (but only for this congregation; we do not judge another congregation by the customs of our own: Matthew 18:15–20).

Nearly all church divisions and quarrels originate when a power-hungry person seeking followers puts mere apostolic practice or human customs (levels 2 or 3) at the very top level as law.

## Help Each New Church to Reproduce

Each new church should send extension workers to reproduce daughter churches, as did the Antioch church (Acts 13:1–3). The longer you wait to mobilize a church for multiplication, the harder it is to reprogram its thinking. Teach your elders the joy of sacrificing to separate their strongest tithers and leaders, in the power of the Holy Spirit as in Antioch, to extend Christ's kingdom. After prayer, perhaps fasting, hold a formal separation service with laying on of hands, as they did. Remember, it is not the individuals that reproduce, but congregations that pray and are moved by the Holy Spirit. Let each new church be a link in the chain. The individual extension worker is only an arm of his church.

## Show Each New Believer How to Witness to Friends and Relatives

The Holy Spirit flows readily through the bonds that exist between family members and close friends (Acts 10:24, 44). Keep new converts in a loving relationship with them (don't pull them out of their circle to put them in a same Christian environment, or those very bonds that aid the spread of the gospel become barriers).

We prepared simple gospel studies (mostly Bible

The commands of Jesus take precedence over any human organization's rule.

stories) that even illiterates could use at once to share their new faith. We accompanied them to show them how to do it, modeling it all in a way they could immediately imitate.

## Pray for Reproduction Power

Each new church in a chain, like a grain of wheat, has the same potential to start the reproduction all over again. Christ's parables in Matthew 13, Mark 4, and John 15 compare the growth and reproduction of His churches to that of plants. An obedient, Spirit-filled church *has* to reproduce at home or abroad. It's her very nature; she is the body of the risen, life-giving Son of God. 🗗

---

*Mission is that dimension of our faith that refuses to accept reality as it is and aims at changing it.*

David Bosch

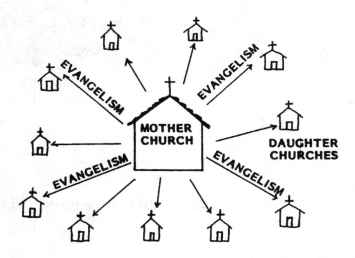

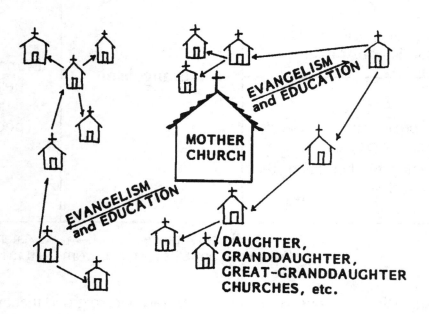

One of the several extension chains we have in Honduras has reproduced over five generations and twenty churches.

# REGULAR MISSIONS and FRONTIER MISSIONS

| | Target Group for Evangelist | |
|---|---|---|
| **Evangelism Type (with examples)** | Reached People Groups | Unreached People Groups |
| **E-3**<br>1. Anglos reaching traditional Hopis in Arizona.<br>2. Brahmin Christian from India reaching Muslims in Pakistan. | **II. Regular Missions** | **III. Frontier Missions** |
| **E-2**<br>1. Navajo Christians working with Mongolians.<br>2. American working with Brazilian middle class. | | |
| **E-1**<br>1. Sharing Christ with your unsaved neighbors.<br>2. Chaplain ministering to U.S. soldiers in Saudi Arabia. | **I. Evangelism** | (Evangelism by initial believers in an unreached people group) |
| **E-0**<br>1. Revivalist preaching to unbelievers in a church congregation.<br>2. Sunday school teacher sharing the gospel with class. | | |

*Evangelist's Cultural Distance from Potential Convert — Greater Distance / Less Distance*

Less Distance ⟷ Greater Distance
Potential Convert's Distance from Culturally Nearest Church

I. **Evangelism:** Ministry to one's own (or very similar) people group that already has a sound indigenous church.

II. **Regular Missions:** Cross-cultural evangelism (ideally in association with Christians of the target culture) to a people group that already has a sound, indigenous church.

III. **Frontier Missions**: Cross-cultural evangelism to a people group that does **not** have a sound indigenous church.

Adapted from Ralph D. Winter B-181 *Perspectives Reader.*

# THE TWO TASKS OF ACTS 1:8

"Ye shall be witnesses to Me **both** in Jerusalem, and in all Judea and Samaria, **and** unto the ends of the earth." Acts 1:8b YLT

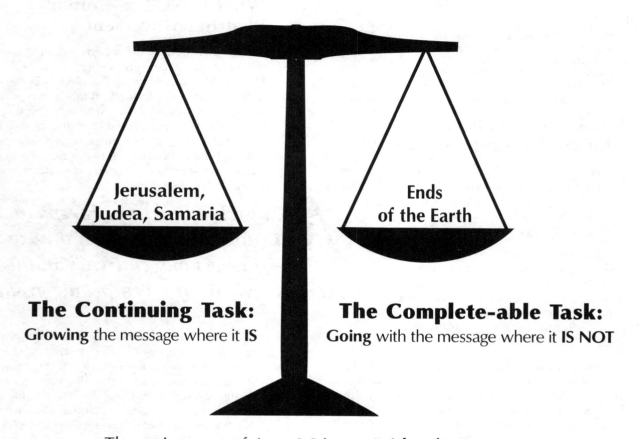

**Jerusalem,
Judea, Samaria**

**Ends
of the Earth**

**The Continuing Task:**
**Growing** the message where it **IS**

**The Complete-able Task:**
**Going** with the message where it **IS NOT**

The assignment of Acts 1:8 is not **"either/or"**;
it is not any part ahead of another; it is not a progression. It is **"both/and."**

# Church Planting Movements

*David Garrison*

David Garrison served the Southern Baptist International Mission Board as their Associate Vice President for Global Strategy. He has lived in Hong Kong, Japan, Germany, France, England, Egypt, Tunisia, and India. He is recognized around the world as a pioneer in understanding Church Planting Movements.

## Key Components of a Church Planting Movement

What is a Church Planting Movement? A simple, concise definition of a Church Planting Movement (CPM) is *a rapid and exponential increase of indigenous churches planting churches within a given people group or population segment.*

There are several key components to this definition. The first is *rapid*. As a movement, a Church Planting Movement occurs with rapid increases in new church starts. Saturation church planting over decades and even centuries is good but doesn't qualify as a Church Planting Movement.

Secondly, there is an *exponential* increase. This means that the increase in churches is not simply incremental growth—adding a few churches every year or so. Instead, it compounds exponentially—two churches become four, four churches become sixteen and so forth. Exponential multiplication is only possible when new churches are being started by the churches themselves—rather than by professional church planters or missionaries.

Finally, they are *indigenous churches*. This means they are generated from within rather than from without. This is not to say that the gospel is able to spring up

> **A** *Church Planting Movement is not an end in itself. The end of all of our efforts is for God to be glorified.*

intuitively within a people group. The gospel always enters a people group from the outside; this is the task of the missionary. However, in a Church Planting Movement the momentum quickly becomes indigenous so that the initiative and drive of the movement comes from within the people group rather than from outsiders.

## What Is NOT a Church Planting Movement

If this definition isn't enough, we might also clarify what a Church Planting Movement is *not*. A Church Planting Movement is more than "evangelism that results in churches." Evangelism that results in churches is a part of a Church Planting Movement, but the "end-vision" is less extensive. A church planter might satisfy himself with the goal of planting a single church or even a handful of churches, but fail to see that it will take a *movement* of churches planting churches to reach an entire nation of people.

> **A** *Church Planting Movement is a rapid and exponential increase of indigenous churches planting churches within a given people group.*

A Church Planting Movement is also more than a revival of preexisting churches. Revivals are highly desirable, but they're **not** Church Planting Movements. Evangelistic crusades and witnessing programs may lead thousands to Christ, and that's wonderful, but it isn't the same as a Church Planting Movement. Church Planting Movements feature churches rapidly reproducing themselves.

Perhaps the closest thing to a Church Planting Movement that still is **not** a Church Planting Movement is when local church planters are trained and deployed to plant multiple churches among their own people. This is a highly productive method of spreading churches across a population segment or people group, but the momentum remains in the hands of a limited group of professional church planters rather than in the heart of each new church that is begun.

Finally, a Church Planting Movement is *not an end in itself.* The end of all of our efforts is for God to be glorified. This occurs whenever individuals enter into right relationship with Him through Jesus Christ. As they do, they are incorporated into churches that enable them to continue to grow in grace with other like-minded believers. Any

Garrison, David. (1999) *Church Planting Movements*. Pg. 7–10; 16–17; 21–23. A booklet published by the International Mission Board, Southern Baptist Convention, Richmond, Va. To order call 1-800-866-3621 time people come to new life in Jesus Christ, God is glorified. Any time a church is planted—no matter who does it—there are grounds for celebration.

So why is a Church Planting Movement so special? Because *it seems to hold forth the greatest potential for the largest number of lost individuals glorifying God by coming into new life in Christ and entering into communities of faith.* (Italics mine. Editor.)

> **A Church Planting Movement occurs when the vision of churches planting churches spreads into the churches themselves.**

However, a Church Planting Movement is not simply an increase in the number of churches, even though this also is positive. A Church Planting Movement occurs when the vision of churches planting churches spreads from the missionary and professional church planter into the churches themselves, so that by their very nature they are winning the lost and reproducing themselves.

Let's review some key points. Missionaries are capable church planters, but they will always be limited in number. Local church planters hold more promise simply because there is a larger pool of them available. Church Planting Movements hold an even greater potential because the act of church planting is being done by the churches themselves, leading to the greatest possible number of new church starts.

## The Setting: A Region in China

China in the early 1990s was reeling from enormous social upheaval. Economic boom had left gross disparities between the haves and have-nots. Rapid urbanization was dismantling ancient family and communal alliances. The entire country anxiously awaited a successor to the Maoist doctrines that had held the collective mind for almost four decades.

New ideas were sweeping through the country and were viewed with a mixture of enthusiasm and rejection. The suppressed student democracy movement, culminating in the clash with government forces in Tiananmen Square in 1989, had left many youth despairing of political reform, yet still searching for some new hope for a better future.

## What happened

Into this setting, the International Mission Board assigned a strategy coordinator in 1991 to a region we'll call "Yanyin." During a year of language and culture study, the missionary conducted a thorough analysis of Yanyin. It consisted of about seven million people clustered in five different people groups living in a variety of rural and urban settings. He mapped their population centers and began several evangelistic probes. After a few false starts, the strategy coordinator developed a reproducing model of indigenous church planting that he implemented to great effect.

In his initial survey, the strategy coordinator found three local house churches made up of about 85 Han* Chinese Christians. The membership was primarily elderly and had been slowly declining for years, with no vision or prospects for growth. Over the next four years, by God's grace, the strategy coordinator helped the gospel take fresh root among this people group and sweep rapidly across the Yanyin region.

## Mobilizing local workers

Aware of the enormous cultural and linguistic barriers that separated him from the people of Yanyin, the missionary began by mobilizing Chinese Christian co-laborers from across Asia. Then, partnering these ethnic Chinese church planters with a small team of local believers, the group planted six new churches in 1994. The following year, seventeen more were begun. The next year, fifty more were started. By 1997, just three years after starting, the number of churches had risen to one hundred ninety-five and had spread throughout the region, taking root in each of the five people groups.

> **Aware of the enormous cultural and linguistic barriers, the missionary began mobilizing Chinese Christian co-laborers from across Asia.**

At this point the movement was spreading so rapidly that the strategy coordinator felt he could safely exit the work. The next year, in his absence, the movement nearly tripled as the total number of churches grew to 550 with more than 55,000 believers.

---

* Han Chinese are the majority people group of China.

## The Setting: The Bholdari of India

In the congested interior of India there is a people group we'll call the Bholdari. The name refers to their language, which claims nearly 90 million speakers living in more than 170,000 villages stretched across four Indian states. The population includes all four castes and the classless untouchables. The majority of the people group are extremely impoverished, illiterate, and dependent upon subsistence agriculture and a barter economy for their livelihood.

The region is also home to several important Hindu holy sites, and the Brahmin, or priestly, caste is well represented among the Bholdari. More than 85 percent of the Bholdari are Hindu, the remainder being Muslim or animist. Within this region there also are four large cities, with more than 1 million people each.

## What happened

In 1989 Southern Baptists sent a strategy coordinator to the Bholdari people. Following a year of language and culture acquisition, the missionary launched a strategy of working through some of the local churches that had embraced his vision for planting new churches. To his horror, the first six Indian church planters, using methods common to church planting in the more tolerant environment of south India, were brutally murdered in separate events as they began their missionary work.

## Finding the "Man of Peace"

In 1992 the tide turned, however, as the missionary strategist implemented a new approach to church planting. Drawing on the teachings of Jesus found in Luke 10, in which Jesus sent out disciples two by two into the villages of Galilee and instructed them to find a "man of peace," the Bholdari evangelist church planters began to do the same. Before opening his mouth to proclaim the gospel, each Bholdari missionary would move in with a local man of peace and begin discipling the family (even before they became believers) into the Christian faith using chronological storying of the Bible.* As these initial converts came to faith, they led their families to the Lord, baptized them, and forged them into the nucleus of a new church in each village.

In 1993 the number of churches grew from twenty-eight to thirty-six. The following year saw forty-two more churches started. A training center ensured that

there would be a continuing stream of evangelist/church planters spreading the word. Along the way, churches began multiplying themselves. In 1996 the number of churches climbed to 547, then 1,200 in 1997. By 1998 there were 2,000 churches among the Bholdari. In seven years more than 55,000 Bholdari came to faith in Jesus Christ. ⬚

*T*he Bholdari church planters began to move in with a local man of peace, discipling the family into the Christian faith.

*Mary Filidis, YWAM*

**Baluch:** The Baluch of Pakistan are Sunni Muslims in a country dominated by a Shiite Muslim majority. These nomadic peoples have been known as great fighters for centuries. About 75% of the four and a half million Baluch live in the Baluchistan province, although the poverty there has caused many to migrate to Karachi, the county's largest city.

Other Baluch are located in southeastern Iran, in Turkmenistan, and in the Gulf States, and a few thousand are in Sweden. The New Testament, completed in Baluchi in 1900, needs revision. Very little work is taking place among this people, and there are only ten known Baluch Christians in the world.

---

* Chronological storying of the Bible: Introducing Jesus by telling the story of the Bible beginning with Creation as opposed to teaching specific doctrines about Him.

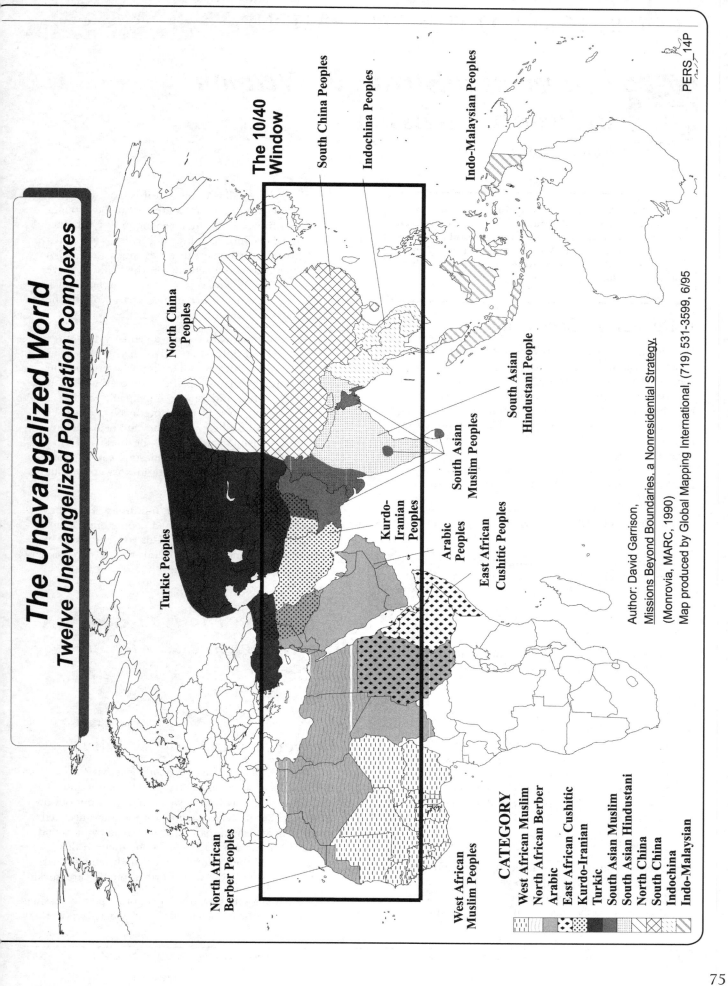

# The Unevangelized World
## Twelve Unevangelized Population Complexes

The 10/40 Window

South China Peoples

Indochina Peoples

Indo-Malaysian Peoples

North China Peoples

South Asian Hindustani People

Turkic Peoples

Kurdo-Iranian Peoples

Arabic Peoples

South Asian Muslim Peoples

East African Cushitic Peoples

North African Berber Peoples

West African Muslim Peoples

### CATEGORY

West African Muslim
North African Berber
Arabic
East African Cushitic
Kurdo-Iranian
Turkic
South Asian Muslim
South Asian Hindustani
North China
South China
Indochina
Indo-Malaysian

Author: David Garrison,
Missions Beyond Boundaries, a Nonresidential Strategy.
(Monrovia, MARC, 1990)
Map produced by Global Mapping International, (719) 531-3599, 6/95

PERS_14P

75

# Prayer as a Strategic Weapon in Frontier Missions

### John D. Robb

> John D. Robb is the Chair of the International Prayer Council, a network of regional and national prayer ministries and networks around the world. He also serves as Director for World Vision International, encouraging deeper integration of transformational prayer into that organization.

## A Revealing Case Study

One of the greatest illustrations of prayer as a strategic weapon in frontier missions is found in the experience of J. O. Fraser, the pioneer missionary to the Lisu tribe of southwest China. In the early 1900s, he preached Christ for several years among the far-flung mountain villages of this people with almost no outward results. Fraser's few converts fell back into the clutches of demonism, and he himself, attacked by severe depression and suicidal despair, almost gave up his mission. Breakthrough occurred when two things happened:

1. The Spirit of God enabled him to pray "the prayer of faith" for several hundred Lisu families to come to Christ.

2. He succeeded in forming a prayer support group of eight to ten Christians in his home country to back up the work in ongoing prayer.

His wife later wrote about the difference this prayer effort made in Fraser's work:

> He described to me how in his early years he had been all but defeated by the forces of darkness arrayed against him.... He came to the place where he asked God to take away his life rather than allow him to labor on without results. He would then tell me of the prayer forces that took up the burden at home and the tremendous lifting of the cloud over his soul, of the gift of faith that was given him and how God seemed suddenly to step in, drive back the forces of darkness, and take the field. [1]

Fraser himself said:

> Work on our knees. I am feeling more and more that it is after all just the prayers of God's people that call down blessing upon the work, whether they are directly engaged in it or not. Paul may plant and Apollos water, but it is God who gives the increase, and this increase can be brought down from heaven by believing prayer, whether offered in China or in England.... If this is so, then Christians at home can do as much for foreign missions as those actually on the field. I believe it will only be known on the last day how much has been accomplished in missionary work by the prayers of earnest believers at home...

> We are not dealing with an enemy that fires at the head only—that keeps the mind only in ignorance—but with an enemy who uses poison gas attacks that wrap the people around with deadly effect and yet are impalpable, elusive... Nor would it be of any more avail to teach or preach to Lisu here while they are held back by these invisible forces...But the breath of God can blow away all those miasmic vapors from the atmosphere of a village in answer to your prayers. [2]

In the years that followed, hundreds of families accepted Christ and ultimately a people movement involving tens of thousands of Lisus ensued. Today in southwest China and northern Burma they are a missionary tribe taking the Gospel to other tribes about them.

*Prayer links our efforts to God in His almightiness, without whose help all such efforts are ultimately in vain.*

## Prayer as a Linking Activity

Prayer at its very heart is a *linking* activity. First, prayer links us with God to receive His power and direction as we pray for the world and carry out our own ministries. Secondly, as we pray for the unevangelized world, it links us with particular unreached groups and the Christian workers laboring among them. It links our efforts and their efforts to God in His almightiness, without whose help all such efforts ultimately are in vain.

Yet having said this, prayer can often be the missing link in our efforts on behalf of the unevangelized world.

Robb, J. D. (1991). "Prayer as a Strategic Weapon in Frontier Missions." *International Journal of Frontier Missions*, B(1), 23–31.

As important as good organization, planning, and strategy are in world evangelization, in our busyness for God we may have neglected to link up with His power and direction to carry out that particular part of His mission given to us. And that is a crucial omission!

World evangelization above all is an issue to be decided by spiritual power, the power of the Holy Spirit released in response to the prayers of His people.

Arthur Matthews, the late former missionary of the China Inland Mission, put his finger on the reason that we often do not emphasize prayer enough:

> The concept that treats prayer as if it were a supplemental booster in getting some project off the ground makes the project primary and the prayer secondary. Prayer was never meant to be incidental to the work of God. It is the work. [3]

## Victory in the Spiritual Realm Is Primary

King Jehoshaphat relied on the weapons of united fasting and prayer, public worship, and praise, which brought God's intervention against the invading armies of Israel's enemies. Bible teacher Derek Prince writes:

> These weapons, scripturally employed by Christians today, will gain victories as powerful and dramatic as they gained for the people of Judah in the days of Jehoshaphat.... *Victory in the spiritual realm is primary.* It is to be obtained by spiritual weapons. Thereafter its outcome will be manifested in every area of the natual and material realm. [4]

> **G**od gave dominion of the earth to humankind. We can exercise our God-given right to influence the affairs of this world through intercessory prayer.

## God Requires Intercession

Why does God desire and require His people's intercession? Most likely because God originally gave dominion of the earth to humankind. That dominion has never been revoked by God. Satan's dominion achieved through rebellion against the Creator is a false, illegitimate, usurped dominion. Redeemed through Christ, we can exercise our God-given right to influence the affairs of this world through the exercise of intercessory prayer. Like Kuwait's request for the multinational force to come against the illegitimate dominion of Iraq, so we, in prayer as God's redeemed children, pray that His will be done, His kingdom come on earth.

## Prayer Extends the Outreach of the Church

Prayer is mentioned over thirty times in the book of Acts alone, and generally it is mentioned as occurring just before major breakthroughs in the outward expansion of the early Christian movement. For the apostles, extended times of united prayer and waiting on God together were pivotal in their mission to the unreached.

The whole European side of the modern Protestant missionary enterprise grew out of Pietism, a revival movement that was steeped in earnest prayer. From its influence the Danish-Halle Mission to India went forth and the Moravian movement under Count Zinzendorf emerged. The prayer meeting that the Moravians began in 1727 went on 100 years! This prayer effort kindled their desire to proclaim Christ to the unreached, and from this one small village, over 100 missionaries went out in twenty-five years.

> **T**he Moravians' prayer meeting began in 1727 and went on 100 years! From one small village, over 100 missionaries went out in 25 years.

Prayer in the power of the Holy Spirit breaks through the false dominion of the enemy and clears the way for His deliverance and *shalom* to come to all peoples.

In the dramatic events in Eastern Europe, God has used the prayers of His people to shake the nations. He can do the same thing in the unevangelized world. He is seeking those who will stand before Him in the gap for the 2,000 major unreached peoples, the 1,000 unevangelized cities, and the 30 unevangelized countries.

## Revivals Impact Frontier Missions

It has been said that "all the mighty spiritual revivals that constitute the mountain peaks of missionary annals had their roots in prayer." [5] Jonathan Goforth, missionary revivalist in the Far East at the beginning of this century, described the powerful revivals and awakenings that took place in Korea and China, and not only revived the church but brought tens of thousands from unreached peoples to Christ. It all began with small bands of believers deciding to pray together regularly for an outpouring of God's Spirit upon them and upon the unconverted.

Goforth later discovered it was not only the missionaries who had been praying but someone in his home country.

> When I came to England, I met a certain saint of God. We talked about the revival in China, and she gave me certain dates when God specially pressed her to pray. I was almost startled on looking up these dates to find that they were the very dates when God was doing his mightiest work in Manchuria and China...I believe the day will come when the whole inward history of that revival will be unveiled and will show that it was not the one who speaks to you now but some of God's saints hidden away with Him in prayer who did most to bring it about.[6]

In Hawaii the revival known as the "Great Awakening" (1837–43) began in the hearts of missionaries who were moved strongly to pray. At their annual meetings in 1835 and 1836

> ...they were powerfully moved to pray and were so deeply impressed with the need of an outpouring of the Spirit that they prepared a strong appeal to the home churches, urging Christians everywhere to unite with them in prayer for a baptism on high.[7]

There were soon signs of growing interest in spiritual things among non-Christians, and then in 1837 so sweeping a spiritual awakening occurred that the missionaries had to labor night and day to accomodate multitudes anxiously seeking the assurance of salvation. In one day over 1,700 converts were baptized, and in six years, 27,000 were added to the church.

J. Edwin Orr, the late historian of revivals, observed that the 19th-century spiritual awakenings "revived all the existing missionary societies and enabled them to enter other fields...[and] practically every missionary invasion was launched by men revived or converted in the awakenings."[8]

## God's Children Possess Their Inheritance, the Peoples

In the history of missions, great ingatherings into the church of Christ appear to be linked to strong, persistent praying. John Hyde, missionary to northern India, became known as "the apostle of prayer," since God raised up scores of national workers in answer to his prayers.

*Mary Filidis, YWAM*

**Uzbek:** Descendants of Genghis Khan, the Uzbeks are Sunni Muslims who lived seventy years under Communist domination. Now, like other peoples in Central Asia, including the Tadjiks, the Khyrgyz, the Kazakhs, and the Turkmen, they have established an independent republic. Some of these people are experiencing renewed interest in the Islamic faith, which was suppressed under the Soviets. Other Uzbeks are more open to new ideas.

Sixteen million Uzbeks live in Uzbekistan. Others are located in Saudi Arabia, Afghanistan, Pakistan, and Turkey, with a few in Europe and the United States. With the current of nationalistic fervor strong, it is especially vital to develop a church movement that will fit appropriately within the Uzebeki culture.

Elsewhere in India, prayer has also proved to be key to great ingatherings among unreached peoples. Missionaries working among the Telugu outcastes were discouraged to the point of almost abandoning the work because of the lack of response. However, the last night of 1853 a missionary couple and three Indian helpers spent the night in prayer for the Telugus on a hill overlooking the city of Ongole. When the first light of day dawned, they all shared a sense of assurance that their prayers had prevailed. Gradually the opposition broke over the next few years, and a mighty outpouring of the spirit brought 8,000 Telugus to Christ in only a six-week period. In one day over 2,200 were baptized, and this church became the largest in the world![9]

> **God is waiting on the prayers of His people to turn Muslim zealots around as He did the apostle Paul, so they can become missionaries.**

In 1902 two lady missionaries with the Khassia Hills Mission were challenged by the need to pray, and Khassian Christians also began to pray for their unconverted fellows. In a few months over 8,000 were added to the church in that section of India.[10]

## Effective Strategies Come from Research and Prayer

Joshua was one of the original "researchers" who spied out the land of promise in Numbers 13. Because he knew the facts about the land and its peoples so well, he was prepared to be the great military strategist that he later became during the conquest. However, in the book of Joshua, we see him continually seeking God for His guidance in the development of effective strategies. He did not lean on his own understanding, but he relied upon God's direction given through prayer.

The principle is still the same. I am becoming more and more convinced that coupling research findings concerning the people group we are trying to reach with ongoing, persevering prayer is an unstoppable combination in the process of developing effective mission strategy. John Dawson's recent book *Taking Our Cities for God: How to Break Spiritual Strongholds* insightfully ties together ministry-related research and intercessory prayer.

## Prayer Is the Supernatural Way of Sending Out Workers

Jesus did not tell the disciples to go all out and round up as many Christian workers as possible or to raise a million dollars for mission. Instead He said that prayer to the One who owns the harvest was the priority because He can call, equip, and send those workers who will be best able to reap the harvest.

I am convinced that the mightiest missionaries to the Muslims are not even converted yet. But God is waiting upon the prayers of His people to turn Muslim zealots around as he did the apostle Paul, so they become missionaries to their people. I am convinced that as prayer networks are formed, focusing on particular peoples, cities, and countries, we will see God raise up armies of new workers.

In 1880, when the China Inland Mission had only 100 workers, and then again in 1887, when additional workers were required, Hudson Taylor and his associates spent protracted time in prayer until they received the assurance of faith that the number required would be granted. Both times, after an appeal for 70 new missionaries in 1880 and 100 in 1887, the full number reached China within the specified time and with all their support supplied.[11]

## Prayer Opens Closed Doors for Christian Presence

Don McCurry, Ministries to Muslims International, recently gave me a striking illustration in this regard. Some years ago he visited the West African country of Guinea. Sekou Toure, a Marxist leader, had just kicked out all the missionaries except two and was busy torturing political prisoners. The two remaining missionaries, McCurry, and twelve national pastors met to intercede for the country.

First they interceded with God for the removal of this Marxist tyrant who had closed the door to further mission efforts when most of the people groups still remained unoccupied by the church. Then they put up maps around the room in which they were meeting and together laid their hands upon those areas of the country and groups that had no Christian presence. They prayed and agreed together for a breakthrough and the establishment of Christian ministries in them. Within a year Sekou Toure was gone, replaced by a benign leader who opened the door to missions once again, and today every one of the people groups they prayed for are now occupied by a national or missionary effort!

## Spiritual Warfare Breaks the Control of Darkness

Chains of spiritual darkness and bondage often link unreached peoples, cities, and countries to principalities and powers who seek to control the affairs of humankind. At present, in the missions world, we are undergoing a rediscovery that the issue in reaching the unreached is one of *spiritual power*. If we are going to see missionary breakthroughs in peoples, cities and countries, we will need to learn how to use the offensive weapon of prayer to dislodge the powers of darkness.

Francis Frangipane, writing about the strongholds the powers of darkness maintain over groups of people, takes a similar line of thinking:

There are satanic strongholds over countries and communities; there are strongholds which influence churches and individuals.... These fortresses exist in the thought patterns and ideas that govern individuals...as well as communities and nations. Before victory can be claimed, these strongholds must be pulled down, and Satan's armor removed. Then the mighty weapons of the Word and the Spirit can effectively plunder Satan's house.[12]

A study of the belief systems of pagan peoples attest to the reality of spirit beings portrayed in Ephesians 6, the book of Daniel, and elsewhere. The Burmese believe in supernatural beings called *nats* arranged hierarchically with control over natural phenomena, villages, regions, and nations. Their link with these beings is maintained through witches or mediums, at least one of whom is found in each village.[13]

A book on the African country of Zimbabwe reveals that every region, city, and village is thought to be under the control of territorial spirits.[14] In Nigeria an Assemblies of God leader, who was a high-ranking occult practitioner before his conversion, said that Satan assigned him control of twelve spirits, each of which controlled 600 demons. He testified, "I was in touch with all the spirits controlling each town in Nigeria, and I had a shrine in all the major cities."[15]

Could it be that whole peoples we have written off as being "resistant" are in themselves really not resistant at all but are in the grip of spirit beings that are the source of the resistance?

## Prayer Must Be Mobilized

There are enormous prayer resources within the Body of Christ that by and large are not being tapped for the unevangelized world because we have thus far failed to develop practical mechanisms to link these resources with the need of the unreached. Probably the most strategic thing we can do for frontier missions is to stimulate the formation of ongoing prayer and spiritual warfare networks focused on particular unreached peoples, cities and countries. 🔲

*Probably the most strategic thing we can do for frontier missions is to stimulate the formation of ongoing prayer and spiritual warfare networks focused on unreached peoples.*

## End Notes

1   Mrs. J.O. Fraser, *Fraser and Prayer*, (London: Missionary Fellowship, 1963), pp. 11–12.

2   Ibid., p. 26.

3   Arthur Mathews, *Born for Battle*, (Robesonia, Pennsylvania: Overseas Missionary Fellowship, 1978), p. 42.

4   Derek Prince, *Shaping History through Prayer and Fasting* (Old Tappan, N.J.: Flemming Revell Company, 1973), pp. 93, 95.

5   Robert H. Glover, *The Bible Basis of Missions*, (Chicago: Moody Press, 1946), p. 180.

6   Johnathan Goforth, *By My Spirit*, (New York: Harper and Brothers, 1930), p. 182.

7   Ibid., pp. 180–181.

8   J. Edwin Orr, *The Flaming Tongue: The Impact of 20th Century Revivals*, (Chicago: Moody Press, 1973), p. xiii.

9   Glover, p. 181.

10  Goforth, p. 184.

11  Glover, p. 183.

12  Francis Frangipane, *The Three Battle-grounds*, (Marion, Iowa: River of Life Ministries, 1989), pp. 15, 21.

13  Melford Spiro, *Burmese Supernaturalism*.

14  From a conversation with Jim Montgomery of DAWN Ministries.

15  Peter Wagner, "Territorial Spirits," Academic Symposium on Power Evangelism, Fuller Seminary, December 13–15, 1988, p. 10.

## Changing Plans for Action

Strategies provide an overall game plan. They give light to our path and help establish our destination. Once a strategy is established, tactical plans can be made to carry it out. Our traditional paradigm for reaching all nations is redesigned by developing "people group" thinking.

Imagine our task as if we were planting a lawn. The ground is prepared and watered. Then a tiny piece of living sod is transplanted into large squares of earth. Each tiny transplant, nourished and cared for, has the ability within itself to grow until it covers all the ground.

In the same way, God's new life needs to be placed into each people group and nourished. A vibrant, growing church can spread rapidly to the far reaches of its own group. This releases us from the impossible burden of winning every person alive on the planet. Our strategic question is "How can we see the Good News planted in each group?"

## New Ways of Thinking

This strategic research helps reform our thinking.

- ▶ The church in some form exists in nearly every geopolitical nation.

- ▶ There is a critical difference between people who are "unsaved" and peoples who are "unreached."

- ▶ Our focus must change from geography to ethnicity.

- ▶ The cross-cultural work force must build a new strategic outlook.

- ▶ Church planting movements are vital to completing the task.

- ▶ Prayer is an imperative foundation for finishing this work.

As we look at the five major blocs of unreached peoples, each with thousands of groups, many groups comprised of millions of individuals, we may feel like grasshoppers in our own eyes (Num. 13:33). Our world may appear to be full of giants, both geographically and spiritually. Yet our resources, both personally and corporately, are finite.

## New Sources of Workers

However, alongside this enormous task, we see the extent of the global labor force. Churches and agencies from many nations are building strategic partnerships. Together, they hope to see unreached groups blessed with the gospel. Research shows new openings for workers. Whole new networks of prayer are being formed. Most of all, like Joshua and Caleb, we see the greatness of God and *the invincibility of His purpose*. Like Caleb, we say, "We should go up and take possession of the land, for we can certainly do it." (Num. 13:30 NIV).

Many changes in our world are requiring us to reassess former paths. Urbanization, migration of peoples, and globalization in a post-modern atmosphere all impact strategic planning. What worked in the past may have to be re-evaluated for the present or the future. God is moving on. His people need to move with Him.

## It Can Be Done

Of course there are giants facing us! What greater way for our God to demonstrate His power, might, and love? He took an enslaved rabble and made them into a nation to reach all nations. He can do the same in our day. Our generation is positioned to be able to complete this assignment, if, like Joshua and Caleb, we have the will to believe and obey the Lord.

Now, with a foundation of Biblical and historic insights, we move on to consider the barriers that keep us from communicating appropriately with the peoples to whom we go. We *must* examine the issues of culture and cultural differences and how they affect our ability to proclaim the Story.

# 4 Cultural Paths

## HOW CAN THEY BE HEARD?

### Reaching All Peoples

Our path received light from many insights. First, God's desire is to reach all nations with His truth. Next, He is working through the ages toward that end and desires that His people connect with the remaining unreached peoples. Now we come to the challenge of culture.

Each of the peoples who need to receive God's message has their own unique way of life, their own distinct mode of operating, and their own ideas and stories. From their history, circumstances, and experiences, they have developed their particular culture. Simply reciting John 3:16 in their language will not suffice.

Missionaries shared this verse with the Navajo people, but Navajos were not concerned about love. They were concerned about protection from the spirit world, and until their needs were addressed, the message was not of interest. When the Navajo learned that Jesus had power over the spirit world, the message got their attention.

### Understanding Each Culture

People have little understanding of their own culture. They accept it, but seldom give it much thought. Culture is largely unconscious. Each culture assumes that the way they do things is the *right* way. This is "ethnocentrism," and no culture escapes it. Only intentional effort can recognize and surmount it.

Shining a spotlight on our own cultural biases is a first step. As that flicker begins, new questions come to light:

- ▶ How can this story be told so that it will be heard?

- ▶ What elements might make it difficult to understand?

- ▶ Which parts of the story address the needs of that particular people?

- ▶ What barriers must be crossed to make God's goodness known to them?

### Levels of Culture

Culture exists on many levels. It is all-encompassing for each people. Some of it is on the surface. Underlying that, there is a more significant, deeper level called "worldview." Unless worldview changes, the people will not really change. If the gospel affects only surface levels, the result is "syncretism" or a mixing of external shifts with unchanged cultural foundations.

When Spain colonized Latin America, many tribes were forced to convert or be killed. In fear, these groups changed outwardly and began using Christian words and ceremonies. However, underneath they still worshipped their former gods and feared the dark spirits. No deeper level changes resulted. This is an example of syncretism.

# HOW CAN THEY BE HEARD?

## Barriers to the Message

There are two barriers to the light of God's message: barriers of understanding and barriers of acceptance. Sometimes the message may be true, but it is proclaimed in a way that people do not understand. A Hindu woman was told, "Jesus has come to give you eternal life," but from her point of view, believing in continual reincarnation she replied, "But I want to get OUT of eternal life." This is a barrier of understanding.

Many people understand the message, but for various reasons reject it. Some Jewish people believe that if they become Christians they betray their own people. To them, joining a religion that has persecuted and accused them of killing Jesus Christ cannot be considered. The message is alien to them. This is a barrier of acceptance. Such barriers hinder the growth of the Kingdom.

When Jewish people were told of Y'eshua the Messiah and were encouraged to continue the celebration of their holidays and Sabbaths, they were far more open. Now Messianic Jewish congregations reach out to their own people. The larger Body of Christ is enriched by their music alone!

## Cultural Challenges and Values

Cross-cultural workers face many tests in shining the light into dissimilar cultures. The complex problems they deal with are real and indisputable. Understanding such problems will help both those who go—and the churches that send them—to plan and pray more effectively.

Every culture, including our own, has beauty and value in God's eyes as well as ungodly elements that are under His judgment. Every culture has neutral elements that can remain undisturbed. The Lord must help us understand which is which.

**Rajasthani:** India, 200 years after William Carey, is a mixture of opportunities and challenges. Constitutionally a secular state and a democracy, the rise of militant Hinduism is threatening the long-standing freedom of witness.

Anticonversion laws in some states and extreme pressure on converts are challenges for the Christians, a minority mainly from the lower classes. India contains one of the largest and most accessible Muslim communities, but very few efforts have been launched to reach them.

Rajputs, the higher-caste Hindus, who live in Rajasthan have shown no response to the Gospel. They are unlikely to respond to the lower caste and tribal Christians. Special strategies must be devised to reach these proud Hindu upper-class peoples, whose whole lives are entwined with the Hindu way of life.

The hold of entrenched spiritual powers must be broken over the peoples of North India. Radio and literature ministries have laid an excellent foundation on which other workers might build. Indian Christians from other nations may be the best source of workers to penetrate the largely unreached Hindu peoples.

# Understanding Culture
## Lloyd E. Kwast

**Lloyd Kwast** taught for eight years in a college and theological school in Cameroon, West Africa, under the North American Baptist General Missionary Society. He taught missions at Talbot and in the School of Intercultural Studies at Biola University from 1972 until his death in 1996.

What is a culture, anyway? For the student just beginning the study of missionary anthropology, this question is often a first response to a confusing array of descriptions, definitions, comparisons, models, paradigms, etc. There is probably no more comprehensive word in the English language than the word "culture" and no more complex a field of study than cultural anthropology. Yet, a thorough understanding of the meaning of culture is prerequisite to any effective communication of God's good news to a different people group.

The most basic procedure in a study of culture is to become a master of one's own. Everyone has a culture. No one can ever divorce himself from his culture. While it is true that anyone can grow to appreciate various different cultures, and even to communicate effectively in more than one, one can never rise above his own, or other cultures, to gain a truly supracultural perspective. For this reason, even the study of one's own culture is a difficult task. And to look objectively at something that is part of oneself so completely is nearly impossible.

One helpful method is to view a culture, visualizing several successive "layers," or levels of understanding, as one moves into the real heart of the culture. In doing so, the "man from Mars" technique is useful. In this exercise one simply imagines that a man from Mars has recently landed (via spaceship) and looks at things through the eyes of an alien space visitor.

## Behavior

The first thing that the newly arrived visitor would notice is the people's *behavior*. This is the outer, and most superficial, layer of what would be observed by an alien. What activities would he observe? What is being done?

When walking into a classroom, our visitor may observe several interesting things. People are seen entering an enclosure through one or more openings. They distribute themselves throughout the room seemingly arbitrarily. Another person enters dressed quite differently than the rest and moves quickly to an obviously prearranged position facing the others and begins to speak.

As all this is observed, the question might be asked, "Why are they in an enclosure? Why does the speaker dress differently? Why are many people seated while one stands?" These are questions of *meaning*. They are generated by the observations of behavior. It might be interesting to ask some of the participants in the situation why they are doing things in a certain way. Some might offer one explanation; others might offer another. But some would probably shrug and say, "It's the way we do things here." This last response shows an important function of culture, to provide "the patterned way of doing things," as one group of missionary anthropologists defines it. You could call culture the "superglue" that binds people together and gives them a sense of identity and continuity that is almost impenetrable. This identity is seen most obviously in the way things are done—behavior.

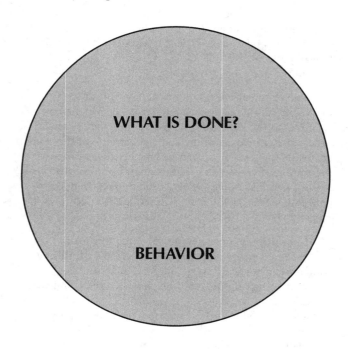

Kwast, L. E. (1992). *Understanding Culture*. In R. D. Winter & S. C. Hawthorne (Eds.). *Perspectives on the World Christian Movement: A Reader* (rev.ed.) (pp. C3–C6). Pasadena: William Carey Library.

## Values

In observing the inhabitants, our alien begins to realize that many of the behaviors observed are apparently dictated by similar choices that people in the society have made. These choices inevitably reflect the issue of cultural *values*, the next layer of our view of culture. These issues always concern choices about what is "good," what is "beneficial," or what is "best."

If the man from Mars continued to interrogate the people in the enclosure, he might discover that they had numerous alternatives to spending their time there. They might have been working or playing instead of studying. Many of them chose to study because they believed it to be a better choice than play or work. He discovered a number of other choices they had made. Most of them had chosen to arrive at the enclosure in small four-wheel vehicles because they view the ability to move about quickly as very beneficial. Furthermore, others were noticed hurrying into the enclosure several moments after the rest had entered and again moving out of the room promptly at the close of the meeting. These people said that using time efficiently was very important to them. Values are "preset" decisions that a culture makes between choices commonly faced. It helps those who live within the culture to know what "should" or "ought" to be done in order to "fit in," or conform to the pattern of life.

## Beliefs

Beyond the questions of behavior and values, we face a more fundamental question in the nature of culture. This takes us to a deeper level of understanding, that of cultural *beliefs*. These beliefs answer for that culture the question, "What is true?"

Values in culture are not selected arbitrarily but invariably reflect an underlying system of beliefs. For example, in the classroom situation one might discover, upon further investigation, that "education" in the enclosure has particular significance because of their perception of what is true about man, his power to reason, and his ability to solve problems. In that sense, culture has been defined as "learned and shared ways of perceiving," or "shared cognitive orientation."

Interestingly, our alien interrogator might discover that different people in the enclosure, while exhibiting similar behavior and values, might profess totally different beliefs about them. Further, he might find that the values and behaviors were opposed to the beliefs that supposedly produced them. The problem arises from the confusion within the culture between operating beliefs (beliefs that affect values and behavior) and theoretical beliefs (state creeds that have little practical impact on values and behavior).

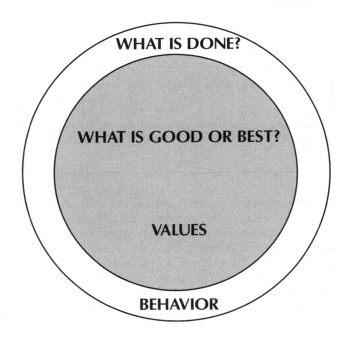

## Worldview

At the very heart of any culture is its *worldview*, answering the most basic question, "What is real?" This area of culture concerns itself with the great "ultimate" questions of reality, questions that are seldom asked but to which culture provides its most important answers.

Few of the people our man from Mars questions have ever thought seriously about the deepest assumptions about life, which result in their presence in the classroom. Who are they? Where did they come from? Is there anything or anyone else occupying reality that should be taken into consideration? Is what they see really all there is, or is there something else, or something more? Is right now the only time that is important? Or do events in the past and the future significantly impact their present experience? Every culture assumes specific answers to these questions, and those answers control and integrate every function, aspect, and component of the culture.

This understanding of worldview as the core of every culture explains the confusion many experience at the level of beliefs. One's own worldview provides a system of beliefs that are reflected in his actual values and behavior. Sometimes a new or competing system of beliefs is introduced, but the worldview remains unchallenged and unchanged, so values and behavior reflect the old belief system. Sometimes people who share the gospel cross-culturally fail to take the

problem of worldview into account and are therefore disappointed by the lack of genuine change their efforts produce.

This model of culture is far too simple to explain the multitude of complex components and relationships that exist in every culture. However, it is the very simplicity of the model that commends it as a basic outline for any student of culture. 

# MAJOR BLOCKS OF UNREACHED PEOPLE

**HINDU**

**2,700 Groups**

**BUDDHIST**

**1,000 Groups**

**MUSLIM**

**3,700 Groups**

**TRIBAL**

**2,000 Groups**

USCWM

# Culture and Cross-Cultural Differences
*Paul G. Hiebert*

Paul G. Hiebert was Professor of Missions and Anthropology at Trinity Evangelical Divinity School until his death in March 2007. He worked six years in India under the Mennonite Brethren and wrote numerous articles and books including Cultural Anthropology, Anthropological Insights for Missionaries, and Anthropological Reflections on Missiological Issues. Most recently, he co-authored Incarnational Ministry with his daughter, Eloise Hiebert Meneses.

One of the first shocks a person experiences when he or she leaves his home country is the foreignness of the people and their culture. Not only do they speak an incomprehensible language, but they also dress in strange clothes, eat unpalatable foods, organize different kinds of families, and have unintelligible beliefs and values. How do these differences affect the communication of the Gospel and the planting of churches in other societies?

## The Concept of Culture

In ordinary speech we use the term "culture" to refer to the behavior of the rich and elite. It is listening to Bach, Beethoven, and Brahms, having the proper taste for good clothes, and knowing which fork to use when at a banquet.

But anthropologists in their study of all humankind, in all parts of the world and at all levels of society, have broadened the concept and freed it from value judgments such as good or bad. There has been a great deal of discussion on how to define the term. For our purposes we will define culture as *the integrated system of learned patterns of behavior, ideas, and products characteristic of a society*.

## Patterns of learned behavior

The first part of this definition is "learned patterns of behavior." We begin learning about a culture by observing the behavior of the people and looking for patterns in the behavior. For example, we have all seen two American men on meeting grasp each other's hand and shake it. In Mexico we would see them embrace. In India each puts his hands together and raises them toward his forehead with a slight bow of the head—a gesture of greeting that is efficient, for it permits a

person to greet a great many others in a single motion, and clean, for people need not touch each other. The latter is particularly important in a society where the touch of an untouchable used to defile a high-caste person and force him to take a purification bath. Among the Siriano of South America, men spit on each other's chests in greeting.

Probably the strangest form of greeting was observed by Dr. Jacob Loewen in Panama. On leaving the jungle on a small plane with the local native chief, he noticed the chief go to all his fellow tribesmen and suck their mouths. When Dr. Loewen inquired about this custom, the chief explained that they had learned this custom from the white man. They had seen that every time he went up in his plane, he sucked the mouths of his people as magic to ensure a safe journey. If we stop and think about it a minute, Americans, in fact, have two types of greeting, shaking hands and sucking mouths, and we must be careful not to use the wrong form with the wrong people.

Like most cultural patterns, kissing is not a universal human custom. It was absent among most primitive tribesmen and considered vulgar and revolting to the Chinese, who thought it too suggestive of cannibalism.

> **W**e will define culture as the integrated system of learned patterns of behavior, ideas, and products characteristic of a society.

Not all behavior patterns are learned. A child touching a hot stove jerks his hand away and yells, "Ouch!" His physical reaction is instinctive, but the expletive is culturally learned.

## Ideas

Culture is also the ideas people have of their world. Through their experience of it, people form mental pictures of maps of this world. For instance, a person living in Chicago has a mental image of the streets around his home, those he uses to go to church and work, and the major arteries he uses to get around town. Obviously there are a great many streets not on his mental map, and as long as he does not go to these

Hiebert, P. G. (1992). *Culture and Cross-Cultural Differences.* In R. D. Winter & S. C. Hawthorne (Eds.). *Perspectives on the World Christian Movement: A Reader* (rev.ed.) (pp. C9–C17; C19–C23). Pasadena: William Carey Library.

areas, he has no need for knowing them. So also people develop conceptual schemes of their worlds.

Not all our ideas reflect the realities of the external world. Many are the creations of our minds, used to bring order and meaning in our experiences. For example, we see a great many trees in our lifetime, and each is different from all others. But it would be impossible for us to give a separate name to each of them, and to each bush, each house, each car—in short, to each experience we have. In order to think and speak, we must reduce this infinite variety of experiences into a manageable number of concepts by generalization. We call these shades of color red, those orange, and that third set yellow. These categories are the creations of our mind. Other people in other languages lump them into a single color or divide them into two, or even four, colors. Do these people see as many colors as we? Certainly. The fact is, we can create as many categories in our minds as we want, and we can organize them into larger systems for describing and explaining human experiences.

In one sense, then, a culture is a people's mental map of their world. This is not only a map of their world but also a map for determining action (Geertz 1972:169). It provides them with a guide for their decisions and behavior.

## Products

A third part of our definition is "products." Human thought and actions often lead to the production of material artifacts and tools. We build houses, roads, cars, and furniture. We create pictures, clothes, jewelry, coins, and a great many other objects.

Our material culture has a great effect on our lives. Imagine, for a moment, what life in America was like a hundred years ago when there were no cars or jets. The invention of writing and more recently of computers has and will have an even more profound effect upon our lives, for these permit us to store up the cultural knowledge of past generations and to build upon it.

## Form and meaning

Behavior patterns and cultural products are generally linked to ideas or meanings. Shaking hands means "hello." So does kissing in certain situations. We also assign meaning to shaking our fists, to frowning, to crying, to letters of the alphabet, to crosses, and to a great many other things. In fact, human beings assign meaning to almost everything they do and make.

It is this linkage between an experienceable *form* and a mental *meaning* that constitutes a symbol. We see a flag, and it carries the idea of a country, so much so that men in battle will even die to preserve their flags. A culture can be viewed as the symbol systems, such as languages, rituals, gestures, and objects, that people create in order to think and communicate.

*Julie Bosacker, YWAM*

**Khmer:** The country of Cambodia, with rich agricultural potential, has been decimated by the savage slaughters perpetrated by the Khmer Rouge. This extremist Marxist insurgency murdered almost all military personnel, civil servants, and educated or wealthy people and turned the nation into an immense forced-labor camp. Though they were ousted by the Vietnamese army in 1978, the Khmer Rouge are still trying to overthrow the elected government, offering bounties for the murder of foreigners.

The Khmer, the majority people of Cambodia, welcomed Buddhism in the 15th century. Though most Buddhist monks were massacred in the "killing fields," there is a revival of Buddhism today. Most of the Christians were martyred as well. Some survived and are working to build the church, even under continued government restrictions.

Many Khmer fled to refugee camps, where there was a great harvest for Christ. Others have been reached in overseas relocation sites. Now some are returning to share their faith in their ravaged homeland. This nation's infrastructure is so seriously damaged that it cannot recover without expatriate help. This could provide an opportunity for Christian professionals.

## Integration

Cultures are made up of a great many patterns of behavior, ideas, and products. But it is more than the sum of them. These patterns are integrated into larger cultural complexes and into total cultural systems.

*Culture is a peoples' mental map of their world. It provides them with a guide for their decisions and behavior.*

To see this integration of cultural patterns, we need only observe the average American. On entering an auditorium to listen to a musical performance, he looks until he finds a chair on which to perch himself. If all these platforms are occupied, he leaves because the auditorium is "full." Obviously there are a great many places where he can sit on the floor, but this is not culturally acceptable, at least not at the performance of a symphony orchestra.

At home the American has different kinds of platforms for sitting in the living room, at the dining table, and at his desk. He also has a large platform on which he sleeps at night. When he travels abroad, his greatest fear is being caught at night without a platform in a private room, so he makes hotel reservations well ahead of time. People from many parts of the world know that all you need is a blanket and a flat space in order to spend the night, and the world is full of flat places. In the airport, at three in the morning, the American traveler is draped uncomfortably over a chair rather than stretched out on the rug. He would rather be dignified than comfortable.

Not only do Americans sit and sleep on platforms, they build their houses on them, hang them on their walls, and put fences around them to hold their children. Why this obsession with platforms? Behind all these behavior patterns is a basic assumption that the ground and floor are dirty. This explains their obsession for getting off the floor. It also explains why they keep their shoes on when they enter the house and why the mother scolds the child when it picks a potato chip off the floor and eats it. The floor is "dirty," even though it has just been washed, and the instant a piece of food touches it, the food becomes dirty.

On the other hand, in Japan the people believe the floor is clean. Therefore they take their shoes off at the door and sleep and sit on mats on the floor. When we walk into their home with our shoes on, they feel much like we do when someone walks on our couch with their shoes on.

At the center, then, of a culture are the basic assumptions the people have about the nature of reality and of right and wrong. Taken together, they are referred to as the people's *worldview*.

This linkage between cultural traits and their integration into a larger system have important implications for those who seek to introduce change. When changes are made in one area of culture, changes will also occur in other areas of the culture, often in unpredictable ways. While the initial change may be good, the side effects can be devastating if care is not taken.

## Cross-Cultural Differences

In their study of various cultures, anthropologists have become aware of the profound differences between them. Not only are there differences in the ways people eat, dress, speak, and act, and in their values and beliefs, but also in the fundamental assumptions they make about their world. Edward Sapir pointed out that people in different cultures do not simply live in the same world with different labels attached, but in different conceptual worlds.

Edward Hall points out just how different cultures can be in his study of time (1959). When, for example, two Americans agree to meet at ten o'clock, they are "on time" if they show up from five minutes before to five minutes after ten. If one shows up at fifteen after, he is "late" and mumbles an unfinished apology. He must simply acknowledge that he is late. If he shows up at half past, he should have a good apology, and by eleven he may as well not show up. His offense is unpardonable.

In parts of Arabia, the people have a different concept or map of time. If the meeting time is ten o'clock, only a servant shows up at ten—in obedience to his master. The proper time for others is from ten forty-five to eleven fifteen, just long enough after the set time to show their independence and equality. This arrangement works well, for when two equals agree to meet at ten, each shows up, and expects the other to show up, at about ten forty-five.

*A culture can be viewed as the symbol systems, such as languages, rituals, gestures, and objects, that people create in order to think and communicate.*

The problem arises when an American meets an Arab and arranges a meeting for ten o'clock. The American shows up at ten, the "right time" according to him. The Arab shows up at ten forty-five, the "right time" according to him. The American feels the Arab has no sense of time at all (which is false), and the

Arab is tempted to think Americans act like servants (which is also false).

## Cross-cultural misunderstandings

Some missionaries in Zaire had trouble in building rapport with the people. Finally one old man explained the people's hesitancy to befriend the missionaries. "When you came, you brought your strange ways," he said. "You brought tins of food. On the outside of one was a picture of corn. When you opened it, inside was corn, and you ate it. Outside another was a picture of meat, and inside was meat, and you ate it. And then when you had your baby, you brought small tins. On the outside was a picture of babies, and you opened it and fed the inside to your child."

*When changes are made in one area of culture, changes will also occur in other areas of the culture, often in unpredictable ways.*

To us the people's confusion sounds foolish, but it is all too logical. In the absence of other information, they must draw their own conclusions about our actions. But we do the same about theirs. We think they have no sense of time when, by our culture, they show up late. We accuse them of lying when they tell us things to please us rather than as they really are (although we have no trouble saying, "Just fine!" when someone asks, "How are you?"). The result is cultural misunderstanding, and this leads to poor communication and poor relationships.

Cultural misunderstandings often arise out of our subconscious actions. Hall illustrates this (1959) in the way people use physical space when they stand around talking. North Americans generally stand about four or five feet apart when they discuss general matters. They do not like to converse by shouting to people twenty feet away. On the other hand, when they want to discuss personal matters, they move in to about two or three feet and drop their voices. Latin Americans tend to stand about two or three feet apart in ordinary conversations and even closer for personal discussions.

Misunderstandings arise only when a North American meets a Latin American. The latter subconsciously moves in to about three feet. The former is vaguely uneasy about this and steps back. Now the Latin American feels like he is talking to someone across the room, and so he steps closer. Now the North American is again confused. According to his spacial distance, the Latin American should be discussing personal matters, like sharing some gossip or arranging a bank robbery. But in fact he is talking about public matters, about the weather and politics. The result is the North American thinks Latin Americans are pushy and

always under his nose; the Latin American concludes that North Americans are always distant and cold.

Misunderstandings are based on ignorance about another culture. This is a problem of knowledge. The solution is to learn to know how the other culture works. Our first task in entering a new culture is to be a student of its ways. Even later, whenever something seems to be going wrong, we must assume that the people's behavior makes sense to them and reanalyze our own understandings of their culture.

## Ethnocentrism

Most Americans shudder when they enter an Indian restaurant and see the people eating curry and rice with their fingers. Imagine going to a Thanksgiving dinner and diving into the mashed potatoes and gravy with your hand. Our response is a natural one, to us. Early in life each of us grows up in the center of our own world. In other words, we are egocentric. Only with a great deal of difficulty do we learn to break down the circle we draw between I and You and learn to look at things from the viewpoint of others. We also grow up in a culture and learn that its ways are the right ways to do things. Anyone who does differently is not quite "civilized." This ethnocentrism is based on our natural tendency to judge the behavior of people in other cultures by the values and assumptions of our own.

But others judge our culture by their values and assumptions. A number of Americans went to a restaurant with an Indian guest, and someone asked the inevitable question, "Do people in India really eat with their fingers?" "Yes, we do," the Indian replied, "but we look at it differently. You see, we wash our hands carefully, and besides, they have never been in anyone else's mouth. But look at these spoons and forks, and think about how many other people have already had them inside their mouths!"

*Cultural misunderstandings often arise out of our subconscious actions.*

If cross-cultural misunderstandings are based on our knowledge of another culture, ethnocentrism is based on our feelings and values. In relating to another people, we need not only to understand them but also to deal with our feelings that distinguish between "us" and "our kind of people" and "them" and "their kind of people." Identification takes place only when "they" become part of the circle of people we think of as "our kind of people."

## Premature judgments

We have misunderstandings on the cognitive level and ethnocentrism on the affective level, but what can go wrong on the evaluative level? The answer lies in premature judgments. When we relate to other cultures, we tend to judge them before we have learned to understand or appreciate them. In so doing, we use the values of our own culture, not of some metacultural framework. Consequently, other cultures look less civilized.

> *The price of adopting total cultural relativism is the loss of truth and righteousness.*

**Cultural Relativism.** Premature judgments are usually wrong. Moreover, they close the door to further understanding and communication. What then is the answer?

As anthropologists learned to understand and appreciate other cultures, they came to respect their integrity as viable ways of organizing human life. Some were stronger in one area such as technology and others in another area such as family ties. But all "do the job," that is, they all make life possible and more or less meaningful. Out of this recognition of the integrity of all cultures emerged the concept of cultural relativism: the belief that all cultures are equally good—that no culture has the right to stand in judgment over the others.

The position of cultural relativism is very attractive. It shows high respect for other people and their cultures and avoids the errors of ethnocentrism and premature judgments. It also deals with the difficult philosophical questions of truth and morality by withholding judgment and affirming the right of each culture to reach its own answers. The price we pay, however, in adopting total cultural relativism is the loss of such things as truth and righteousness. If all explanations of reality are equally valid, we can no longer speak of error, and if all behavior is justified according to its cultural context, we can no longer speak of sin. There is then no need for the gospel and no reason for missions.

What other alternative do we have? How can we avoid the errors of premature and ethnocentric judgments and still affirm truth and righteousness?

**Beyond Relativism.** There is a growing awareness that no human thought is free from value judgments. Scientists expect one another to be honest and open in the reporting of their findings and careful in the topics of their research. Social scientists must respect the rights of their clients and the people being studied. Businessmen, government officials, and others also have values by which they live. We cannot avoid making judgments, nor can a society exist without them.

On what basis, then, can we judge other cultures without being ethnocentric? We have a right as individuals to make judgments with regard to ourselves, and this includes judging other cultures. But these judgments should be well informed. We need to understand and appreciate other cultures *before* we judge them. Our tendency is to make premature judgments based on ignorance and ethnocentrism.

As Christians we claim another basis for evaluation, namely, Biblical norms. As divine revelation they stand in judgment on all cultures, affirming the good in human creativity and condemning the evil. To be sure, non-Christians may reject these biblical norms and use their own. We can only present the gospel in a spirit of redemptive love and let it speak for itself. Truth, in the end, does not depend on what we think or say, but on reality itself. When we bear witness to the truth, we do not claim a superiority for ourselves but affirm the truth of the gospel.

But what is to keep us from interpreting the Scripture from our own cultural point of view and so imposing many of our own cultural norms on the people? First, we need to recognize that we have biases when we interpret the Scriptures and thus be open to correction. We also need to let the gospel work in the lives of new Christians and through them in their culture, recognizing that the same Holy Spirit who leads us is at work in them and leading them to the truth.

> *Our first task in entering a new culture is to be a student of its ways. When something seems to be wrong we must reanalyze our own understandings of their culture.*

Second, we need to study both the values of the culture in which we minister and those of our own. By this approach, we can develop a metacultural framework that enables us to compare and evaluate the two. The process of genuinely seeking to understand another system of values goes a long way in breaking down our monocultural perspectives. It enables us to appreciate the good in other systems and be more critical of our own.

Since even in the formulation of a metacultural system of values our own cultural biases come into play, we need to involve Christian leaders from other cultures in the process. They can detect our cultural blind spots better than we can, just as we often see their cultural prejudgments better than they.

*There is much in every culture that is worthwhile and should not only be retained but encouraged. Much, too, is "neutral" and need not be changed.*

We will find that there is much in every culture that is worthwhile and should not only be retained but encouraged. For instance, most cultures are much better than ours in human relationships and social concern, and we can learn much from them. Much, too, is "neutral" and need not be changed. In most settings wood houses serve as well as mud or brick ones, and a dress is not better than a sari or sarong. Some things in all cultures, however, are false and evil. Since all people are sinners, we should not be surprised that the social structures and cultures they create are affected by sin. It is our corporate sins, not only our individual sins, that God seeks to change.

Now back to the discussion of translation. Beginning in Genesis we read, "In the beginning God…" The question is, how shall we translate the word "God"? In Telugu, a south Indian language, we can use the words "Isvarudu," "Devudu," "Bhagavanthudu," or a number of others. The problem is that each of these carries the Hindu connotation that gods have exactly the same kind of life as human beings, only more of it. They are not categorically different from people. There is no word that carries the same connotations as the Biblical concept of God.

This also raises the problem of translating the Biblical concept of "incarnation." In the Biblical setting, incarnation is seen as an infinite God crossing the great gulf between Himself and human beings and becoming a person. In other words, He crossed from one category to another. In the Indian setting, gods constantly become incarnate by moving down within the same category to the level of people. Obviously this concept of incarnation is fundamentally different from the Christian one. To use it is to lose much of the meaning of the Christian message. But how then can we translate the Biblical concepts of God and incarnation in Telugu or other Indian languages?

We might coin a new word for "God" or "incarnation," but then the people will not understand it. Or we can use one of the Telugu words, but then we face the danger that the Biblical message will be seriously distorted. Often the best we can do is use a word with which the people are familiar but then teach them

the meaning we are giving to it. It may take years and even generations before the people understand the new meanings and the total Biblical worldview within which these meanings make sense.

This process may seem to take too long. What about the illiterate peasant who accepts Christ at an evening service? Do not his concepts and worldview change immediately? Obviously not. But his salvation is not dependent on whether he has a Christian worldview or not, but on whether he accepts Christ's salvation however he understands it and becomes His follower. However, for the long-range building of the church, the people and their leaders must have an understanding of the Biblical concepts and worldview if the message is to be preserved over the generations.

## Implications of Cultural Differences for Missions

It is clear that cultural differences are important to a missionary who must go through culture shock, learn to overcome misunderstandings and ethnocentric feelings, and translate his message so that it is understood in the local language and culture. But there are a number of other important implications that need to be touched briefly.

### The Gospel and culture

We must distinguish between the Gospel and culture. If we do not, we will be in danger of making our culture the message. The Gospel then becomes democracy, capitalism, pews and pulpits, Robert's Rules of Order, clothes, and suits and ties on Sunday. One of the primary hindrances to communication is the foreignness of the message, and to a great extent the foreignness of Christianity has been the cultural load we have placed upon it. As Mr. Murthi, an Indian evangelist, put it, "Do not bring us the Gospel as a potted plant. Bring us the seed of the Gospel and plant it in our soil."

*One of the primary hindrances to communication is the foreignness of the message.*

The distinction is not easy to make, for the Gospel, like any message, must be put into cultural forms in order to be understood and communicated by people. We cannot think without conceptual categories and symbols to express them. But we can be careful not to add to the Biblical message our own.

A failure to differentiate between the Biblical message and other messages leads to a confusion between cultural relativism and Biblical absolutes. For example, in many churches where it was once considered sinful for women to cut their hair or wear lipstick, or for people to attend movies, these are now acceptable. Some, therefore, argue that today premarital sex and adultery are thought to be sinful, but that in time they too will be accepted.

It is true that many things we once considered sin are now accepted. Are there then no moral absolutes? We must recognize that each culture defines certain behavior as "sinful" and that as the culture changes, its definitions of what is sin also change. There are, on the other hand, certain moral principles in the Scriptures that we hold to be absolute. However, even here we must be careful. Some Biblical norms, such as leaving the land fallow every seventh year and not reaping the harvest (Leviticus 25) or greeting one another with a holy kiss (1 Thessalonians 5:26) seem to apply to specific cultural situations.

## Syncretism versus indigenization

Not only must we separate the Gospel from our own culture, we must seek to express it in terms of the culture to which we go. The people may sit on the floor, sing songs to native rhythms and melodies, and look at pictures of Christ who is Black or Chinese. The Church may reject democracy in favor of wise elders, or turn to drama to communicate its message.

But as we have seen, translation involves more than putting ideas into native forms, for these forms may not carry meanings suitable for expressing the Christian message. If we, then, translate it into native forms without thought to preserving the meaning, we will end up with *syncretism*—the mixture of old meanings with the new so that the essential nature of each is lost.

If we are careful to preserve the meaning of the Gospel even as we express it in native forms, we have *indigenization*. This may involve introducing a new symbolic form, or it may involve reinterpreting a native symbol. For example, bridesmaids, now associated with Christian weddings, were originally used by our non-Christian ancestors to confuse the demons who, they thought, had come to carry off the bride.

## Conversion and unforeseen side effects

Since cultural traits are linked together into larger wholes, changes in one or more of them lead often to unforeseen changes in other areas of the culture. For example, in one part of Africa, when the people became Christians, their villages also became dirty. The reason for this was that they were now not afraid of evil spirits, which they believed hid in the refuse. So they no longer had to clean it up.

Many cultural traits serve important functions in the lives of the people. If we remove these without providing a substitute, the consequences can be tragic. In some places husbands with more than one wife had to give up all but one when they became Christians. But no arrangements were made for the wives who were put away. Many of them ended up in prostitution or slavery.

## Theological autonomy and world Christianity

As Christianity becomes indigenous in cultures around the world, the question of the unity of the church arises. There is an increasing stress that the church in each cultural setting become autonomous: self-supporting, self-administering, and self-propagating. But how do we cope with theological variety? How do we react when the churches we help plant want theological autonomy and call for a socialist or even Marxist evangelical Christianity?

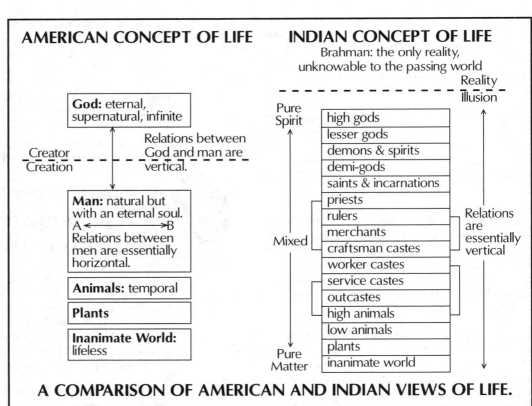

**A COMPARISON OF AMERICAN AND INDIAN VIEWS OF LIFE.**

It is clear that cultures vary a great deal. As the Gospel becomes indigenous to them, their theologies—their understandings and applications of this Gospel—will also vary. What, then, does it mean to be a Christian? And how can Christians who disagree in some points of theology have true fellowship with one another?

> # *Many cultural traits serve important functions in the lives of the people. If we remove these without providing a substitute, the consequences can be tragic.*

Here we must remember two things. In the first place, we need to understand the nature of human knowledge and recognize its limitations. People experience an infinitely varied world around them and try to find order and meaning in their experiences. They discover the order that exists in the world itself, and they impose a mental order on it. They create concepts that allow them to generalize, to lump a great many experiences into one. They also act like a movie editor, linking certain experiences in order to make sense of them. For example, experiences in the same classroom on different days are put together and called Introduction to Anthropology. A different set is thought of as "church activities."

When we read the Scriptures, we must remember that we interpret them in terms of our own culture and personal experiences. Others will not interpret them in exactly the same way. We must, therefore, distinguish between the Scriptures themselves and our theology or understanding of them. The former is the record of God's revelation of Himself to humankind. The latter is our partial, and hopefully growing, understanding of that revelation. If we make this distinction, we can accept variations in interpretation and yet find fellowship with those who are truly committed followers of Christ.

In the second place, we must never forget that the same Holy Spirit who helps us to understand the Scriptures is also interpreting them to believers in other cultures. It is He and not we who is responsible for preserving divine truth and revealing it to us. We must make certain that we are committed followers of Jesus Christ and open to the instruction of His Spirit. ◉

## References

1972. Clifford Geertz. "Religion as a Cultural System." In *Reader in Comparative Religion*, edited by W. A. Lessa and E. Z. Vogt. 3rd ed. New York: Harper and Row.

1959. Edward T. Hall. *Silent Language*. Greenwich, Conn.: Fawcett.

# THE URBAN CHALLENGE
## In God's World...

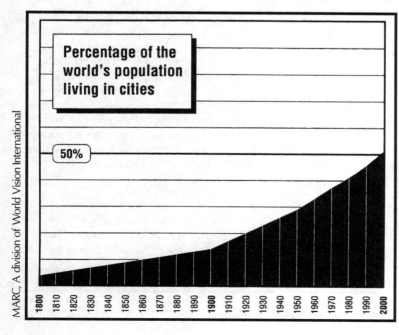

**Percentage of the world's population living in cities**

50%

1800 1810 1820 1830 1840 1850 1860 1870 1880 1890 1900 1910 1920 1930 1940 1950 1960 1970 1980 1990 2000

MARC, A division of World Vision International

- 21% of all urban dwellers live in the least evangelized part of the world, for which there are no city-wide evangelistic campaigns.

- 62% of all Christians—over one billion people—live in urban settings.

- By 2025 more than one-quarter of the world's population will be poor and living in the squatter settlements of the Two-thirds World.

- There are over 1.3 billion urban poor, of which 520 million are slum dwellers; their numbers increase by 70 million a year.

- There are more than 100 million street children in today's world-class cities—25% of whom both work and sleep in the streets.

**Sources:** Population Crisis Committee, 1991; Barrett and Johnson; Our Globe, 1990

# The Viable Missionary: Learner, Trader, Storyteller

*Donald N. Larson*

**Donald Larson** was Director for Intercultural Living and Learning at Link Care Center from 1982 until his death in June 2000. He was professor of Anthropology and Linguistics at Bethel College in Minnesota and the Director of the Toronto Institute of Linguistics. He formerly served as Director of the Inter-Church Language School in the Philippines, as well as developing language school programs in Thailand and Indonesia.

When my interest in the mission of the Christian church first awakened, I was too old to be acceptable to my denomination as a candidate. But for the past twenty years I have worked behind-the-scenes in mission, helping people to deal with the problems of language and culture learning. From this position off-stage, I have observed missionaries, sending agencies, local missionary communities, and national Christians and non-Christians in several fields. From these observations, I have concluded that there is often a wide gap in the missionary's conception of his role and how it is viewed by the non-Christians of his adopted community. The purpose of this paper is to examine this gap and propose ways and means of closing it.

By way of example, I recently met a young man heading for a short term of missionary service in southeast Asia and asked him what he was going to be doing there. He replied in all seriousness that he was "going to teach the natives to farm." I pressed him with a question: "Don't they know how to farm there?" He thought for a moment and then replied, "Well, I really don't know. I haven't got a very clear picture of things yet." Imagine what the non-Christian of his adopted community would think of him if they should hear him say such things! Whether this young man knows it or not, these Asians were farmers long before the Pilgrims landed at Plymouth Rock and even long before there were Christians anywhere.

Unfortunately, such statements as those made by the young man are not limited to short-termers. Career missionaries are sometimes unaware of the experience, background, and worldview of the members of their host communities and how they themselves are viewed. This gap between missionaries and non-Christians in their local communities generates communication problems of many different kinds.

## Typical Encounter Models

In an encounter with the missionary, whom he views as an outsider, the local non-Christian tends to view their relationship in one of three ways. He uses the schoolhouse, the marketplace, and the courtroom as backdrops to his encounters with the missionary. As if they were at school, he sees the missionary as teacher and himself as student. The purpose of their encounter is to transmit information to be learned. As if they were in the marketplace, he sees the missionary as seller and himself as buyer. The purpose of their encounter is to buy and sell something. As if in the courtroom, he sees the missionary as an accuser and himself as the accused. Their encounter deals with judgment. In the schoolhouse the teacher says, "I will teach you something." In the marketplace the merchant says, "I have something to sell you." In the courtroom the judge says, "I will measure you by this standard." Depending on the scene, the national views his need differently. In the schoolhouse he asks himself whether he needs to learn what the teacher has to teach. In the marketplace he asks himself whether he needs to buy what the merchant has to sell. In the courtroom he asks himself whether he needs to take the judge's accusation seriously.

But can an outsider teach or sell or accuse an insider? Does the non-Christian need what the missionary presents? Is the missionary able to communicate the Gospel through the roles of seller, teacher, or accuser? Are they effective? These are serious questions.

Schoolhouse

Marketplace

Courtroom

Local Non-Christian

Missionary

Larson, D. N. (1992). The Viable Missionary: Learner, Trader, Storyteller. In R. D. Winter & S. C. Hawthorne (Eds.). *Perspectives on the World Christian Movement: A Reader* (rev.ed.) (pp. C99–C106). Pasadena: William Carey Library.

Of course, there are other ways to look at the non-Christian's encounter with the missionary than through the three analogies used above.

**T**he typical missionary today may be paying too little attention to the viability of his role.

## Viable Role Dimensions

The typical missionary today may be paying too little attention to the *viability* of his role. If I were volunteering for missions today and hoped to be productive and happy, I would make certain that my role was viable from four perspectives: (1) the community in which I reside, (2) its missionary residents, (3) the agency that sends me, and (4) myself.

To elaborate, my role must allow me to be myself, to be my own person. It must also be viable in the local missionary community. If the local missionary community doesn't recognize my role and its importance, I won't be able to survive for long. My role must also be viable from the standpoint of the sending agency. I need their support and encouragement. I cannot survive for long if they do not give me an important place in their community. Finally, my role must be viable from the point of view of the local community. I do not want to parade myself around in this community as some kind of a freak, or a misfit, or a spy, or useless. This matter of community viability is often overlooked. It should not be. It is important, for I must have positive experiences in order to continue. Local residents must feel good about my presence in their community. My contribution must reinforce and complement the ongoing missionary program. The sending agency must have a solid rationale underlying its programs and the opportunities it provides for me. So the new missionary must look for roles that are simultaneously legitimate to these four parties: me, my host community, its missionary community, and the sending agency.

**T**he missionary must become an insider if he hopes to avoid negative reactions to his presence.

To the non-Christian, the roles of teacher, seller, or accuser may or may not be viable. The non-Christian may expect the outsider to learn the insider's viewpoint before he can teach effectively about the outside. He may expect him to survive on the level of insiders and depend on the local market before he can sell important goods. He may expect him to measure himself by their own laws before he accuses insiders in terms of an outside standard.

A principle of order seems to be important: learner before teacher, buyer before seller, accused before accuser. An outsider may have to follow this order before he can be viable in these roles to the insider.

Outsiders cannot live on the edge of a community without coming to the attention of insiders in a negative way. The term "outsider" has negative connotations. So the missionary must become an insider, at least to some extent, if he hopes to avoid these negative reactions to his presence and become a valuable person in the community.

If the insider is reluctant to learn from an outside teacher or buy from an outside seller or accept the accusations of an outside accuser, the outsider cannot hope to accomplish much until he finds new roles or redesigns the old ones.

## Three Roles

As I see it, there are three roles that the missionary can develop in order to establish viability in the eyes of the national non-Christian: learner, trader, and storyteller. I would first become a learner. After three months I would add another: trader. After three more months, I would add a third: storyteller. After three more months, while continuing to be learner, trader, and storyteller, I would begin to develop other roles specified in my job description.

Let me elaborate. From his position as an outsider, the missionary must find a way to move toward the center if he hopes to influence people. Some roles will help him to make this move. Others will not. His first task is to identify those that are most appropriate and effective. Then he can begin to develop ways and means of communicating his Christian experience through these roles in which he has found acceptance.

## Learner

More specifically, as learner my major emphasis is on language, the primary symbol of identification in my host community. When I try to learn it, they know that I mean business—that they are worth something to me because I make an effort to communicate on their terms. I learn a little each day and put it to use. I talk to a new person every day. I say something new every day. I gradually reach the point where I understand and am understood a little. I can learn much in three months.

I spend my mornings with a language helper (in a structured program or one that I design on my own) from whom I elicit the kinds of materials that I need to talk to people in the afternoons. I show him how to drill me on these materials and then spend a good portion of the morning in practice. Then in the afternoon I go out into public places and make whatever contacts are natural with local residents, talking to them as best I can with my limited proficiency—starting the very first day. I initiate one conversation after another, each of which says both verbally and nonverbally, "I am a learner. Please talk with me and help me." With each conversation partner, I get a little more practice and a little more proficiency, from the first day on.

*I add a role of trader: trading experience and insight with people of my adopted community.*

At the end of my first three months, I have established myself with potentially dozens of people and reached the point where I can make simple statements, ask and answer simple questions, find my way around, learning the meaning of new words on the spot, and most importantly, experience some measure of "at-homeness" in my adopted community. I cannot learn the "whole language" in three months, but I can learn to initiate conversations, control them in a limited way, and learn a little more about the language from everyone whom I meet.

## Trader

When my fourth month begins, I add a role—that of trader, trading experience and insight with people of my adopted community—seeing ourselves more clearly as part of mankind, not just members of different communities or nations. I prepare for this role by periods of residence in as many other places as I can, or vicariously, through course work in anthropology and related fields. I also come equipped with a set of 8 x 10 photos illustrating a wide range of ways to be human.

During the second three months I spend mornings with my language helper learning to talk about the photos in my collection. Thus I build on the language proficiency developed in the first month. I practice my description of these pictures and prepare myself as best I can to answer questions about them. Then in the afternoon I visit casually in the community, using the photos as part of my "show and tell" demonstration. I tell as much as I can about the way others live, how they make their livings, what they do for enjoyment, how they hurt, and how they struggle for survival and satisfaction.

At the end of this second phase, I establish myself not only as a learner but as one who is interested in other people and seeks to trade one bit of information for another. My language proficiency is still developing.

I meet many people. Depending upon the size and complexity of the community, I establish myself as a well-known figure by this time. I become a bridge between the people of the local community and a larger world—at least symbolically.

## Storyteller

When I begin my seventh month, I shift emphasis again to a new role. Now I become a storyteller. I spend mornings with my language helper. Now it is to learn to tell a very simple story to the people whom I meet and respond to their inquiries as best I can. The stories that I tell are based on the wanderings of the people of Israel, the coming of Christ, the formation of God's new people, the movement of the church into all the world and ultimately into this very community, and finally, my own story of my encounter with Christ and my walk as a Christian. During the mornings I develop these stories and practice them intensively. Then in the afternoon I go into the community, as I have been doing for months but now to encounter people as storyteller. I am still language learner and trader, but I have added the role of storyteller. I share as much of the story with as many people as I can each day.

At the end of this third phase, I have made acquaintances and friends. I have had countless experiences that I will never forget. I have left positive impressions as learner, trader, and storyteller. I am ready for another role, and another and another.

## Viability Reconsidered

With this profile in mind, let's examine this activity in the light of our earlier discussion of viability. The figure on the following page helps to focus on the issues: the plus sign (+) means that the role is unquestionably viable. The question mark (?) means that some further discussion and clarification are probably necessary before viability can be established.

From the standpoint of local residents, an outsider who is ready, willing, and able to learn probably has an entree. Furthermore, the average person in these communities probably has a natural curiosity about people in other places. This curiosity can probably be tapped and traded by a sensitive approach. Finally, storytelling and the reporting of incidents are common in every community. Everyone does it. Of course there are rules that must be respected. I assume that someone who has already established himself as learner and trader can share stories and experiences of his own with other people. Local residents will probably listen and perhaps even help him to get it told.

I find these roles viable. I enjoy learning and know how to go about it. I have a general understanding of different ways that people live and appreciate the possibilities inherent in the trader role. I love to tell stories and enjoy listening to them, especially when the teller is deeply involved in them himself.

## DIMENSIONS

| ROLES | Local Residents | Missionary Community | Sending Agency | Missionary |
|---|---|---|---|---|
| Learner | + | ? | ? | + |
| Trader | + | ? | ? | ? |
| Storyteller | + | + | + | + |

But from the standpoint of the sending agency and the local community, these roles may be questionable. Of the three, the storyteller role is perhaps the easiest one to develop, though one often finds missionaries to be sermonizers, theologizers, or lecturers, not storytellers. The viability of the learner role is open to question. A new missionary, expected to be a learner as far as the affairs of his local missionary organization are concerned, is not always given the time or encouraged to get to know local residents intimately. The viability of the trader role is largely untested, though I believe that sending agencies and local missionary communities should consider its importance carefully.

Why not exploit the learner role to the fullest? Most people who live as aliens sooner or later realize its importance. Why not get the new missionary off on the right foot—especially if it has increasing payoff in his second and third phases? Furthermore, the learner role symbolizes a number of important things to local residents that are important in the communication of the Gospel. The learner's dependence and vulnerability convey in some small way the messages of identification and reconciliation that are explicit in the Gospel. Coming to be known as a learner can certainly do the local missionary community no harm. It may be able to do some good.

The viability of the trader role is perhaps more difficult to establish—partly because of its newness. It seems to be too "secular." Yet from the community's standpoint, a secular role may be much more natural and acceptable for the alien. Coming as some sort of "sacred specialist," the outsider generates all sorts of questions, objections, and barriers. But there is still another consideration: this role reinforces the idea of the Gospel as something for all people. Except for anthropologists, demographers, and a few other specialists, Christians probably have a wider

understanding of human variation than any other group of people, simply because of our multiethnic, multiracial, and multilingual characteristics. The trader role complements the more formal presentation of the Gospel through the sharing of essentially "secular knowledge" about peoples of the world.

There are obvious implications here for the selection, orientation, and evaluation of missionaries. A discussion of them, however, is beyond the scope of this paper.

## Conclusion

We face a difficult situation today as the star of colonialism continues to fall and as the star of maturing national churches continues to rise. Missionaries become more and more frustrated as the viability of their role is questioned. We must take this situation seriously. The biblical mandate challenges the Christian to become one with those to whom he brings the Word of Life. Furthermore, history shows that vulnerability and flexibility are themselves powerful witnesses to the working of the Spirit within man. Finally, if the mission movement is to continue, new roles must be added and old ones must be redesigned.

Any new missionary can prepare himself in rather simple and straightforward fashion to meet the demands of these three roles. Insofar as these roles are viable from the point of view of the local community, the new missionary should begin with them. Unfortunately, sending agencies and local missionary communities may not be ready to buy these ideas. The let's-get-on-with-the-job mentality militates against getting bogged down in learning, trading, and storytelling. But this get-on-with-the-job mentality needs to be challenged, for if it implies roles that insulate the missionary from local residents, alternatives must be developed.

**The trader role reinforces the idea of the Gospel as something for all people.**

Some months ago at a language and culture learning workshop in East Africa, a missionary asked me if I knew anything about elephants. When I replied that I did not, she asked more specifically if I knew what happens when a herd of elephants approaches a water hole that is surrounded by another herd. I replied that I did not know what would happen. She then proceeded to explain that the lead elephant of the second group turns around and backs down toward the water hole. As soon as his backside is felt by the elephants gathered around the water hole, they step aside and make room for him. This is then the signal to the other elephants that the first herd is ready to make room for them around the hole.

When I asked what point she was trying to make,

she stated simply and powerfully, "We didn't back in." The continuing movement of mission in the world today may require missionaries to "back in" to their host communities. The roles of learner, trader, and storyteller may not be appropriate in a headfirst approach, but they may be necessary in an approach that emphasizes "backing in." ◉

## DIVIDING THE RESOURCES

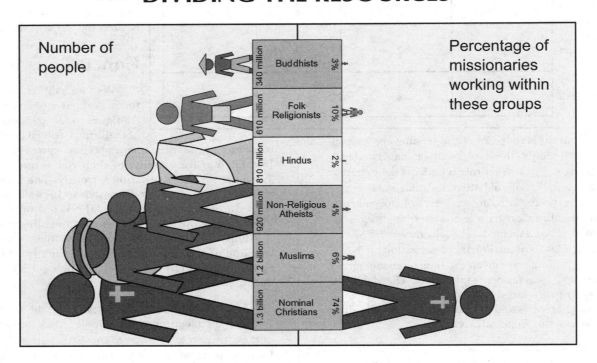

| Number of people | | Percentage of missionaries working within these groups |
|---|---|---|
| 340 million | Buddhists 3% | |
| 610 million | Folk Religionists 10% | |
| 810 million | Hindus 2% | |
| 920 million | Non-Religious Atheists 4% | |
| 1.2 billion | Muslims 6% | |
| 1.3 billion | Nominal Christians 74% | |

## In God's world...

▸ Christians are allocating only 1.2% of their mission funding to the 1.6 billion people who live in the least-evangelized world.

▸ Only 1% of the Scripture distribution is directed toward the least-evangelized world.

▸ Only 10% of all foreign missionaries and 6% of the full-time Christian workers are directed toward the least-evangelized world.

*MARC, a division of World Vision, Intl.*

# Concept Fulfillment
*Don Richardson*

When a missionary enters another culture, he is conspicuously foreign, and that is to be expected. But often the gospel he preaches is labeled foreign. How can he explain the gospel so it seems culturally right?

The New Testament way seems to be through concept fulfillment. Consider: The Jewish people practiced lamb sacrifice. John the Baptist proclaimed Jesus as the perfect, personal fulfillment of that sacrifice by saying, "Behold the *Lamb of God* who takes away the sin of the world!"

This is concept fulfillment.

> *When a missionary enters another culture, he is conspicuously foreign. How can he explain the gospel so it seems culturally right?*

Nicodemus, a Jewish teacher, knew that Moses had lifted up a serpent of brass upon a pole so that Jews, when dying of snakebite, could look at it and be healed. Jesus promised, "As Moses lifted up the serpent in the wilderness, even so must the Son of Man be lifted up, that whoever believes in Him should not perish, but have everlasting life."

This too is concept fulfillment.

A Jewish multitude, recalling that Moses had provided miraculous manna on a six-day-a-week basis, hinted that Jesus ought to repeat His miracle of the loaves and fishes on a similar schedule. Jesus replied, "Moses gave you not the *true* bread from heaven. The true bread from heaven is He who comes down from heaven and gives life to the world...I am that Bread of Life!"

Once again, concept fulfillment.

When some charged that Christianity was destroying the Jewish culture, the writer to the Hebrews showed how Christ actually fulfilled all the central elements of Jewish culture—the priesthood, tabernacle, sacrifices, and even the Sabbath rest. Let's call these *redemptive analogies*—looking for their fulfillment in Christ. Their God-ordained purpose was to precondition the Jewish mind to recognize Jesus as Messiah.

## Application Today

The strategy of concept fulfillment can be applied by missionaries today—if only we learn to discern the particular redemptive analogies of each culture.

Consider the advantage: when conversion is accompanied by concept fulfillment, the individuals redeemed become aware of the spiritual meaning dormant within their own culture. Conversion does not deny their cultural background, leaving them disoriented. Rather they experience heightened insight into both the Scriptures and their own human setting and are thus better prepared to share Christ meaningfully with other members of their own societies. See how concept fulfillment has worked in other cultures:

## Examples in Other Cultures

### The Damal and "Hai"

Less than one generation ago, the Damal people of Irian Jaya were living in the Stone Age. A subservient tribe, they lived under the shadow of a politically more powerful people called the Dani.

What hope could there be, you may ask, of finding a redemptive analogy in such a Stone Age setting? And

> *The writer to the Hebrews showed how Christ actually fulfilled all the central elements of Jewish culture.*

yet the Damal talked of a concept called *hai*. *Hai* was a Damal term for a long-anticipated golden age, a Stone Age utopia in which wars would cease, men would no longer oppress one another, and sickness would be rare.

Richardson, D. (1976). Excerpted from "How Missionaries Enrich Cultures," *Moody Monthly Magazine*, June 1976, Moody Magazine: Chicago, Illinois.

# HOW CAN THEY BE HEARD?

Mugumenday, a Damal leader, had yearned to see the advent of *hai*. At the end of his life, Mugemenday called his son Dem to his side and said, "My son, *hai* has not come during my lifetime. Now you must watch for *hai*. Perhaps it will come before you die."

**W**hen conversion is accompanied by concept fulfillment, the individuals redeemed become aware of the spiritual meaning dormant within their own culture.

Years later, Gordon Larson, John Ellenburger, Don Gibbons, and their wives entered the Damal valley where Dem lived. After tackling the Damal language, they began to teach the gospel.

The people, including Dem, listened politely. Then one day...

"O my people!" Dem, now a mature adult, had risen to his feet. "How long our forefathers searched for *hai*. How sadly my father died without seeing it. But now, don't you understand, these strangers have brought *hai* to us! We must believe their words, or we will miss the fulfillment of our ancient expectation."

A breakthrough began. Virtually the entire population welcomed the gospel. Within a few years congregations sprang up in nearly every Damal village.

But that was not the end.

## The Dani and "Nabelan-Kabelan"

The Dani, haughty overlords of the Damal, were intrigued by all the excitement. Curious, they sent Damal-speaking representatives to inquire. Learning that the Damal were rejoicing in the fulfillment of their ancient hope, the Dani were stunned. They too had been waiting for the fulfillment of something they called *nabelan-kabelan*—the belief that one day immortality would return to mankind. Was it possible that the message that was *hai* to the Damal could also be *nabelan-kabelan* to the Dani?

By then Gordon and Peggy Larson had been assigned to work among the Dani. Dani warriors now recalled that they often mentioned "words of life" and a man named Jesus, who not only could raise the dead but also rose again Himself.

Suddenly everything fell into place for the Dani as it had for the Damal. The word spread. In valley after valley, the once barbarous Dani listened to the words of life. A church was born.

Concept fulfillment.

## The Karen and a black book

The Karen tribe in Burma had a legend that one day a teacher of truth would appear and he would carry a black object tucked under his arm. This first missionary to come among them always carried a black, leather-covered Bible tucked under his arm. The Karen listened with rapt attention every time he took the Bible out from under his arm and preached.

Triggered by this catalyzing cultural element, a great moving of the Spirit of God soon swept thousands of Karen into the church of Jesus Christ. Yet some studies of the phenomenal growth of the church among the Karen fail to mention this detail.

## The Asmat and a new birth

When Jesus told Nicodemus he must be born again, Nicodemus was astounded. Even though he was well educated, he met Jesus' assertion with a naively literal, almost childish objection:

"How can a man be born when he is old? Can he enter into his mother's womb a second time and be born?"

Surely, if a theologian like Nicodemus had that hard a time comprehending the meaning of "new birth," then a naked, illiterate, stone-age cannibal would have a thousand times more difficulty.

On the contrary, one part of Irian Jaya's Asmat tribe have a way of making peace that requires representatives from two warring villages to pass through a symbolic birth canal formed by the bodies of a number of men and women from both villages. Those who pass through the canal are considered *reborn* into the kinship systems of their respective enemy villages. Rocked, lullabied, cradled, and coddled like new-born infants, they become the focus of a joyful celebration. From then on they may travel freely back and forth between the two formerly warring villages, serving as living peace bonds.

**T**heir peace-making custom has impressed deeply upon the Asmat mind a vital concept: True peace can come only through a new birth experience!

For no one knows how many centuries, this custom has impressed deeply upon the Asmat mind a vital concept: *True peace can come only through a new birth experience!*

Suppose God called you to communicate the gospel to these Asmat people. What would be your logical starting point? Let us assume you have learned their language and are competent to discuss the things dear to their hearts.

One day you visit a typical Asmat man—let's call him Erypeet—in his longhouse. First you discuss with him a former period of war and the new birth transaction that brought it to an end. Then…

Converts among such tribes then find, along with their personal redemption, that they become resistant to apathy, the great destroyer of indigenous peoples overcome by culture shock.

"Erypeet, I too am very interested in new birth. You see, I was at war with an enemy named God. While I was at war with God, life was grim, as it was for you and your enemies.

"But one day my enemy God approached me and said, 'I have prepared a new birth whereby I can be born in you and you can be born again in Me, so that we can be at peace….'"

By this time Erypeet is leaning forward on his mat, asking,

"You and your people have a new birth, too?" He is amazed to find that you, an alien, are sophisticated enough to even *think* in terms of a new birth, let alone *experience* one!

"Yes," you reply.

"Is it like ours?"

"Well, Erypeet, there are some similarities, and there are some differences. Let me tell you about them…."

Erypeet understands.

What makes the difference between Erypeet's and Nicodemus's responses? Erypeet's mind has been preconditioned by an Asmat redemptive analogy to acknowledge man's need for a new birth. Our task is simply to convince him that he needs *spiritual* rebirth.

Do redemptive analogies like these occur by mere coincidence? Because their strategic use is foreshadowed in the New Testament, and because they are so widespread, we discern the grace of God working. Our God, after all, is far too sovereign to be merely lucky.

But has anyone found a culture lacking concepts suitable for redemptive analogies?

## The Yali and "Osuwa"

A formidable candidate for this grim distinction was the cannibal Yali culture of Irian Jaya. If ever a tribe needed some Christ-foreshadowing belief a missionary could appeal to, it was the Yali.

By 1966 missionaries of the Regions Beyond Missionary Union had succeeded in winning about twenty Yali to Christ. Priests of the Yali god Kembu promptly martyred two of the twenty. Two years later they killed missionaries Stan Dale and Phillip Masters, driving about one hundred arrows into each of their bodies. Then the Indonesian government, also threatened by the Yali, stepped in to quell further uprisings. Awed by the power of the government, the Yali decided they would rather have missionaries than soldiers. But the missionaries could find no analogy in Yali culture to make the gospel clear.

Last year another missionary and I conducted a much belated "culture probe" to learn more about Yali customs and beliefs. One day a young Yali named Erariek shared with us the following story from his past:

"Long ago my brother Sunahan and a friend named Kahalek were ambushed by enemies from across the river. Kahalek was killed, but Sunahan fled to a circular stone wall nearby. Leaping inside it, he turned, bared his chest at his enemies, and laughed at them. The enemies immediately lowered their weapons and hurried away."

Yali culture instinctively echoes the Christian teaching that man needs a place of refuge.

I nearly dropped my pen. "Why didn't they kill him?" I asked.

Erariek smiled. "If they had shed one drop of my brother's blood while he stood within that sacred stone wall—we call it an *osuwa*—their own people would have killed them."

Yali pastors and the missionaries working with them now have a new evangelistic tool. Christ is the spiritual *Osuwa*, the perfect place of refuge. For Yali culture instinctively echoes the Christian teaching that man needs a place of refuge. Ages earlier they had established a network of *osuwa* in areas where most of their battles took place. Missionaries had noticed the stone walls but had never ferreted out their full significance.

### Redemption and Resistance

Concepts like the Damal's *hai*, the Dani's *nabelan-kabelan*, the Asmat new birth, and the Yali *osuwa* form the very heart of their cultural life. When outsiders obliterate distinctives like these, something dies within the hearts of the people. But the gospel preserves these concepts. Converts among such tribes then find, along with their personal redemption, that they become resistant to *apathy*, the great destroyer of indigenous peoples overcome by culture shock.

Hundreds of areas remain where response to the gospel has been unsatisfactory or even nonexistent. In many of these areas, sensitive culture probes may discover undreamed-of possibilities for spiritual penetration through concept fulfillment. Discouraged missionaries or national pastors may gain fresh confidence in their ability to make the gospel understood. ◎

# THE SUCCESS OF THE MODERN MISSION MOVEMENT

## Percent of the World's Christians Living in the Two-Thirds World *

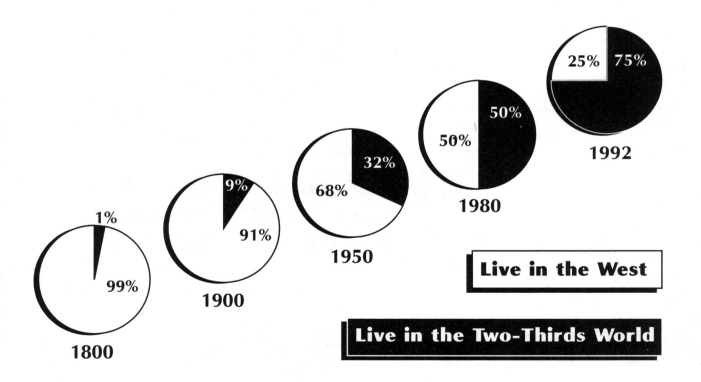

\* Includes Asia, Africa, Latin America, the South Pacific, and the Middle East

# The Missionary's Role in Culture Change
### Dale W. Kietzman and William A. Smalley

**Dale Kietzman**, a member of Wycliffe Bible Translators since 1946, worked with the Amahuaca Indians of Peru. He served in a number of administrative roles, including United States Division Director. He also served as President of World Literature Crusade/Every Home for Christ and more recently as Chairman of the Communications Division of William Carey International University.

**William A. Smalley** was Professor Emeritus of Linguistics at Bethel College in St. Paul, Minnesota. Smalley worked for twenty-three years for the United Bible Societies and as a consultant to the Bible societies in his retirement. He was also active in the formation of the Toronto Institute of Linguistics. He was editor of the journal *Practical Anthropology* from 1955 to 1968. Smalley died in 1997.

## How Change Occurs

The important thing for the missionary to note is that change is almost always initiated by someone within the cultural community. Even though the idea may have been sparked by contact with another culture, it still must be introduced from within to be accepted. The alternative to this scheme is change forced upon a people through superior might, whether moral or physical. This is the sort of change that missions have often been responsible for and that resulted in such unfortunate reaction.

The real agent of the Holy Spirit in any society for the changes in the culture of that society is the church, the body of believers (*not* necessarily the organized church of any particular denomination). The church is the salt working through the whole dish. It is that part of the society that has a new relationship to God yet reacts in terms of the attitudes and presuppositions of that society. It understands, in an intuitive, unanalyzed way, motives and meanings as the missionary cannot. It must make the decisions.

## The Missionary's Part

What, then, can missionaries do about culture change? Are they only to be evangelists preaching a noncultural gospel without making value judgments? This is an impossibility, even if it were desirable.

There cannot be preaching except in cultural terms, and no human being can or should try to escape value judgments. Missionaries cannot legitimately force or enforce any culture change. Nor do they have an adequate basis for advocating specific changes in a culture unless they have a profound knowledge of the culture.

Missionaries do, however, have an extremely important function in the tactful, thoughtful, serious presentation of alternate forms of cultural behavior to the Christians in a society. On the basis of their knowledge of history, their understanding of the church elsewhere, and above all, their knowledge of the tremendously varied ways in which God deals with people, as recorded in the Scriptures, they can make it clear to them that there are alternative ways of behavior to their own and help them in prayer and study and experiment to select those cultural forms that would be the best expression for their relationship to God in their culture.

The missionary's basic responsibility is to provide the material upon which the native Christian and church can grow "in grace and knowledge" to the point where they can make reliable and Spirit-directed decisions with regard to their own conduct within the existing culture. This involves a complete freedom of access to the Word of God, with such encouragement, instruction, and guidance in its use as may be necessary to obtain a healthy and growing Christian community.

The missionary's role in culture change, then, is that of a catalyst and of a source of new ideas, new information. It is the voice of experience, but an experience based on his own culture for the most part and therefore to be used only with care and understanding. Part of the value of anthropological study, of course, is that it gives at least vicarious experience in more than one cultural setting, for by study in this field missionaries can gain awareness of the much wider choice of alternatives than their own culture allows.

It is the church that is the legitimate agency in which the missionary should work. It is the people who must make the decisions based on the new ideas that they have received. It is they who must reinterpret old needs and expressions, examined now in the light of their relationship to God and to their fellow men in Christ Jesus.

Kietzman, D. W. & Smalley, W. A. (1992). From "The Missionary's Role in Culture Change" by permission of the authors. In R. D. Winter & S. C. Hawthorne (Eds.). *Perspectives on the World Christian Movement: A Reader* (rev.ed.) (pp. C160–C161). Pasadena: William Carey Library.

## How can they be heard?

## Distinctions of Distances

Understanding the people group concept, it become clear that taking the Story to others is about more than geographical distance. Even more formidable than oceans and mountain ranges is cultural distance. Messengers must not only overcome their own cultural biases but also learn the cultural cues and rules of people to whom they go. At the same time, the messengers must take the Story from the Hebrew culture in which it was recorded and find ways to make it relevant and understandable in the target culture.

To the Dog Rib Indians of northern Canada, the idea of a sheep is unknown. How does one teach about the Lamb of God or the Good Shepherd? To the people of Thailand, snow is an alien concept. How does one communicate that sins can be washed "white as snow"?

Even the idea of sin is different in every culture. Is it a sin for women to eat bananas, as in some South Sea Island cultures? Is it a sin to make a minor mistake in a ritual performance, as in many animistic cultures? Or is it a sin to fail to recycle newspapers, as currently practiced in some Western cultures? All cultures present the messengers with challenge.

## The Role of the Messengers

Entering the culture in ways that help messengers to become "belongers" is vitally important. To have humility, like that of the Lord Himself, is essential. Learning the language and learning the culture are critical first steps. Yet they are not sufficient to compete the work. Messengers must also seek to understand the culture at the level of its worldview and seek the Holy Spirit to effect changes at that level.

With proper regard for the culture and great respect for the new believers, messengers may wisely allow changes to be developed by the mature national leaders. Messengers can offer examples from other cultures but acknowledge the experience and wisdom within each people group to make their own decisions, guided by Scripture. They must decide what form a church should take to make it fit naturally within their world. The church that looks to the local people like it "belongs" to them is the church that can grow within the native soil.

Must men and women sit together in worship times? Must hands be folded to pray, or can they be lifted up with open palms? Must elders be chosen by a vote, or can the community use their own ways of selecting leaders? These issues may seem small, but the sum of them can be very significant in producing a church that "feels right" to the national believers.

## Contextualizing Without Compromising

The one consistent element of culture is that *culture is constantly changing*. Coca-Cola, movies, the Internet, cell phones, Nike, and McDonalds are contributing to changes in cultures around the globe. Nearby cultures influence each other. Of course, the arrival of the Kingdom Story will inevitably change cultures, too.

However, messengers want to bring change for the welfare, not the detriment, of the culture they love and serve. Whatever can be preserved of the culture should be kept. In a continual, living interaction with Scripture and the Holy Spirit, many changes can be considered and the local culture can determine which are appropriate. Some will be discarded, some will be adjusted, and some will be adapted or adopted.

The goal is finding suitable *contextualization* of the message without compromising the key essentials. No simple answers are available. Every culture will offer distinctive problems. In loving relationship with the people, God's Story can be interwoven with their story. When this happens, God will be exalted in their nation.

## Paying the Price

Sometimes realizing the intricacies and hazards inherent in taking the Gospel to other cultures is overwhelming. Could we rely on technology—radio, film, the Internet, computers—to do the work? Must messengers still pay the price, face the dangers, and endure the afflictions needed to proclaim God's ways?

Yes, they must. No technology will ever replace the need for God's own people to go. The message must take on flesh for it to be embraced and understood. Only people—not things—can rightly bring in the presence of the living God. King David learned this lesson when he was transporting the Ark of the Covenant (2 Sam 6): God's presence must only be transported on the shoulders of His priests. As a royal priesthood (1 Peter 2:10) we too are God's instruments to bring His presence where He is not yet known.

Printed materials, DVDs, and radio all support the work in valuable ways. However, they can never take the place of committed, loving, visible witnesses. As individuals, churches, and agencies, we must send and we must go until the Lord returns. That alone will incarnate God's Story to the watching nations. We must never cease to present ourselves for His service, wherever He may choose to deploy us. Like our Father, we must send our very best!

In Jesus' final command to disciple the nations, we are particularly reassured of his ever-present involvement. As we set ourselves to go out, He promises, "Lo, I am with you always, even to the end of the age." (Matthew 28:20b NIV). This is certainly what it means to know Him in the power of His resurrection and the fellowship of His sufferings. Let us press on to this high calling!

**Fulani:** Fulanis, who originated in Senegal, number possibly 29 million in ten western and central African countries. Originally a nomadic and pastoral people, the lives of many of them revolve around their cattle. They have been Muslim since the fourteenth century and pride themselves on being propagators and perpetuators of Islam.

Ten million Fulanis live in northern Nigeria. Some form the ruling class of that country who strongly contend against every Christian advance, even killing believers and destroying churches. Others comprise the nomadic cattle herders who roam the Sahel. Finding ways to build communities of believers in a nomadic culture is a special challenge. The conversion of the Fulani would have profound effects throughout West Africa.

Julie Bosacker, YWAM

# 5 Partnership Paths

## TELLING THE STORY TOGETHER

### Uniting as World Christians

Understanding the story helps us in our role as *World Christians*. David Bryant, founder of Concerts of Prayer, defines World Christians as

> day-to-day disciples for whom Christ's global cause has become the integrating, overriding priority....
> (They are) Christians whose life directions have been solidly transformed by a world vision.
> [Bryant 1992: D-306]

Once God's heart for the nations is understood, we are constrained by love to communicate His truth (2 Cor. 5:14).

### Responding as a Worldwide Church

It is encouraging to embrace the global dimensions of our citizenship in the Kingdom. As John Stott reminds us, the church is "a multi-national, multi-ethnic community, under orders to evangelize until Christ returns" (Pg. 4). We aren't in this alone! Maybe we feel that simply shining simple the little lantern of our church or our fellowship is very limited. Instead, we can catch sight of a mighty spotlight as we stand with an international fellowship of truth! Linking arms with others gives us great optimism.

Both *evangelism and development* contribute to telling the story. We must display deeds of love alongside words of truth. In the unreached world, the story must also be validated by demonstrations of God's power. Only prayer can bring that about.

This by no means implies a termination of responsibilities for the Western church. How tragic if any part of the body should cease to send its sons and daughters out in the service of the King! Now we also perceive older believers making major active contributions as well.

If there is humility and sensitivity, the Western world can contribute experience, resources, and practical wisdom to multi-cultural partnerships. The non-Western world has a nearer comprehension of poverty and oppression. They show courage in suffering, being beaten and imprisoned, even laying down their lives. Together we can support and sustain one another. Together we can *press on to closure*, seeing a living church movement expanding among every people!

### Tough Questions, Challenging Choices

Is it a violation of respect for cultures to proclaim the only true way to God? We must be prepared to respond to these charges both factually and Biblically. The answers confound our critics!

How can we strategically invest our personal gifts and abilities in kingdom commitment? Knowing the variety of roles that play a part in the work can direct us to places of significant service. Valuing one another's indispensable contributions gives each person a sense of their global significance. Cooperation and partnership are not just practical; they are vital.

It would be futile to try to *complete world evangelization* without dedicated, ardent prayer. Unless prayer is the core of all we do, nothing lasting will result. We may multiply activity, but it will amount to nothing.

With prayer, we stay ready to hear His voice when He gives new strategies. While we seek to please the Lord and see Him glorified, prayer joins us with one another. In His power alone will we be able to tell the story together. His unassailable light gives direction to our Path.

# Evangelism as Development
## Edward R. Dayton

Development is a many-meaning word. For some it has a sense of Western imperialism: the "developed" country is attempting to impose their own values and desires on "lesser developed" countries. "Developed to what?" they ask. For what? There is a built-in assumption that things are better when they are "developed."

of *community* development. The assumption is that if we can deal with an entire community that is still intact in its community setting, development is possible. There are many who agree that this is the right approach. We do too.

> **T**he U.S.A.I.D. finally concluded that there was little hope for replicating the developed West through massive doses of technology. It was a somber, but wise, conclusion.

Development has about it the ring of human progress. *Human* progress. It can find its roots in the Age of Enlightenment, when for the first time in history, a large segment of society began to believe that they really could control their destinies. The humanists of the seventeenth and eighteenth centuries were stimulated in their thinking by the great discoveries (for the West!) of the Americas and the African continent. What we can now see were often coincidences of history worked together to convince them that by dint of hard work and high ideals man could triumph over his situation. The stories of Horatio Alger became the everyday coin of our belief. The Calvin-inspired Protestant ethic became an end in itself. "Progress" was measured by acquisition.

Once the West was won, those who were a part of the grand adventure naturally concluded that what they had been able to accomplish should be a possibility for others. They looked with compassion, mixed with a good degree of superiority, at their neighbors in less "developed" countries and set about to help them develop. Failures outnumbered successes at every turn. The American State Department's Agency for International Development finally concluded that there was little hope for replicating the developed West through massive doses of Western technology. It was a somber, but wise, conclusion.

We are now involved in a fall-back situation of operating on the principle that our mistake was one of scale. To attempt to develop an entire nation was beyond our scope, but there still remains the possibility

Now, the goal of community development always was and still remains to bring a group to a place of self-reliance or self-sufficiency: they find within themselves all that is needed to maintain life at a desired level. The fly in the ointment is that the underlying premise of those involved in micro-development, namely, given the right circumstances and resources, mankind is capable of creating for himself a *good* society. The premise is false.

The premise is wrong because man's values are flawed. The natural man is turned in on himself, concerned for himself and his own welfare. Given a choice between his own welfare and the welfare of his society, he will usually erroneously conclude that his own best ends are served by serving himself. This is particularly true if he follows the model of the West. For the model of the West is, "*You* can do it! Look at me. *I* did it!" Or, to put it in the title of a not-so-old popular tune, "I Did It *My* Way."

> **T**he goal of community development is to bring a group to a place of self-reliance or self-sufficiency.

And so it is quite easy for us to become involved in *valueless* community development. We can look with Christian compassion on a group of people living on the edge of poverty and conclude that if they had a better water system, better farming methods, and basic preventive medicine, they would be all right. Community development is possible. But along with those changes in material standards, there needs to be a change in spiritual standards. There needs to be the announcement

Dayton, E. R. (1992). *Evangelism as Development*. In R. D. Winter & S. C. Hawthorne (Eds.). *Perspectives on the World Christian Movement: A Reader* (rev.ed.) (pp. D210–D212). Pasadena: William Carey Library. MARC, a division of World Vision, International.

of the gospel of the Kingdom, the possibility of a radical change at the core of one's being.

It's not a question of material development that is accompanied by the gift of eternal life found in Christ. It's a question of the basic motivation to want to change, to want to find a new relationship with one's neighbor, to want to put spiritual values before material values. Evangelism is at the core of true development. It is the catalyst that makes the rest of the mix take form.

> *It's a question of the basic motivation to want to change, to want to find a new relationship with one's neighbor. Evangelism is at the core of true development.*

Perhaps an extreme example will make the point. World Vision is currently involved in an area of the world that has recently been resettled by the government. Each family has been given a plot of ground, half of which is to be used for a cash crop controlled by the government and the other half of which can be used for personal use. People have come from many different settings to take advantage of this offer. They each have a means of livelihood. Their material needs are met, but there is a great deal of unrest, strife, and social upheaval. Our "development" solution is to support the establishment of a Christian community center that will bring a common value system to the community. The anticipation is that as people become one in Christ, they will relate to one another in a new way. Helping to plant a church that will provide the missing values turns out to be the key element of development.

Christians have been uniquely equipped to do development. First, we come to the task with the right motivation. The love of Christ constrains us. The demands of righteousness and justice are upon us.

Second, Christians come to the task with an ability to work out our lives in the midst of the tension that, while we believe we are called upon to work against the forces of evil we find in our world, at the same time we believe that only in Christ's return will that evil be permanently defeated.

But Western Christians live in the midst of what a recent writer has called the *Culture of Narcissism*, a culture in which the individual is turning in on himself to find a fulfillment or self-understanding or self-awareness or a host of other in-words. We tell ourselves that the society is out of control. Our leaders are found incompetent or corrupt. Our technology threatens to overcome us rather than save us. History loses its meaning for us. What was right seventy years ago is no longer important. Today's problems, we reason, are so different that we will have to make up the rules as we go along. And without recognizing what is happening, we Christians easily follow the same path. We adjust our theology to fit the circumstances we can't change. And therefore it becomes easy for us to conclude that what one values, what one holds most important, probably varies for everyone. And who are we to tell someone else how to live? And that's about the way non-Christian development approaches the task.

The message of the gospel is a radical message. It not only says, "Change your mind about things," it also demands, "Let Christ change your life—think about your sister and your brother. What's important is not how much you acquire but how you live out your life." Salvation is not just eternity. Salvation begins now with a new mind in Christ.

> *The message of the gospel is a radical message. What's important is not how much you acquire but how you live out your life.*

Let's listen again to that message—daily. And if we really believe that Christ changed our life, let's believe that evangelism is a key part of development.

> ## If we will do the possible,
> ## God will do the impossible.
> *John Rowell*

# Biblical Development
*Bob Moffitt*

**Bob Moffitt** is the founder and president of Harvest Foundation, an organization involved in curriculum development for leadership training in Two-Thirds World Churches. He is the author of *Adventures in God's Kingdom* and the *Leadership Development Training Program*.

## Secular and Biblical Development

What is development? How is it defined? What are its characteristics? Secular and Christian development each provide different answers to these questions.

**Secular Development** is designed to improve living conditions. It supports and encourages a higher quality of life. It believes that people, individually and corporately, can improve their quality of life through intentional human effort. In the Two-Thirds World, secular development works primarily to meet physical and social needs—health, water, housing, agriculture, economic enterprise, education, etc. Good secular development has two key characteristics: it helps people help themselves, and it is sustainable (it can be continued without ongoing external support.)

**Biblical Development** affirms much of this but with a radically different orientation. This difference is critical. Secular development is man-centered: for man, by man, limited to what man can do for himself. Biblical development is God-centered: from God, seeking to honor God, and relying on Him as the principal participant in the development process. Biblical development does not exclude man but sees him cooperating under God in the process of man's healing.

In Biblical development, "quality of life" is determined by God's intentions for His people. It is not limited to the tangible and visible arenas of man's need, but includes the healing of areas of emotion and spirit. It is not limited to what man can do for himself but is as limitless as God's power, love, and mercy.

## The Goal of Development Is God's Intentions

Development must have a goal, an objective, an agenda. The Christian objective and agenda are directed by God's intentions. Secular development asks, "What are your needs?" Biblical development asks, "What are God's intentions for you and this particular need?" The answer sets the goal for Biblical development.

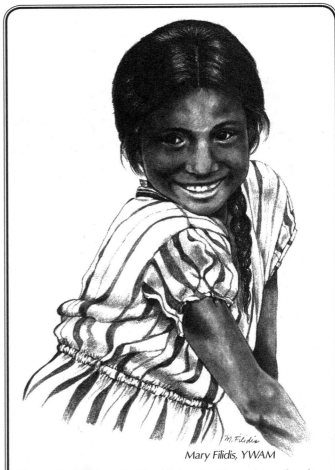

*Mary Filidis, YWAM*

**Durango Nahuatl:** Combining its Hispanic and Indian heritage, Mexico is filled with an intense nationalism and a search for identity. Latin America's fourth largest country is struggling with serious social, economic, and political problems. Mexican evangelicals are growing in numbers while undergoing many types of persecution. Around 8 million of her people are descendants of ancient cultures, including Aztec, Mayan, and Zapotecan. One hundred fifty-four groups are poorly reached and 25 are entirely unengaged.

The Durango Nahautl people conserve what is thought to be one of the oldest forms of the Aztec language. They live as subsistence farmers, hunting and gathering foods in the wild canyons of Durango and Nazarit. Their worldview is a Christo-pagan mix: a thin veneer of folk Catholicism over an animistic pre-Columbian religion. One new believer, as the result of a dramatic power encounter, is quietly sharing his newfound life with his fellow tribesmen. A Bible translation project is in beginning stages.

Moffitt, B. (1994). *Leadership Development and Training Curriculum.* Tempe, Ariz.: Harvest Foundation.

Felt needs are legitimate concerns in development works, but they are not the only concern. Heroin addicts feel the need for heroin. Some women express a felt need for abortion on demand. A teenager may express a need for a car. These represent real feelings; however, responding to them may actually hinder development. Therefore the question must be, "What is the root need beyond the felt need?" Unless the felt need is life-threatening—lack of food for a starving child—development work is best directed toward the root need.

Christians realize root needs are related to underlying spiritual causes. Scripture describes the relationships between all these needs, and God's solutions. Before setting goals, Christians ask, "Father, what is Your perspective of this need, its root, and Your solution?"

## Jesus' Development Models God's Intentions

Jesus, though divine, was also man, and He is our model for development. To understand God's intentions, Luke 2:52 is a good starting point. Luke, a medical doctor, described Jesus' development in four domains—wisdom, physical, spiritual, and social. "And Jesus grew in wisdom and stature, and in favor with God and men" (NIV).

If Jesus needed to develop in all these areas, so do all men. God is concerned about the *whole man*. Development must reflect this *wholistic* or *balanced* concern to represent God's intentions. The purpose of Jesus' development was to honor God, to serve and give His life for others. Man also should grow in order to love and honor Him, to love and serve others. Biblical development will promote this.

It is well to note that Jesus' development was in the context of *adequacy* rather than *affluence*. God made sure Jesus had the necessary resources to grow in wisdom—a simple synagogue school in which the study of God's law was the focus. He had the necessary resources to grow physically—shelter, clothing, food, water, sanitation, physical labor, etc. He had the necessary resources to grow spiritually—a God–fearing home and ability to read the Scriptures. And, He had the necessary resources to grow socially—a loving, functional family who modeled appropriate relationships in the family and community. Jesus' development took place in an environment of adequacy, or even relative poverty, rather than in an affluent, technically advanced environment.

## The Primary Resource for Development Is God

God is the originator of development. He created all things. He sustains all things. All resources come from Him. As stewards of talents and resources God provides, development workers prayerfully and courageously invest them to advance God's goals.

As Creator, God deals in the supernatural. He is not limited to the existing material world. His principles can and do produce blessing and change. Because development workers are servants of the living God, they are not limited to visible material resources. In the face of insurmountable difficulties, they can take confidence in God's promise to those who walk in His righteousness: He will heal the people and their land.

Ten years ago I visited an impoverished village in central Mexico. Village leaders, recently converted, committed to live God's way. They weren't particularly interested in development. Yet now the village has been transformed from a place where families were killing each other in blood feuds to one where they serve one another in love. In an area where pigs once roamed freely through mud huts, there are now tidy wooden houses. (The first seven houses were built for village widows.) In a place that had only a small stream and not one latrine, there is now running water and sanitation. In the once empty and deserted schoolhouse, children now attend classes.

Ten years ago, the prospect for development in this village looked bleak. However, God's intervention was

*Biblical development is not limited to what man can do for himself, but is as limitless as God's power, love, and mercy.*

not limited to visible resources. The people of this village entered into a pact of righteousness with God—a pact in which they sought and followed His intentions. Leaders in the village regularly went to the forest to study Scripture and pray for several days. They stayed till they reached agreement on what God wanted them to do. Then they put their convictions into practice. I marveled as He moved to "heal their land."

## The Local Church: Active Participant in Development

The local church is the most visible and permanent representation of God's Kingdom in any community. More than any other institution, it can reflect God's concern in each domain of man's need. Other Christian institutions have a particular focus—evangelism, education, health, economic development. They are limited by organizational mandate in their ability to represent God's concern for the whole person.

Where there is a local church, it should be actively involved in servant leadership in development. Thereby local churches grow their ability to proclaim and demonstrate God's intentions for the people of their respective communities. The potential for sustainability of the work will increase as well.

## Development: Required of the Poor as Well as the Rich

The parable of the talents (Matthew 25:14–30) teaches that *no one* is exempt from the responsibility to courageously risk their resources for the Kingdom of God. Damage results if the poor are regarded as too poor to play a part. Unless the issue is survival, the appeal to outside resources often reinforces a sense of powerlessness. If provided before local people learn to value and invest the resources God had entrusted to them, long-term dependency on outside financial, material and technical aid may occur. The history of modern development is replete with examples of well-intended efforts that actually inhibited rather than advanced development.

God multiplies the gifts of the poor. In biblical accounts of the widow of Zarephath, the feeding of the 5,000, and the widow's mite, God acted in response to sacrificial commitment of resources. Even the poor must demonstrate God's love to those around them. This is their gift from God.

In India, a village church realized they had a responsibility to invest the little they had to demonstrate God's love to their Hindu neighbors. They went out to see what needs existed. They discovered that some Hindu women owned only one sari. Every other day, when the sari was being washed, they could not leave their homes for shopping or other necessities.

The pastor asked if any in the congregation with three saris would give one to help these Hindu women. The result? All the saris needed (about twelve) were given and delivered. At the same time, Hindu women requested Christians to come and pray for the protection of their unborn children. Matching needs with resources has become part of the Sunday worship experience of these Indian Christians. A church that had seen itself as too poor to make a difference now entered a much fuller dimension of outreach.

## Development: More Than Technology

Development includes technology, but it is much more than technology. Western Christians tend to assume technology is the first requirement for adequate development. Other cultures may see it quite differently. Valson Thampu, a Christian professor in New Delhi, writes:

The danger is...a reductive idea of resources as only that which is brought in from abroad. This can breed a psychology of dependence and culture of corruption.

Providing care for AIDS victims, for example, the temptation is for westerners to set up a chain of hospices on models and standards feasible only in the West. The enormous potential that the joint family system in Asia and Africa has for providing care can be lost. The emphasis will be exclusively on technology-intensive caring institutions and not on the caring capacities of people.[1]

God has made all people valuable. Being in His image, they are resourceful. Biblical development will reflect that understanding.

> **G**od has made all people valuable and resourceful. Biblical development will reflect that understanding.

## Development: All Must Give

Encouraging sacrificial stewardship for the poor in no way exempts those whose resources are abundant. In John 12:28 Jesus says, "You will always have the poor among you, but you will not always have Me" (NIV). This is often quoted to excuse indifference to the plight of the poor. In fact, Jesus was quoting Deuteronomy 15:11, which gives a very different conclusion: "Therefore I command you to be openhanded toward your brothers and toward the poor and needy in your land" (NIV).

The responsibility exempts no Christian. If the poor are held accountable for this, how much more will the rich be expected to use all they have to bless others, honor God, and expand the Kingdom!

God requires compassionate and liberal sharing with those in need. *All* people are to risk their resources for the Kingdom. Isaiah 58, Matthew 25, Luke 10:25–37, James 2:14, and 1 John 3:16–18 make it clear that it is impossible to love one's neighbors without being open to promote all God's intentions for them. Lovingly done, this is Biblical development.

## End Notes

1   Thampu, V. (1994) "The Indian America Connection: A critique of mission partnerships." *World Christian.* Nov/Dec (p. 23).

# Do Missionaries Destroy Cultures?

*Don Richardson*

When Fray Diego de Landa, a Catholic missionary accompanying Spanish forces in the New World, discovered extensive Mayan libraries, he knew what to do. He burned them all, an event, he said, the Maya "regretted to an amazing degree, and which caused them much affliction." The books, in his opinion, were all full of "superstition and lies of the devil." And so, in 1562, the poetry, history, literature, mathematics, and astronomy of an entire civilization went up in smoke. Only three documents survived de Landa's misguided zeal.

Magnificent totem poles once towered in Indian villages along Canada's Pacific coast. By 1900 virtually all such native art had been chopped down, either by missionaries who mistook them for idols or by converts zealously carrying out the directives of missionaries.

These incidents and many more show that we missionaries have sometimes acted in a culture-destroying manner. Whether through misinterpreting the Great Commission, pride, culture shock, or simple inability to comprehend the values of others, we have needlessly opposed customs we did not understand. Some, had we understood them, might have served as communication keys for the gospel!

The world has been quick to notice our mistakes. Popular authors like Herman Melville, Somerset Maugham, and James Michener have stereotyped missionaries as opinionated, insensitive, neurotic, sent to the heathen because they were misfits at home.

Michener's austere Abner Hale, a missionary in the novel *Hawaii*, became the archetype of an odious bigot. Hale shouts hellfire sermons against the "vile abominations" of the pagan Hawaiians. He forbids Hawaiian midwives to help a missionary mother at the birth of "a Christian baby." The mother dies.

Hale even forbids Hawaiians to help his wife with housework lest his children learn the "heathen Hawaiian language." His wife works herself into an early grave.

When Buddhist Chinese settle in Hawaii, Michener has Hale barging into their temples to smash their idols.

Interesting literary grist, to be sure.

Unfortunately for naive readers, "Abner Hale" came to mean "missionary." We've been carrying him on our backs ever since.

Anthropologist Alan Tippett of the Fuller Seminary School of World Mission once researched hundreds of

*Mary Filidis, YWAM*

**Parsee:** The Parsees are a minority religion in the mosaic of India and surrounding countries. Zoroastrians who fled Muslim persecution in Iran, they number about 3 million. Their commitment to "good thoughts, good words, good deeds" has led to a reputation for excellence in business, medicine, law, and the arts.

Only those born Parsees are allowed to be Zoroastrians. Not even a person who marries one may join their faith. Most Parsees in India are prosperous and educated. They are well thought of, having started over a thousand charities for the needy of other races.

Little or no work has been undertaken among these people. They are representative of many smaller religious sects like the Sikhs, the Druzes, the Mormons, the Jains, the Sokka Gakai, and others whose divergent belief systems make them into unique people groups. In each case, special strategies will be needed. Almost every nation and every major religion has such groups, but few are concentrating on ways to engage and win them.

Richardson, D. (1992). "Do Missionaries Destroy Cultures?" In R. D. Winter & S. C. Hawthorne (Eds.). *Perspectives on the World Christian Movement: A Reader* (rev.ed.) (pp. C137–C148). Pasadena: William Carey Library.

early missionary sermons stored in the Honolulu archives. None had the ranting style Michener suggests as typical. Critics seem to suggest, naively, that if only missionaries stayed home, primitive people would be left undisturbed to fulfill the myth of Rousseau's "noble savage."

> *Critics suggest naively that, if only missionaries stayed home, primitive people would be left undisturbed.*

The fact is, commercial exploiters or other secular forces have already wrought havoc with indigenous cultures on an awesome scale. Livingstone was preceded by Arab slave traders. Amy Carmichael was preceded by victimizers who dragged boys and girls away to temples, where they faced the terrors of child prostitution.

Secular forces such as these have sometimes destroyed entire peoples. In North America not only the famous Mohicans but also the Hurons and possibly as many as twenty other Indian tribes were pushed into extinction by land-hungry settlers. Pioneers on one occasion sent a tribe wagonloads of gift blankets known to be infected with smallpox.

In Brazil only 200,000 Indians remain from an original population estimated at 4 million. In the past seventy-five years more than one tribe per year has disappeared. Readers may assume that Brazil's missing tribes have been absorbed into society, but this is not the case. Thousands have been brutally poisoned, machine-gunned, or dynamited from low-flying aircraft. Other thousands succumbed to a slower, more agonizing death by *apathy*. As encroachment caused their cultures to disintegrate, Indian men have even been known to cause their wives to miscarry. They refused to bring children into a world they could no longer understand.

Prior to 1858, India's Andaman Islands were the home of at least 6,000 pygmy negritoes. Then the British established a penal colony in the islands and victimization began. Today a scant 600 negritoes remain.

Similar tragedies are unfolding throughout the Philippines, Asia, and Africa.

Concern is widespread today—and justly so—for endangered animal species. But hundreds of our own human species are in even greater danger! A yearly loss of ten linguistically distinct tribes may be a conservative figure.

Only a few of the world's governments have established agencies to protect their ethnic minorities. Brazil, the Philippines, and India are three examples. Secular agencies, however, suffer from severe budget restrictions.

Furthermore, other arms of government may interfere with the programs. For example, not long after Brazil's National Foundation for the Indian established Xingu National Park as a reserve for endangered tribes, roadbuilders obtained permission to blast a modern highway through the center of it! As a result two of Xingu's "protected" tribes were destroyed by measles and influenza introduced by construction crews.

Clearly, the "enlightened" policy of "leave-them-alone" isn't working. What, then, can halt their march toward extinction? Grants, land, and secular welfare programs may help on the physical level (though sometimes godless officials introduce alcoholism or other vices, undermining whatever good their programs may accomplish).

But the greatest danger to aboriginals is one that such programs cannot deal with—the breakdown of the aboriginal's sense of "right" relationship with the supernatural. Every aboriginal culture acknowledges the supernatural and has strict procedures for "staying right" with it. When arrogant outsiders ridicule a tribe's belief, or shatter its mechanisms for "staying right," severe disorientation sets in. Tribesmen believe they are under a curse for abandoning the old ways. They become morose and apathetic, believing they are doomed to die as a people. Materialistic social workers or scientists cannot help such people. The tribesmen *sense* even an unspoken denial of the supernatural and become even more depressed.

Who then can best serve such people as spiritual ombudsmen? None other than the very ones popularly maligned as the number one enemy: the Bible-guided, Christ-honoring missionary. Consider some case histories:

Less than a generation ago, according to Robert Bell of the Unevangelized Fields Mission, Brazil's Wai Wai

> *Commercial exploiters or other secular forces wrought havoc with indigenous cultures on an awesome scale.*

tribe had been reduced to its last sixty members. This had come about largely through foreign diseases and by the Wai Wai custom of sacrificing babies to demons to try to prevent those diseases.

Then a handful of UFM missionaries identified themselves with the tribe, learned their language, gave it an alphabet, translated the Word of God, and taught Wai Wai to read. Far from denying the supernatural world, the missionaries showed the Wai Wai that a God of love reigned supreme over it. And that God had prepared for them a way of "staying right" on a far deeper level than they had ever dreamed of.

The Wai Wai now had a rational—even delightful—basis for *not* sacrificing babies to demons, and the tribe began to grow. Today the Wai Wai are fast becoming one of Brazil's most populous tribes. And optimistic Wai Wai Christians are teaching other dwindling groups of Indians how to cope with the twentieth century through faith in Jesus Christ.

Repentance and faith in Jesus Christ *can* solve many of the survival problems of endangered peoples. The help given to the Wai Wai, furthermore, is only a very recent example of a long heritage of helping beleaguered peoples.

Near Stockbridge, in what is now Massachusetts, early American missionary John Sargent and his associates established a community to preserve Indian rights, preparing them for survival among encroaching Europeans. Before ethnocentrism was named as a social evil, and before the birth of anthropology as a science, Sargent and his helpers unpatronizingly tilled the soil side by side with their Indian friends. Practicing what anthropologists now call "directed change," they also shared their Christian faith. The Indians received it as their own.

That faith, and the love of their spiritual paracletes, sustained the tribe through more than a century of suffering. Greedy settlers soon decided that the land was too good for "mere Indians" and evicted them. After protesting unsuccessfully, Sargent obtained guarantees of land farther west. A few years later the community was uprooted again by other settlers. And again. Fifteen times they were forced to move. Each time the missionaries moved with them, wresting concessions for new land and holding the community together. At last the community settled in Michigan, where it was allowed to rest and survives to this day. As a side benefit, such missionary experiments helped convince scholars that a science of anthropology was necessary.

In both cases just cited, missionaries introduced culture change, but not arbitrarily and not by force. They brought only changes required by the New Testament or required for the survival of the people. Often the two requirements overlap (for example, the cessation of Wai Wai child sacrifices).

Once an interviewer reproached me (perhaps facetiously) for persuading the Sawi tribe in Indonesia to renounce cannibalism.

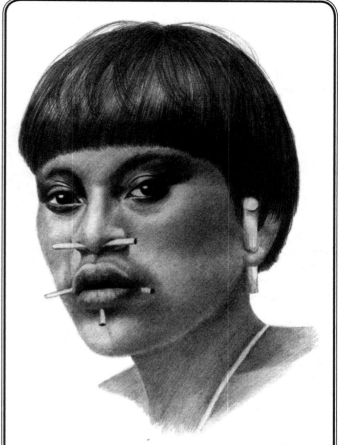

*Julie Bosacker, YWAM*

**Yanomamo:** The Indian tribes of the Amazon jungle are in great danger. Unscrupulous land developers, settlers, and gold seekers have murdered Indians and taken what they wanted from their territories. To build the Transamazon road, Brazilians demolished whole villages with bulldozers and bombed others. Many tribes are losing their cultural identities, even if some of their people survive these depredations.

The Yanomamo, a semi-nomadic people with a subsistence agriculture, supplemented by hunting and fishing, have no written language. They live in northwest Brazil and Venezuela in the Orinoco River area. Exceptionally warlike, they seldom even trade with other tribes. Their animistic practices make use of a hallucinogenic snuff called *ebene*.

Besides the Yanomamo, there are some 50 known tribal groups, such as Parkana, Zuruaha, Himarima, and Cinta—Larga, unreached by the Gospel. Perhaps 100 more groups have been absorbed, fully or partially, into Brazilian society. Brazil has restricted access of workers to many of these groups, even when the tribe requested missionary help. Some tribes hide deeper in the jungle; others commit suicide; others have wasted away in apathetic depression. Brazilian Christians are attempting to find and reach them while there is still time.

"What's wrong with cannibalism?" he asked. "The Sawi practiced it for thousands of years. Why should they give it up now?"

I replied, "Can a people who practice cannibalism survive in the world today? No, they cannot. The Sawi are now citizens of the Republic of Indonesia. The Indonesian

*Wai Wai Christians are teaching other dwindling groups of Indians how to cope with the 20th century through faith in Jesus Christ.*

Republic does not permit its citizens to eat other people. Therefore, part of my task was to give the Sawi a rational basis for *voluntarily* renouncing cannibalism before the guns of the police decided the issue."

On another level Sawi culture entertained a dark compulsion to venerate dead relatives by handling, or even *eating*, the rotting flesh of their corpses. Yet when the Sawi received the Christian teaching of the resurrection, they immediately abandoned such procedures, almost with a sigh of relief. The gospel cured them of this strange compulsion.

The Sawi are among perhaps 400 black-skinned Melanesian tribes just emerging from the stone age in Irian Jaya. Thirteen years ago the Netherlands ceded Irian Jaya (then New Guinea) to Indonesia. Today an estimated one hundred thousand Indonesians have migrated to Irian Jaya. Will the tribal people be prepared to cope with their more enterprising migrant neighbors? Or will they become extinct?

Scattered throughout Irian Jaya, more than 250 evangelical missionaries (all too few) are ministering the gospel to both races. Knowledgeable in Indonesian as well as many of Irian's 400 tribal languages, they are helping members of clashing cultures understand each other. With the sympathetic help of the Indonesian government, they are optimistic that major culture shock may be averted. Already, through faith in Christ, tens of thousands of Irianese have begun a smooth transition into the twentieth century.

Surely ethnic crises of this magnitude are far too sensitive to be left to the dubious mercy of purely commercial interests. Missionaries whose hearts overflow with the love of Christ are the key. Yet still the secular media tend to promote an anti-missionary agenda. The following article is an example of this.

## Cultural Imperialism?

*"Guilty as Charged!" according to Australian journalist Hamish McDonald and the* Washington Post. *After he visited Irian Jaya, Indonesia, to cover the effects of a severe earthquake in June 1976, Hamish McDonald quickly turned his attention to the relationship between Irianese tribespeople and missionaries. His opinions appeared in the following article in the* Washington Post *on August 3, 1976.*

JAYAPURA, Irian Jaya—Fundamentalist Christian missionaries are provoking hostile and occasionally murderous reactions from primitive tribespeople in mountain areas south of here. In the most savage of recent incidents, about eighteen months ago, thirteen local assistants of a mission were killed and eaten as soon as the European missionary went away on leave.

The missionaries are also coming under attack by anthropologists and other observers for attempting the almost total destruction of local cultures in the areas they evangelize. This is seen as the basic cause of recent violent outbreaks, and is contrasted with the more adaptive policies of Roman Catholic and mainstream Protestant missionary groups.

The fundamentalists are working in the remote Jayawijaya mountains where they are now carrying the brunt of relief work following recent severe earthquakes believed to have killed as many as a thousand people.

They belong to five missionary groups—the Christian and Missionary Alliance, the Unevangelized Fields Mission, the Regions Beyond Missionary Union, The Evangelical Alliance Mission, and the Asia-Pacific Christian Mission—banded together in an organization called The Missionary Alliance. They are joined by a

*Sargent and his helpers tilled the soil side by side with their Indian friends practicing "directed change."*

technical missionary group, the Missionary Aviation Fellowship, an efficient air service with fifteen light aircraft and a helicopter—essential in a territory where the longest paved road is the 25-mile drive from Jayapura, the provincial capital, to the airport. They are well backed by Congregationalist, Baptist, and nondenominational Bible groups in North America, Europe, and Australia, although most members and funds come from the United States.

Sometimes rejecting the label "fundamentalist," they describe themselves as "orthodox" or "faith" Christians. Their central characteristic is belief in the literal truth of the Bible.

In recent years they have set up several missions in the Jayawijaya mountains, an unmapped and little-known area that had its first outside contact only about twenty years ago. The Melanesian people there learned the use of metal only recently. They live on sweet potatoes, sugar cane, and bananas, supplemented by pork and occasional small marsupials or birds that they hunt with bows and arrows.

Their only domestic animals are their pigs, which they regard as having souls. When I asked an anthropologist there why they ate such close friends, he said: "It doesn't matter. They eat people, too."

The men wear only the *koteka*, a penis gourd, and the women small tufts of grass fore and aft. Divided by rugged terrain and language from even close neighbors, they feud periodically in set-piece confrontations.

Although their culture recognizes personal and family property, they are remarkable for their willingness to share. Tobacco is their only vice, imported from the coast somehow in the forgotten past. Cowrie shells are the only currency resembling money.

Their culture and traditional religion express the most basic human concepts. They and the other 900,000 people in Irian Jaya produce dazzling works of art in traditional carvings and handicrafts.

Typically, a new missionary arriving builds his house by itself, next to a grass airstrip. One told me: "The first thing is to move in and live with the people. You must prove that you want to help them, by giving them food, medicine, and shelter, teaching them, and learning their

**Y**ou are looking for the key that unlocks the culture and opens the way for the gospel.

language. Often it takes two to four years to learn the language. I guess what you are looking for is the cultural key, the key that unlocks the culture and opens the way for the gospel."

But many missionaries appear to regard the gospel as totally incompatible with the traditional culture, in which they see no deep value. One missionary from the Papua New Guinea border region referred to the old men who stayed aloof from his mission as "having no interest in spiritual things." The first action of a missionary who stayed awhile recently in Valley X was

to hand out shirts to tribesmen. At Nalca Mission, women have been persuaded to lengthen their grass skirts to knee length, apparently to satisfy missionary modesty.

Smoking tobacco is condemned and forbidden as sinful. Until recently, the mission air service searched baggage and refused to fly anyone found carrying tobacco or alcohol.

In 1968 two Western missionaries were killed on the south slope of the Jayawijaya range. Three months ago an American missionary was virtually chased out of the Fa-Malinkele Valley because of his manner.

**M**issionaries are helping members of clashing cultures understand each other.

The incident of cannibalism occurred at a mission called Nipsan, where the Dutch missionary had been using local Irianese assistants from the longer evangelized area near Wamena, farther west. When the missionary went on leave, the tribespeople turned on fifteen assistants, killing and eating thirteen. Two escaped to the jungle. An Indonesian army unit later entered but dropped the case because of the baffling problems of law involved.

The Dutch missionary subsequently made a fund-raising tour of Europe and North America to buy a helicopter from which he proposed to conduct aerial evangelization through a loudspeaker. But the first time this was tried, a month ago, volleys of arrows reportedly greeted the airborne preacher.

The fundamentalists are compared unfavorably with the Roman Catholic missionaries who operate on the southern side of Irian Jaya under a territorial division initiated by the Dutch and maintained by the Indonesians after the 1963 transfer of administration.

"The difference between them is quite simple," said one source at Jayapura. "The Protestants try to destroy the culture. The Catholics try to preserve it."

At a mission called Jaosakor near the southern coast, the Catholics recently consecrated a church largely designed by the local people and incorporating traditional Asmat carvings around the walls. Bishop Alphonse Sowada, of the Nebraska-centered Crosier Fathers, carried out the ceremony in episcopal robes accompanied by local leaders in full regalia of paint, tooth necklaces, and nose-bones. The method of dedication was to scatter lime, made from fired seashells, from bamboo containers over walls, floors, and altars in the way the Asmat people inaugurate their own communal buildings.

Nearly all Catholic missionaries in Irian Jaya are required to hold degrees in anthropology before beginning their calling. Many have published articles and writings on the local peoples. "The basis of our approach is that we believe God is already working through the existing culture, which follows from the belief that God created all things and is present in all of them," one priest said.

*How would you respond to McDonald's assertions? On September 21, 1976, I sent the following open letter to the* Post, *but it never appeared in its "letters to the editor" column. It was, however, selected by John H. Bodley for inclusion in his* Tribal Peoples and Development Issues, *a widely used secular anthropology textbook. (Mayfield Publishing Co., Mountain View, Calif. 1988).*

Dear Sirs:

A few weeks ago journalist Hamish McDonald arrived in Irian Jaya to report on the earthquake which recently devastated a mountainous region here. At least that's what he told the missionaries whose help he needed to reach the area.

The earthquake was of particular interest because it struck the habitat of a number of the earth's last remaining stone age tribes, some of whom still practice cannibalism. Triggering literally thousands of landslides, the upheaval wiped out fifteen tribal villages, killed more than a thousand people, and left 15,000 survivors with only 15 percent of their gardens. The missionaries McDonald approached were busy staging an urgent food airlift. Still, they graciously offered him space on one of their overloaded mercy flights from Jayapura into the interior…

The world might never have known that these tribes exist, nor would relief agencies have been informed of their plight, had not a dozen or more evangelical Protestant missionaries explored their uncharted mountainous habitat during the past fifteen years. At risk to their own lives, the evangelicals succeeded in

*T*he question "Should anyone go in?" is obsolete because obviously someone will.

befriending several thousand of these highly suspicious, unpredictable tribesmen. Meticulously, they learned and analyzed unwritten tribal languages, a task so agonizing that less motivated persons would have no time for it. They also carved out the four airstrips which now made relief operations possible and, as a sidelight, enabled

McDonald to carry out his assignment on location.

The missionary aircraft taxied to a halt on one of these airstrips. McDonald leaped out and began snapping pictures…

*T*he most isolated minority cultures must eventually be overwhelmed by the commercial and political expansion of majority people.

There are reasons why the missionaries had to go into isolated areas like Irian Jaya as soon as they could. History has taught them that even the most isolated minority cultures must eventually be overwhelmed by the commercial and political expansion of majority peoples. Naive academics in ivy-covered towers may protest that the world's remaining primitive cultures should be left undisturbed, but farmers, lumbermen, land speculators, miners, hunters, military leaders, road builders, art collectors, tourists, and drug peddlers aren't listening.

They are going in anyway. Often to destroy. Cheat. Exploit. Victimize. Corrupt. Taking, and giving little other than diseases for which primitives have no immunity or medicine.

This is why, since the turn of the century, more than ninety tribes have become extinct in Brazil alone. Many other Latin American, African, and Asian countries show a similar high extinction rate for their primitive minorities. A grim toll of five or six tribes per year is probably a conservative worldwide estimate.

We missionaries don't want the same fate to befall these magnificent tribes in Irian Jaya. We risk our lives to get to them first because we believe we are more sympathetic agents of change than profit-hungry commercialists. Like our predecessor John Sargent, who in 1796 launched a program that saved the Mohican tribe from extinction, and like our colleagues in Brazil who just one generation ago saved the Wai Wai from a similar fate, we believe we know how to precondition tribes in Irian Jaya for survival in the modern world. The question, "Should anyone go in?" is obsolete because obviously someone *will*.

It has been replaced by a more practical question: "Will the most sympathetic persons get there first?" To make the shock of coming out of the stone age as easy as possible. To see that tribals gain new ideals to replace those they must lose in order to survive. To teach them the national language so they can defend themselves in disputes with "civilizados."

And yet produce literature in their own language so it will not be forgotten. To teach them the value of money, so that unscrupulous traders cannot easily cheat them. And better yet, set some of them up in business so that commerce in their areas will not fall entirely into the hands of outsiders. To care for them when epidemics sweep through or when earthquakes strike. And better yet, train some of them as nurses and doctors to carry on when we are gone. We go as ombudsmen who help clashing cultures understand each other.

We missionaries are advocates not only of spiritual truth but also of physical survival. And we have enjoyed astonishing success in Irian Jaya and elsewhere. Among the Ekari, Damal, Dani, Ndugwa, and other tribes,

**W*e missionaries are advocates not only of spiritual truth but also of physical survival.***

more than 100,000 stone-agers welcomed our gospel as the fulfillment of something their respective cultures had anticipated for hundreds of years. The Ekari called it *aji*. To the Damal, it was *hai*. To the Dani, *nabelan-kabelan*—an immortal message which one day would restrain tribal war and ease human suffering.

The result: cultural fulfillment of the deepest possible kind. And it opened the door to faith in Jesus Christ for tens of thousands.

Along with our successes, there have been setbacks. Nearly two years ago one of our colleagues from a European mission, Gerrit Kuijt, left some coastal helpers in charge of a new outpost while he returned to Holland. In his absence, a few of the coastals began to molest the surrounding tribespeople for private reasons. Thirteen coastals were killed in retaliation.

Sympathize. Sometimes it is not easy to find responsible helpers willing to venture with us into these wild areas. At times you have to trust someone; you have no choice.

Earlier, in 1968, two of our buddies, Phil Masters and Stan Dale, died together while probing a new area of the Yali tribe. But then Kusaho, a Yali elder, rebuked the young men who killed them, saying: "Neither of these men ever harmed any of us, nor did they even resist while you killed them. Surely they came in peace and you have made a terrible mistake. If ever any more of this kind of men come into our valley, we must welcome them."

And so a door of acceptance opened through the wounds of our friends. It was a costly victory. Stan's and Phil's widows were each left with five small children to raise alone. Yet neither widow blamed anyone for the death of her husband, and one of them still serves with us in Irian Jaya today.

Ours is a great work, and a very difficult one. It is not subsidized by any government and can succeed only as it has sympathetic support from churches, private individuals, and the public in general. That is where correspondent McDonald could have helped. Instead...

McDonald now transferred to a Mission Aviation Fellowship helicopter loaded with sweet potatoes contributed by Christians from the Dani tribe and rice from Indonesian government stores. Pilot Jeff Heritage thought McDonald seemed surprisingly uninterested in the many tribal hamlets stranded like islands in the midst of uncrossable landslides, their inhabitants on the edge of starvation. After only a few hours in the interior, he returned to the coast and wrote his report.

Wielding the cliché "fundamentalist" with obvious intent to stigmatize and nettle us, McDonald launched a scathing yet baseless attack which appeared as a major article in the *Washington Post* and was relayed by wire service to hundreds of newspapers around the world. Citing the loss of Gerrit Kuijt's thirteen helpers and the murder of Phil and Stan eight years ago, he made the absurd accusation that we are "provoking hostile and occasionally murderous reactions from primitive tribesmen." He continues: "The missionaries are also coming under attack by anthropologists and other observers for attempting the almost total destruction of cultures..."

Who are the anthropologists and other observers? Within our ranks we have a number of men who hold degrees in anthropology, and they have not warned us of any such attack by members of their discipline. We have cooperated with a number of anthropologists in Irian Jaya over the past twenty years and have had good mutual understanding with them.

**W*e have cooperated with a number of anthropologists and had good mutual understanding with them.***

Perhaps McDonald is referring to the three remaining members of a German scientific team he met on one of his helicopter stops in the interior. Some of them, reportedly, have been critical toward us, not on the basis of wide knowledge of our work but because of anti-missionary sentiments they brought with them to Irian Jaya.

Their problem is that they hold to an old school of anthropology, still current in some areas, which favors isolating primitive tribes from all change in zoo-like reserves. A new school, now rising in America, has at last recognized the futility of this approach and advocates

## *We want to stop the intertribal warfare that has gone on for centuries.*

instead that primitive tribes be exposed to survival-related "directed change," in order that they may learn to cope with encroachment, now seen as inevitable.

Directed change is exactly what evangelical missionary John Sargent practiced back in 1796 and what we are practicing in 1976. In fact, missionaries are virtually the only persons who do. Anthropologists don't remain with tribesmen long enough. And humanists aren't sufficiently motivated. But if, indeed, we are under attack, a careful reporter should have asked us for our defense, if any. McDonald did not do this, though he had opportunity. What evidence does he present for his charge that we are "attempting the almost total destruction of local cultures" in Irian Jaya? He writes: "The first action of a missionary…in Valley X recently was to hand out shirts to the tribesmen."

The tribesmen concerned had just lost most of their homes in the earthquake. Indonesian officials had provided shirts to help them stay warm at night in their crude temporary shelters at mile-high elevations. No one wanted a rash of pneumonia cases complicating the relief operation. Johnny Benzel, the missionary, cooperated with the government directive by handing out the shirts.

Nowhere have we ever provided Indonesian or Western-style clothing until demand for it arose among the tribal people themselves. This usually took from seven to fifteen years. Tribal church elders preached in the open or under grass-roofed shelters, wearing their penis gourds, and no one thought anything of it. Even today the vast majority of men still wear gourds and women wear grass skirts.

It is the Indonesian government, not missionaries, which tries to shame tribals into exchanging gourds and grass skirts for shorts and dresses under Operation Koteka. But they do it for understandable reasons. They want the tribesmen to become part of Indonesian society as soon as possible, find employment, etc.

At Nalca, McDonald snapped a photo of a native with a ball-point pen stuck through the pierced septum of his nose. This photo appeared in some newspapers with the ludicrous caption: "Ball-point pen replaces nosebone; fundamentalist preachers destroy culture." A native forages a used ball-point pen out of Johnny Benzel's wastepaper basket, sticks it through his nose, and presto! Johnny is accused of destroying culture. Very tricky, McDonald.

McDonald slams Johnny again: "At Nalca mission, women have been persuaded to lengthen their grass skirts to knee-length…" What actually happens is that families of the Dani tribe follow missionaries to places like Nalca, and over a period of years the Nalca women begin to imitate the style of their Dani counterparts, which happens to be longer.

Do we, then, approve of everything in the local cultures? No, we do not, just as no one in our own Western culture automatically approves of everything in it.

We are out to destroy cannibalism, but so also is the Indonesian government. The difference is, we use moral persuasion, and if we fail, the government will eventually use physical force. Our task is to give the tribals a rational basis for giving it up voluntarily before the guns of the police decide the issue with traumatic effect.

We also want to stop the intertribal warfare that has gone on for centuries. In view of all they have to go through in the next fifty years, it is imperative that the tribes stop killing and wounding each other *now.* Often we are able to stop the fighting by emphasizing little-used peace-making mechanisms within the cultures themselves. Or we simply provide the third-person presence which enables antagonists to see their problems in a new light.

We are against witchcraft, suspicion of which is a major cause of war. Killing by witchcraft is contrary, not only to Christian concepts of goodness but also to the humanist's, isn't it?

## *If it is survival-related directed change, it cannot be faulted on anthropological grounds.*

We are against sexual promiscuity, and not for religious reasons only. In 1903, Chinese traders seeking bird-of-paradise plumes landed on the south coast of Irian Jaya. They introduced a venereal disease called lymphogranuloma venereum among the 100,000-member Merind tribes. Since group sex was widely accepted, the disease spread like wildfire. It wiped out 90,000 lives in ten years.

McDonald attempts to antagonize us still further by comparing our methods unfavorably with "the more adaptive policies of Roman Catholic and mainstream Protestant groups."

Only one "mainstream" Protestant mission works in interior Irian Jaya, and they have experienced the same problems McDonald uses as grounds to incriminate us. For example, that mission's director was seriously wounded with three arrows eight years ago, and eight of his carriers were killed, while trekking through a wild area. Such incidents are merely an occupational hazard and should not be used to levy blame.

As far as I know, Roman Catholic missionaries have not been wounded or slain by tribals in Irian Jaya. This is due, not to "more adaptive policies," but to the fact that they limit their work mainly to areas already well-controlled by the government. But they have counted their martyrs across the border in Papua New Guinea, and this is no shame to them.

If McDonald had taken time to visit Roman Catholic and evangelical Protestant areas of operation and compare them, he would have found the degree of culture change at least as great if not greater in the Roman Catholic areas. For example, in all Roman Catholic areas primitives are expected to give up their tribal names and take Latin names like Pius or Constantius, whereas in evangelical Protestant areas they still use their Irianese name, like Isai or Yana. But here again, if it is survival-related directed change, it cannot be faulted on anthropological grounds.

McDonald continues, "Nearly all Roman Catholic missionaries in Irian Jaya are required to hold degrees in anthropology." Actually, the percentage of Roman Catholic and evangelical Protestant missionaries holding degrees in anthropology is approximately equal, and when it comes to prowess in learning tribal dialects, the evangelicals excel by far. The majority of Roman Catholic priests teach in Indonesian even where it is not understood.

McDonald describes the lime-scattering dedication of a new Catholic church at Jaosakor. Surely if this is the limit of their cultural penetration, our Catholic friends must be far from satisfied. Cultural penetration, to be effective, must go far deeper than mere externals like scattering lime. Not until you come to grips with internal concepts in the category of the Ekari tribe's *aji* or the Dani tribe's *nabelan-kabelan*, are you getting close to the heart of a people. And in matters of this category, we evangelicals have been spot on. As one of our members said to McDonald, "What we are looking for is the cultural key..." McDonald quoted his words, yet failed totally to appreciate them.

Another point of McDonald's article calls for refutation: Gerrit Kuijt raised funds for a helicopter for general service to all tribal peoples in Irian Jaya, not for "aerial evangelism." In fact, it was this helicopter that was on hand just in time to help in the earthquake relief operation and that bore McDonald on his reporting mission. Thank you, Gerrit, for your foresight. The rest of us are not unappreciative like McDonald.

McDonald, your article was erroneous, inept, and irresponsible. You have made a perfect nuisance of yourself. You and the *Washington Post* owe us a printed apology.

Do missionaries destroy cultures? We may destroy certain things "in" cultures, just as doctors sometimes must destroy certain things "in" a human body, if a patient is to live. But surely as we grow in experience and God-given wisdom, we must not and will not destroy cultures themselves.

---

**Minankabau:** Many of the 6 million Minankabau people still live on the West Indonesian island of Sumatra. Women own the land where they work with water buffalo to plant the crops. Rich soil and abundant streams provide excellent conditions for growing rice. Men work in urban areas and bring in outside resources, returning to help with harvest.

To be Minankabau is to be Muslim, yet Minan practices retain many elements of folk animism. Their culture is stable and change-resistant. They have maintained their matriarchal clan lineages in the face of Islamic traditions. Special strategies may need to be developed for reaching matrilineal societies like the Minan. There could be possibilities of reaching the men when they are working in the cities.

Indonesia is the world's largest Muslim nation and is increasingly restrictive of any mission work. Workers from within Christian bodies in Indonesia may be the best hope to take up the challenge. Building a culturally Minankabau church will be necessary for it to survive the many pressures. The New Testament has been translated and some work is under way.

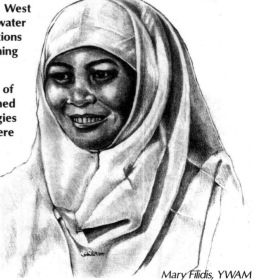

*Mary Filidis, YWAM*

# The Company of the Committed
## Patricia Moore and Meg Crossman

> Patricia Moore is Dean of the offsite graduate program for Northern Arizona University. She has been active in stimulating creative approaches to mission funding. With Julie McDonald, she is the author of *Adventures in Giving*.

*The share of the man who stayed by the supplies is to be the same as that of him who went down to the battle.*

1 Samuel 30:24 NIV

David recognized a critical fact about warfare: support troops are as essential as those who go into battle. He ruled that their reward must be the same. The Lord had earlier ordered that the Israelites were to divide the spoils between the soldiers who took part in the battle and the rest of the community who made it possible for them to go (Numbers 31:27). No army, regardless of their strength, can long survive without support and supply.

> **D**avid recognized a critical fact about warfare: support troops are as essential as those who go into battle.

## Finding Our Roles

While all Christians are called to participate in reaching the nations, only some are sent out cross-culturally. A zeal for the spread of the Gospel can be lived out in many ways. When we strategize to complete the task, the focus of our attention must not only include missionary concerns at the front lines but also go beyond them to support and supply as well. Unless all these roles are filled, worldwide missions quickly grind to a halt.

Every believer can discover roles for which God has equipped them. Paul's examples of the interdependence of the body of Christ in 1 Corinthians 12 show that every believer has a vital part to play. This is as applicable to God's worldwide plans as it is to a local church. Nothing is more energizing to a field worker than the backing of a dedicated sender, mobilizer, welcomer, or intercessor fulfilling his ministry with intensity, focus, perseverance, and sacrifice. All are full participants in the company of the committed. Since churches and biographies often highlight the role of those who go, we will instead begin with the other options.

## Senders

*Now you Philippians know also that in the beginning of the gospel, when I departed from Macedonia, no church shared with me concerning giving and receiving but you only…you sent aid once and again for my necessities.*

Philippians 4:15–16

Paul deeply valued his partnership with the Philippian church, who acted as true senders: backing his missionary endeavors with prayer, concern, involvement, and provision, while actively ministering at home. Paul and the church at Philippi thought of themselves as a team. Without the participation of a team of committed senders—both churches and individuals—no missionary will ever win his target people group. Conservative estimates are that, for one person to go, there needs to be a team of six to thirty active senders.

### It can't be done alone

Individuals are wonderful, but individuals alone are never sufficient. Churches, agencies, and lay people together must embrace the vision. They work in tandem to care both for the missionaries and their target people. Only as a team can they provide the stability, wisdom, guidance, and longevity to persevere to completion. In the days of the Student Volunteer Movement, more than 100,000 volunteered to go to the field. Only about 20,000 actually went, largely because of a lack of senders.

Senders are often unaware of the critical importance of their task. They usually do their work behind the scenes, isolated from one another. Thanks or public recognition seldom comes their way. Effective senders, therefore, operate on an inner conviction that their investments in the Gospel grow out of God's specific call on their lives. They also recognize that sending requires as much discipline and commitment as going.

### Senders are vital

Two key ingredients combine in the ministry of most senders: generosity and intercession. There is constant pressure in our culture to conform lifestyle to income, but senders strive to resist this. Many chose to adopt a lifestyle comparable to that of missionaries on the field, to free more income for support. Some dedicated senders quietly give away half of their income or more for the spread of the Gospel.

Prayer flows out of giving. In Matthew 6:21, Jesus said, "For *where your treasure is,* there your heart will be also." In the Kingdom economy, investment *precedes* heart involvement, not the other way around. Those who invest in others' ministries find it natural to lift those they support and the target people to the Father in prayer. Countless missionaries affirm that the resultant prayer is even more vital to their work than funding.

## Options for senders

Senders' generosity of heart often includes other significant roles such as research and supplies. One whole ministry focuses on shipping needed materials to the field. Others serve as a backup resource to field workers doing needed research through sources available at home, but not on the field, and sending it to the workers. Email and the Internet have opened whole new connections for these services.

A group of computer experts in Florida developed a ministry using their skills by training missionaries on computers and finding donated computers and software suitable for field needs. A dairyman provided cows to indigenous church planters so they could support their families without funding from outside their country. Accountants, teachers, bankers, business consultants, as well as medical and dental professionals use their proficiencies for mission undertakings. Their expertise may provide platforms for workers to enter restricted areas. Their deeds of love confirm the Gospel that full-time workers have been preaching.

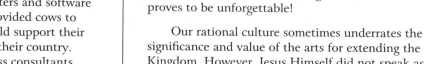

*Seeing people find their place of significant service energizes mobilizers.*

## Mobilizers

*The Lord spoke to Moses, saying: 'Make two silver trumpets for yourself;…you shall use them for calling the congregation and for directing the movement of the camps.'*

Numbers 10:1–2 NKJV

Sending is not the only way to participate in international work from home base. Someone must sound the rallying call. Those who desire to see others trained, prepared, and released to ministry are known as mobilizers. Mobilizers stir other Christians to active concern for reaching the world. They coordinate efforts between senders, the local church, sending agencies, and missionaries on the field.

## Mobilizers are essential

To understand the role of mobilizers, think of World War II as a parallel. Only 10% of the American population went to the war. Of those, only 1% were actually on the firing lines. However, for them to be successful in their mission, the entire country had to be mobilized!

Seeing people find their place of significant service energizes mobilizers. They are often networkers and

trainers. Rather than focusing on a single ministry, they delight to make known a full spectrum of possibilities from which each person can choose.

Often mobilizers provide teaching, practical help, and reassurance, motivating churches and helping them get under way. Mobilizers provide facts for strategic involvement and encouraging God's people as they develop their distinctive roles. Completing our task will call for informed, servant-hearted, diligent mobilizers.

## Drama and the arts

In this increasingly visual age, skits, plays, dramas, paintings, film, videos, puppetry, mime, and even dance are being used to communicate God's mandate to His people. Dramatic presentations can be a powerful mobilizing tool. The story of God's heart for all nations forcefully communicated through these media often proves to be unforgettable!

Our rational culture sometimes underrates the significance and value of the arts for extending the Kingdom. However, Jesus Himself did not speak as a theologian; He told wonderful stories to get His message across. Many drama teams use those same parables as a model for their presentations. Significantly, Scriptural parables transfer across cultures with surprising effectiveness: the story of the prodigal son can tell deep truths to Thais or Berbers or Navajos.

## Welcomers

*The stranger who dwells among you shall be to you as one born among you, and you shall love him as yourself; for you were strangers in the land of Egypt: I am the Lord your God.*

Leviticus 19:34 NKJV

God prepared His own people to be sensitive to the needs of strangers by the lessons of their sojourn in Egypt. Even His own Son lived as a refugee in Egypt in His early years. Welcomers are those stirred by the needs of those ethnic groups who reside in the welcomer's home country. Welcomers seek opportunities to touch the lives of thousands of internationals who come to study, work, or emigrate permanently.

## Welcomers are strategic

Welcomers are especially crucial in reaching populations whose home countries restrict mission work. One missionary is working with a very persecuted population in a highly volatile country in the Middle East. His greatest asset is the help of a vibrant national believer who hated Christians until he became a refugee and was sent to the United States. The Christians loved, helped, and resettled him. They won him to the Lord and took the time to disciple him. As a mature believer, he returned to his home country and now makes an impact the missionary could never have on his own.

The heart of this ministry grows out of the gift of hospitality (GK: *Philoxenia,* meaning "love of strangers"). Welcomers befriend people, demonstrating the love of Christ in very practical ways. They may work with university students, diplomats, technical workers, refugees, military personnel, or immigrants. Instead of fearing new ethnic groups as a threat, Christians see their coming as a strategic opportunity for love and witness.

*Instead of fearing new ethnic groups as a threat, Christians see their coming as a strategic opportunity for love and witness.*

## Churches develop welcoming ministries

The church can develop special strategies, appropriate to each group. A ministry in Chicago works with churches to present each new refugee family with a "Welcome to America" packet within a week after they arrive. Elsewhere, churches develop outreach around teaching English as a Second Language. One group uses the Ann Landers column. The class reads her advice to learn American idioms and discuss ideas. The students are exposed to Christian values (which often take issue with Ann's advice). They express their own ideas, which helps the leaders see where *they* are spiritually.

Effective welcomers learn all they can of the culture and language of their target people. Guest workers from Turkey are being reached in Germany. Christians in the Netherlands work with Indonesians who have relocated there. While living as students in Hungary, Mongolians were won to the Lord. Both language learning and cultural sensitivity contribute to making these ministries effective.

This highly convenient form of cross-cultural ministry also provides fruitful connections for anyone preparing for field service. A small college-age team wanted to explore the possibilities for getting into a closed country in North Africa. They got to know as many students from that country as possible. When they were repeatedly turned down for entry visas, the father of a student they had befriended turned out to be the key they needed. He arranged permission for them to enter for a year!

## Intercessors

*Ask of Me and I will give you the nations for your inheritance and the ends of the earth for your possession.*

Psalm 2:8 NKJV

## Prayer above all

Every one of us must spend time in prayer and intercession, but some are especially called to this ministry. Instead of praying only for individuals you know on the field, how about praying for an unreached people group who has no one to care about them? Many churches are choosing to adopt a particular people group or become advocates for them. By praying specifically for them, researching their culture and history, and networking with others who are interested, they can strategically undergird effective work.

Prayer strategies are multiplying. *Global Prayer Digest* focuses on a different group of unreached peoples in each monthly issue. YWAM produces a 30-day guide to prayer for Muslims during Ramadan, the month the Islamic world fasts. *Operation World* has gathered statistics and prayer guidelines for each nation in the world. Through Wycliffe, prayer teams intercede for Bible-less peoples. The Lydia International Prayer Fellowship has women all over the world praying for specific nations, especially their leaders. Several groups are organizing children to pray, primarily for the unreached.

*Amy Barstad*

## Start with repentance

Serious prayer often begins with serious repentance. Southern Baptists in the U.S. have asked African-Americans to forgive them for the abuses received since the time of slavery. Many groups are asking forgiveness of tribes and minorities in their countries who have been mistreated and despised. At the Global Congress on World Evangelization (GCOWE) in Korea, Arab Christians and Jewish Christians sought each other's forgiveness, Japanese delegates repented before Koreans, and the Orthodox representatives asked the forgiveness of Evangelical believers. Prayer walks retracing the routes of the Crusades request forgiveness from Jews, Muslims, and Orthodox believers for the offenses against them by crusaders.

Through the AD2000 Movement, prayer teams go into countries and cities in the 10/40 window to walk and pray through the very streets where an unreached people lives. By coming to pray, teams do not have to learn a language to make a difference. Children often participate in these prayer walks as well. Not only does this mobilize the sending church to focused prayer, it allows Christians to experience the reality of the needs in a depth no video or story could ever portray.

## Goers

*As the Father has sent Me, I also send you.*

John 20:21 NASB

Some people envision a goer only as a dynamic pioneer who is willing to brave any danger to reach his target group. While these types of entrepreneurial leaders are important, they are not the only persons needed on the field. Greg Livingstone, founder of Frontiers, believes a variety of gifts are important to make a healthy team. He explains the three major categories that should be included.[1]

## Three different roles

Leaders of the entrepreneurial mold get the team motivated to go to the field. Their optimism, enthusiasm, and "can-do" spirit keep people moving forward in spite of obstacles. However, after several years in the culture, a new kind of leader is required. This would be one with a combination of pastoral and administrative gifts, who is skilled in managing team relations and keeping them working well together. The entrepreneur may prefer to move on to envision another team.

A second set of gifts are held by those Livingstone calls "the 'people' people." Friend-makers, generous hosts, teachers, evangelists, pastoral disciplers, and prophets calling for purity are all a part of this

assemblage. Together they make up the heart of the team, befriending the target people, welcoming them into their homes, challenging them with the claims of Christ, then teaching them to obey all He commands.

Finally, the facilitators are a critical component. These are people with marketable skills or a business project that could gain the team entry. A professor of appropriate technology and international development could not leave home permanently but opened the doors for the team with his expertise and credentials. He returned annually to reconnect with the officials and to advise the team on technical matters.

Facilitators would also include those gifted to handle the logistical-practical needs of the team so that they can function well in their location for a number of years. In one area, a couple in their sixties serves, running errands, providing hospitality and wise advice for younger team members, and functioning as un-official team "mentors." One widowed mother joined a team just so she could be with her grandchildren, and she proved to be a blessing to nationals and workers alike.

> *Many churches become advocates for a people group, researching their culture and history and networking with others.*

Leaders, people connectors, and facilitators all contribute to team fruitfulness. These varied kinds of goers often practice their giftedness in welcomer and mobilizer functions before they go to the field. Church planting is the end goal for all these roles, but each team member must learn to assist in their own unique way.

## Joining the Worldwide Team

### Analyze your interests

To test whether sending, mobilizing, welcoming, going, or intercession best utilizes your gifts and abilities, simply try one out. Often, in reality, they overlap and strengthen one another. What burdens and concerns has the Lord given you? Do you have a heart for certain people, tribes, or countries? Are you interested in urban missions, Bible translation, church planting, or supporting nationals in their own cross-cultural outreach? Do you find an affinity with the vision of a certain agency?

Look for opportunities that have a natural fit with your abilities or interests. This is vital, since the satisfaction you gain from following your God-given inclinations will help motivate you to persist in the face of obstacles. Whether you are a corporate executive, a university professor, a housewife, a barber, or a construction worker, you have skills, experience, and a circle of influence that can extend the Kingdom.

## Start right where you are

Service opportunities abound. Could you use your accounting or personnel skills to help a mission agency? Could your whole family work together on a mission project? Could you extend an overseas business trip for a day or two to visit your church's field workers? Could you become the email contact for missionaries your church has sent out?

If you're called to be a sender, don't wait to get rich or find a "windfall." Begin to give, both your time and your finances, and make your giving sacrificial. Look for fresh opportunities to generate funds. Can you sell something? Is there a service you can offer in your spare time or lessons you might teach? One group scours garage sales for antiques, which are then marketed through an antique dealer in their congregation. The dealer even adds her commission to the fund.

## Expect to expand

When your income increases, increase your giving. When your involvement works out well, bring in others. Pray that God will bless you financially, and when it happens, don't forget the purpose for which God gave it. Use your God-given creativity to explore untried options to keep your interests continually lively and stimulating.

## Keep learning

Talk to other Christians who serve effectively in these roles. Ask questions about mission agencies and ministries that interest you. Find friends or fellow church members who are headed for short-term or full-time missions and get involved with them. Spend time with missionaries who visit your church. Choose a country in which you are interested, and specialize in learning its culture, geography, government, economy, history, and present needs and problems. Take the posture of a learner with international friends, asking them to teach you how to cook their food or make their crafts or play their games. And never forget to turn these all into opportunities for more perceptive prayer!

## Try something radical

Do more than you think you can. Don't be afraid to give all your birthday or graduation money, all the money from an unexpected inheritance, 50 percent from your business, 80 percent from your tax refund. Invite an international to live with your family. Even better, consider moving to an area of your town where they live.

The family of an Episcopian priest blessed a student from a closed Muslim emirate as he lived with them. Upon returning, he advanced in leadership in his own country. He recently gave permission for the first Christian church in history to be constructed there. On the other hand, a military officer from Ethiopia was the recipient of haughty, prejudicial treatment when he trained in the U.S. He returned to lead a military coup and ruthlessly persecute the church in his home country for many years.

Start small, but don't expect to stay there. Every gift from God **will** grow if it is put to work. Only the buried "talents" remain unchanged and undeveloped (Matthew 25:14–29). Starting small lets you learn along the way.

## Opportunities available

God holds all Christians accountable to participate in reaching the nations. Whether you go to the field, enable someone else to go, mobilize the Body of Christ, welcome those God brings to your home territory, or intercede for the nations, you can advance His Kingdom. Limitless opportunities exist to participate globally, from those experiencing tremendous success to costly pioneer works persevering in faith.

*Every gift from God will grow if it is put to work.*

Even missionaries can serve in these ways. One couple, working in a very resistant field in France, supported a team in Indonesia because they wanted to have a part in a ministry that was bearing fruit! Another mission couple used their prayer letters to teach and mobilize their team back home.

## Each has a part

There are no superstars in the Kingdom of God. Those on whom the spotlight shines stand on the shoulders of others who sacrifice, pray, train, love, and give to keep them there. Before he left for the field, C. T. Studd gave away his considerable inheritance; part of that helped General Booth start the Salvation Army. George Mueller, who worked with orphans in England, tithed to Hudson Taylor's ministry in China. We work together as partners in a purpose larger than ourselves.

As we serve, each in our assigned place, we prove the truth of David's age-old insight that every warrior is essential to the battle. Along with those who go to the field, we likewise will be found "called, chosen, and faithful" (Revelation 17:14) as each one develops in their particular role. As servants to one another in His Kingdom cause, we, too, will swell the ranks of the company of the committed.

## End Notes

1  Livingstone, Greg. *Planting Churches in Muslim Cities: A team approach.* Grand Rapids, Mich.: Baker Book House, 1993. pp. 101–108.

# LOCAL CHURCH AND MISSION AGENCY RELATIONSHIPS: A MODEL

*Harry Larson*
*Missions Pastor, Emmanuel Faith Community Church*
*Escondido, California*

| The Role of the Local Church | The Role of the Mission Agency |
|---|---|
| • Give vision to church members. | • Give vision to the local church. |
| • Educate members in the Biblical basis of missions, as well as historical, cultural, and strategic issues in world mission. Be aware of needs around the world and challenge agencies to act if necessary. | • Be aware of needs around the world. Develop a clear strategy for finishing the task. Challenge churches to participate if they are not actively involved in world mission. |
| • Seek the Lord fervently in prayer as to the church's involvement in missions. Take initiative in determining priorities. Consider possibility of adopting a specific people group and sending a team to them. | • Seek the Lord fervently in prayer in setting priorities. Target unreached people groups. Nurture growth of established national churches. Encourage church prayer for world mission. Present needs for mission candidates. |
| • Select and approve mission candidates. Help those who are approved select a suitable mission agency. Work with agencies and others to determine appropriate gifts, training, and experience. | • Challenge potential candidates. Encourage candidates to develop within, and be sent out by, their local church. Consult with church during selection and approval process. |
| • Take primary responsibility for candidate training, for developing and confirming gifts, and for providing appropriate ministry experience. | • Work with local church throughout training or internship process. Meet and correspond with both church and candidate regarding progress and need for additional preparation. |
| • Get realistic appraisals of missionary's spiritual and physical needs. Work with agency to provide suitable help. Make appropriate visits to field to encourage and counsel missionary. | • Share realistic picture of how missionary is doing with appropriate church representatives. Suggest ways the church might help. Give honest feedback about the church's participation. |
| • Share in major ministry decisions for missionary. Ensure the missionary is truly in favor of changes. Discuss changes in priorities. | • Inform the church of plans for any major changes in missionary's role *before* plans are finalized. Explain reasons and seek input. |
| • Maintain close relationships with both missionary and agency so that the church can help in appropriate ways if problems develop. | • Inform the church promptly should problems develop. Involve church in process of working through difficulties. Allow church input early before it's "too late" for it to make a difference. |
| • Take responsibility to help the missionary adjust to life at home while on furlough or permanent return. Be especially sensitive to psychological needs of both missionaries and their children as they experience reverse culture shock. | • Inform the church of the mission's policies on furlough time and finances. Seek the local church's help, especially upon permanent return home of missionaries. Suggest ways the church can help with adjustments. Be candid about any negative reasons for separation. |

129

# *Prayer: Rebelling Against the Status Quo*
*David F. Wells*

**David Wells** is presently the Andrew Mutch Distinguished Professor of Historical and Systematic Theology at Gordon-Conwell Theological Seminary in South Hamilton, Massachusetts. Wells is the author of numerous articles and twelve books.

You will be appalled by the story I am about to relate to you. Appalled, that is, if you have any kind of social conscience.

A poor black, living on Chicago's South Side, sought to have her apartment properly heated during the frigid winter months. Despite city law on the matter, her unscrupulous landlord refused. The woman was a widow, desperately poor, and ignorant of the legal system, but she took the case to court on her own behalf. Justice, she declared, ought to be done. It was her ill fortune, however, to appear repeatedly before the same judge, who, as it turned out, was an atheist and a bigot. The only principle by which he abode was, as he put it, that "blacks should be kept in their place." The possibilities of a ruling favorable to the widow were, therefore, bleak. They became even bleaker as she realized she lacked the indispensable ingredient necessary for favorable rulings in cases like these—namely, a satisfactory bribe. Nevertheless, she persisted.

At first the judge did not so much as even look up from reading the novel on his lap before dismissing her. But then he began to notice her. Just another black, he thought, stupid enough to think she could get justice. Then her persistence made him self-conscious. This turned to guilt and anger. Finally, raging and embarrassed, he granted her petition and enforced the law. Here was a massive victory over "the system"—at least as it functioned in his corrupted courtroom.

In putting the matter like this I have not, of course, been quite honest. For this never really happened in Chicago (as far as I know), nor is it even my "story." It is a parable told by Jesus (Luke 18:1–8) to illustrate the nature of petitionary prayer.

The parallel Jesus drew was obviously not between God and the corrupt judge, but between the widow and the petitioner. This parallel has two aspects. First, the widow refused to accept her unjust situation, just as the Christian should refuse to resign himself or herself to the world in its fallenness. Second, despite discouragements, the widow persisted with her case as should the Christian with his or hers. The first aspect has to do with prayer's *nature* and the second with its *practice*.

I want to argue that our feeble and irregular prayer, especially in its petitionary aspect, is too frequently addressed in the wrong way. When confronting this failing, we are inclined to flagellate ourselves for our weak wills, our insipid desires, our ineffective technique, and our wandering minds. We keep thinking that somehow our *practice* is awry, and we rack our brains to see if we can discover where. I suggest that the problem lies in a misunderstanding of prayer's *nature* and our practice will never have that widow's persistence until our outlook has her clarity.

What, then, is the nature of petitionary prayer? It is, in essence, rebellion—rebellion against the world in its fallenness, the absolute and undying refusal to accept as normal what is pervasively abnormal. It is, in this its negative aspect, the refusal of every agenda, every scheme, every interpretation that is at odds with the norm as originally established by God. As such, it is itself an expression of the unbridgeable chasm that separates good from evil, the declaration that evil is not a variation on good but its antithesis.

> *What is the nature of petitionary prayer? It is, in essence, rebellion—rebellion against the world in its fallenness, the absolute and undying refusal to accept as normal what is pervasively abnormal.*

Or, to put it the other way around, to come to an acceptance of life "as it is," to accept it on its own terms—which means acknowledging the *inevitability* of the way it works—is to surrender a Christian view of God. This resignation to what is abnormal has within it the hidden and unrecognized assumption that the power of God to change the world, to overcome evil by good, will not be actualized.

Wells, D. F. Prayer: (1992) "Rebelling Against the Status Quo." In R. D. Winter & S. C. Hawthorne (Eds.). *Perspectives on the World Christian Movement: A Reader* (rev. ed.) (p. A144–147). Pasadena: William Carey Library.

Nothing destroys petitionary prayer (and with it, a Christian view of God) as quickly as resignation. "At all times," Jesus declared, "we should pray" and not "lose heart," thereby acquiescing to what is (Luke 18:1).

**N**othing destroys petitionary prayer (and with it, a Christian view of God) as quickly as resignation.

The dissipation of petitionary prayer in the presence of resignation has an interesting historical pedigree. Those religions that stress quietistic acquiescence always disparage petitionary prayer. This was true of the Stoics, who claimed that such prayer showed that one was unwilling to accept the existent world as an expression of God's will. One was trying to escape from it by having it modified. That, they said, was bad. A similar argument is found in Buddhism. And the same result, although arrived at by a different process of reasoning, is commonly encountered in our secular culture.

Secularism is that attitude that sees life as an end in itself. Life, it is thought, is severed from any relationship to God. Consequently the only norm or "given" in life, whether for meaning or for morals, is the world as it is. With this, it is argued, we must come to terms; to seek some other referent around which to structure our lives is futile and "escapist." It is not only that God, the object of petitionary prayer, has often become indistinct, but that his relationship to the world is seen in a new way. And it is a way that does not violate secular assumption. God may be "present" and "active" in the world, but it is not a presence and an activity that changes anything.

Against all of this, it must be asserted that petitionary prayer only flourishes where there is a twofold belief: first, that God's name is hallowed too irregularly, his kingdom has come too little, and his will is done too infrequently; second, that God himself can change this situation. Petitionary prayer, therefore, is the expression of the hope that life as we meet it, on the one hand, *can* be otherwise and, on the other hand, that it *ought* to be otherwise. It is therefore impossible to seek to live in God's world on his terms, doing his work in a way that is consistent with who he is, without engaging in regular prayer.

That, I believe, is the real significance of petitionary prayer in our Lord's life. Much of his prayer life is left unexplained by the Gospel writers (e.g., Mark 1:35; Luke 5:16; 9:18; 11:1), but a pattern in the circumstances that elicited prayer is discernible.

First, petitionary prayer preceded great decisions in his life, such as the choosing of the disciples (Luke 6:12); indeed, the only possible explanation of his choice of that ragtag bunch of nonentities, boastful, ignorant, and uncomprehending as they were, was that he had prayed before choosing them. Second, he prayed when pressed beyond measure, when his day was unusually busy with many competing claims upon his energies and attention (e.g., Matthew 14:23). Third, he prayed in the great crises and turning points of his life, such as his baptism, the Transfiguration, and the Cross (Luke 3:21; 9:28–29). Finally, he prayed before and during unusual temptation, the most vivid occasion being Gethsemane (Matthew 26:36–45). As the "hour" of evil descended, the contrast between the way Jesus met it and the way his disciples met it is explained only by the fact that he persevered in prayer and they slept in faintness of heart. Each of these events presented our Lord with the possibility of adopting an agenda, accepting a perspective, or pursuing a course that was other than God's. His rejection of the alternative was each time signaled by his petitionary prayer. It was his means of refusing to live in this world or to do his Father's business on any other terms than his Father's. As such, it was rebellion against the world in its perverse and fallen abnormality.

To pray declares that God and his world are at cross-purposes; to "sleep," or "faint," or "lose heart" is to act as if they are not. Why, then, do we pray so little for our local church? Is it really that our technique is bad, our wills weak, or our imaginations listless? I don't believe so. There is plenty of strong-willed and lively discussion—which in part or in whole may be justified—about the mediocrity of the preaching, the emptiness of the worship, the superficiality of the fellowship, and the

**P**etitionary prayer flourishes where there is a twofold belief: first, that God's name is hallowed too irregularly, his kingdom has come too little, and his will is done too infrequently; second, that God himself can change this situation.

ineffectiveness of the evangelism. So why, then, don't we pray as persistently as we talk? The answer, quite simply, is that we don't believe it will make any difference. We accept, however despairingly, that the situation is unchangeable, that what is will always be. This is not a problem about the practice of prayer but rather about its *nature*. Or more precisely, it is about the nature of God and his relationship to this world.

Unlike the widow in the parable, we find it is easy to come to terms with the unjust and fallen world around us—even when it intrudes into Christian institutions. It's not that we are unaware of what is happening, but simply that we feel impotent to change anything. That impotence leads us to strike a truce with what is wrong.

In other words, we have lost our anger, both at the level of social witness and before God in prayer. Fortunately he has not lost his, for the wrath of God is his opposition to what is wrong, the means by which truth is put forever on the throne and error forever on the scaffold. Without God's wrath, there would be no reason to live morally in the world and every reason not to. So the wrath of God, in this sense, is intimately connected with petitionary prayer that also seeks the ascendancy of truth in all instances and the corresponding banishment of evil.

The framework Jesus gave us for thinking about this was the Kingdom of God. The Kingdom is that sphere where the king's sovereignty is recognized, and, because of the nature of our king, that sovereignty is exercised supernaturally. In Jesus, the long-awaited "age to come" arrived; in him and through him, the Messianic incursion into the world has happened. Being a Christian, then, is not a matter of simply having had the right religious experience, but rather of starting to live in that sphere which is authentically divine. Evangelism is not successful because our technique is "right," but because this "age" breaks into the lives of sinful people. And this "age to come," which is already dawning, is not the possession of any one people or culture. God's "age," the "age" of his crucified Son, is dawning in the whole world. Our praying, therefore, should look beyond the concerns of our private lives to include the wide horizon of all human life in which God is concerned. If the Gospel is universal, prayer cannot restrict itself to being local.

It is not beside the point, therefore, to see the world as a courtroom in which a "case" can still be made against what is wrong and for what is right. Our feebleness in prayer happens because we have lost sight of this, and until we regain it we will not persist in our role as litigants. But there is every reason why we should regain our vision and utilize our opportunity, for the Judge before whom we appear is neither an atheist nor corrupt, but the glorious God and Father of our Lord Jesus Christ. Do you really think, then, that he will fail to "bring about justice for his chosen ones who cry to him night and day? Will he keep putting them off?" "I tell you," our Lord declares, "he will see that they get justice, and quickly" (Luke 18:7–8). 

---

*Julie Bosacker, YWAM*

**Bosnian:** The heartbreak of ethnic strife has focused the world's concern on the former nation of Yugoslavia. Sarajevo, the Bosnian capital where the Archduke Ferdinand was assassinated, triggering World War I, has been reduced to ruins. The Serbian forces have made the horror of "ethnic cleansing" an international byword.

Bosnian Muslims are Europe's least evangelized people. Little has been done to give them the Gospel, and there are no known churches. Now it may be even more difficult to reach them, since Christianity is perceived as part of the reason they have been attacked by Catholic Croats and Orthodox Serbians.

Bosnia has fewer Evangelical believers than any European country, so the opportunities for Bosnians to hear are few. Workers in refugee camps may find openings to love, help, and reach these people, especially the women who have been victims of organized rape.

The study of God's story has shown a new light on the path of our lives. It brightens our understanding of Scripture, of history, of peoples, of cultures, and of our own role. The work of God continues in our generation and we have a part to play. Consider these new points of view.

## New View of Scripture and of History

The Old Testament is a factual account of a nation with a purpose: *to glorify God by taking His story to the nations.* The New Covenant extends this call. There are consequences to the response made to that purpose. Will we bless others or keep the blessing for ourselves and those who are like us?

The light of history shows that God is still dealing with peoples and nations to bring them into His Kingdom. It demonstrates consequences on a global scale of extending the blessings or hoarding them. Will we take the blessing to the nations or must they come to us? Will we reach the nations in our midst or be sent to them where they are? Our choices do affect history.

## New View of Strategy and Culture

Seeing our world in terms of people groups instead of geopolitical nations changes the assignment we are carrying out. Church planting movements can make finishing world evangelization a reality. The continual movement of peoples from nation to nation gives us multiplied opportunities to tell them God's story.

The study of culture is fascinating. Cultures not only present barriers to overcome, they also represent the source of enriching insights, beauty, and variety. Each culture needs a unique presentation of His story. As each is welcomed into the Kingdom, we can anticipate a dazzling array of praise from redeemed peoples, tribes, and languages before the throne of the Lamb.

## New View of the Church and Ourselves

The body of Christ, both local and international, contains worldwide dimensions essential to God's ongoing work. Both expressions contribute to the completion of our momentous task. Only with the encouragement and love of our own fellowship dare we go forward. Only with the cooperation and partnership of the church worldwide can we envision eventual victory.

The scope and depth of an all nations perspective gives us new ways of viewing ourselves. Our gifts are both critical and significant. Each one can make a strategic contribution. Our lives have international possibilities. Our experiences are vital to *the World Christian movement.*

As World Christians, we can be settled in our commitment and our confidence. *The relentless purposes of God continue.* We can join Him in His work of love. Valiant brothers and sisters from every nation serve alongside us. Our partnerships are not just a help and a blessing. The very partnerships themselves demonstrate God's story. Peoples and nations *can* joyfully and peacefully work together in God.

## New View of Our Father

Kingdom vision humbles us with awe at the heart of our Father. He will not accept the status quo on this planet and neither should we. The length and breadth and height and depth of His love are beyond description. His loving rule deserves to be advanced and exalted. His infinite righteousness merits universal acceptance. It is our privilege to announce the entry of His reign.

Knowing these truths and knowing Him, World Christians together proclaim, *"Thy Kingdom come!"*

# NOTES

# NOTES

# NOTES

NOTES

# NOTES

# NOTES

NOTES

# NOTES

# NOTES